THE ART OF
OLIVER GOLDSMITH

edited by
Andrew Swarbrick

VISION
and
BARNES & NOBLE

Vision Press Limited
Fulham Wharf
Townmead Road
London SW6 2SB

and

Barnes & Noble Books
81 Adams Drive
Totowa, NJ 07512

ISBN (UK) 0 85478 026 2
ISBN (US) 0 389 20462 5

Printed and bound in Great Britain by
Unwin Brothers Ltd.,
Old Woking, Surrey.
Phototypeset by Galleon Photosetting,
Ipswich, Suffolk.
MCMLXXXIV

Critical Studies Series

THE ART OF
OLIVER GOLDSMITH

Contents

Chronological Table

1730[?]   Born 10 November, probably at Pallas, Co. West-
             meath, second son of the Rev. Charles Goldsmith,
             who shortly afterwards becomes curate-in-charge of
             the parish of Kilkenny West and moves to Lissoy
             where G. spends his childhood.

c. 1737–45   Educated at the Diocesan School at Elphin and at
             schools at Athlone near Lissoy and Edgeworthstown,
             Co. Longford.

1745   Admitted as sizar to Trinity College, Dublin on
             11 June.

1747   Death of his father. G. publicly admonished on 21
             May for his part in a student riot.

1750   Graduates B.A. in February.

1750–52   After failing to obtain ordination in the Church,
             becomes tutor to Flinn family in Co. Roscommon.
             Makes unsuccessful journeys to Cork (perhaps plan-
             ning to emigrate to America) and to Dublin (intend-
             ing to study Law in London).

1752   Enters University of Edinburgh in September to study
             medicine, with financial assistance from his relations.

1754   Leaves Edinburgh about 10 February to study
             medicine at Leyden University, where he remains
             until early 1755.

1755   Journeys across Flanders to Paris apparently to con-
             tinue medical studies, then through Germany and
             Switzerland to Italy (Padua, Venice and Florence)
             returning through France to England. *The Traveller*
             begun in the summer.

1756   Lands at Dover about 1 February and travels to
             London.

1756–57   Various posts held: as an assistant to an apothecary,
             as a physician in Southwark (possibly applying at

7

about this time for a medical degree from Trinity College, Dublin), perhaps as a proof-reader in Samuel Richardson's printing-house, and as usher at the Rev. John Milner's boys' school at Peckham, Surrey.

1757   Contributes articles to the *Monthly Review* whilst living with its editor and proprietor, Ralph Griffiths.

1758   Temporarily returns to Peckham in charge of the school. Translation of Jean Marteilhe's *Mémoires d'un Protestant* published in February. In August promised a post as a civilian physician with the East India Company on the coast of India but fails to reach his destination when on 21 December he cannot obtain post as hospital-mate on ship to India.

1759   Begins contributing to Smollett's *Critical Review* in January. Plan of travelling to India abandoned in March with news of French victories there. Publishes *An Enquiry into the Present State of Polite Learning in Europe* on 2 April. Henceforth known as 'Dr. Goldsmith' and soon included in his increasing literary acquaintance are Percy, Smollett, Murphy, Burke, Young and Johnson. Between 6 October and 24 November writes *The Bee*.

1759–60   Contributes essays to the *Busy Body*, the *Weekly Magazine*, the *Royal Magazine* and *Lady's Magazine*.

1760   On 24 January starts to contribute his 'Chinese Letters' to John Newbery's *Public Ledger* and continues the series until 14 August 1761. In the summer, moves from Green Arbour Court to No. 6 Wine Office Court, off Fleet Street.

1761   Percy describes meeting with G. and Johnson. G. probably meets Joshua Reynolds at this period.

1762   Between January and June contributes essays to *Lloyd's Evening Post* including 'The Revolution in Low Life'. The 'Chinese Letters' published in book form as *The Citizen of the World* on 1 May; this virtually marks the end of G.'s journalistic period and the start of his career as compiler and hack-writer, mainly for Newbery. *The Life of Richard Nash* published 14 October. On 28 October Newbery sells Collins, a Salisbury bookseller, a third share in *The Vicar of Wakefield* which he had bought from Goldsmith, arrested by bailiffs, through Johnson. Late in the year, G. moves to Canonbury House, Islington, to live with Newbery.

1764	A founder member of The Club, with Johnson, Reynolds, Burke, Garrick and others. On 26 June publishes *An History of England in a Series of Letters from a Nobleman to his Son*. During September moves to No. 2 Garden Court in the Temple. Sells his oratorio libretto *The Captivity* to Newbery and Dodsley on 31 October. 19 December publishes *The Traveller, or A Prospect of Society*.
1765	Publishes his *Essays*, collected from earlier publications, on 3 June, and in the same month moves to No. 3 King's Bench Walk in the Temple.
1766	*The Vicar of Wakefield* published at Salisbury on 27 March. In December publishes an anthology, *Poems for Young Ladies*, dated 1767.
1767	Friendship grows with Reynolds and his coterie, including Mrs. Horneck, a widow, and her two daughters. In April publishes his anthology, *The Beauties of English Poesy* and in the spring completes *The Good Natur'd Man*. John Newbery dies in December.
1768	First performance of *The Good Natur'd Man*, produced by Colman at Covent Garden, on 29 January. His brother, Henry, dies in May. Moves to No. 2 Brick Court in the Temple and acquires a cottage at Edgware with a friend, Edward Bott.
1769	In February contracts to write 'a new Natural History of Animals, etc.' for Griffin. *The Roman History* published 18 May. Contracts to write a history of England for Davies on 13 June. In December appointed Professor of Ancient History at the Royal Academy.
1770	*The Deserted Village* published by Griffin on 26 May. His *Life of Parnell* prefixed to an edition of *Parnell's Poems*. In the summer journeys to Paris with the Hornecks. Writes *The Haunch of Venison*, addressed to his friend Lord Clare.
1771	During the summer stays in a cottage near Hyde, working on his *History of England* and a new comedy. On 6 August his *History of England . . . to the Death of George II* is published.
1772	His *Threnodia Augustalis* performed 20 February. By August, seriously ill with a bladder infection.
1773	Contributes to the *Westminster Magazine*, including essays on the theatre, between January and March. *She Stoops to Conquer* produced by Colman at Covent

Garden on 15 March. Completes first volume of *Grecian History* by 22 June.

1774   Early in the year Garrick's satiric epitaph on G. read at a meeting of the club at St. James's Coffee-House provokes G's *Retaliation*, unfinished at his death. On 25 March, seriously ill with kidney trouble and fever. Dies on 4 April at the Temple; buried there five days later. *Retaliation* posthumously published 19 April. *History of the Earth, and Animated Nature* posthumously published 1 July. Abridgement of the *History of England* posthumously published 2 July. The *Grecian History* posthumously published 15 July.

1776   Monument by Nollekens erected in Westminster Abbey with Johnson's epitaph. *The Haunch of Venison* posthumously published.

Introduction

by ANDREW SWARBRICK

Whilst it is true that other writers of his generation are more highly esteemed by the modern age, Oliver Goldsmith hardly needs to be rescued from neglect. From the time his literary reputation began to grow in London to our own day, the nature of his personality and literary achievement has provoked persistent controversy, and more than one commentator has turned in relief to the colourful legends and anecdotes surrounding that elusive figure. Joshua Reynolds, writing shortly after Goldsmith's death, felt obliged to give a deliberately dispassionate account of his friend to counter 'the booksellers [who] have lived upon his reputation, as his friends have lived upon his character, ever since his death'. Still Goldsmith's personality continues to fascinate and perplex. It would seem that try as we might, more than two centuries after his death we find ourselves, when contemplating his work, turning again and again to a man of beguiling paradoxes. Goldsmith needs rescuing not from neglect, but from our own baffled affection for his charming naïvety.

In compiling this volume I have tried to restore serious critical attention to those classics of our literature created by Goldsmith as well as to certain areas of his life and work previously disregarded. For if we are puzzled by his complex personality, equally puzzling is that natural simplicity of his style which critics have noted from his day to our own. Writers as diverse as Johnson, Hazlitt, Scott, Goethe, Henry James and W. B. Yeats have tried to explain that limpid ease and

11

urbane elegance which seem, whilst inimitable, yet representative of their age. An understanding of the nature of Goldsmith's literary achievement is in danger of remaining as elusive as an understanding of the man, and it is as a further step towards such critical enlightenment that these essays have been assembled.

All but one of these studies have been written especially for this volume. (John Montague's essay, unavailable for some twenty years, so fits my purposes that I had no hesitation in departing from my original plan.) They are intended to offer a broad survey of Goldsmith's works—including such comparatively neglected writings as *Animated Nature* and *Retaliation*—whilst undertaking a detailed critical appraisal of particular texts. At the same time, I have tried to balance this literary criticism with studies of more general aspects of Goldsmith: his political inclinations; his classical inheritance; his place within certain eighteenth-century literary traditions and the whole complex business of our fictive 'Goldsmith-the-man'. The essays presented here are not, I hope, weighed down with learning, but have been written to take account of recent studies of Goldsmith. That a good number of contributors are practising poets is not accidental; neither is the fact that many are natives of Ireland, for Goldsmith's Irish origins are part of the very complexity of the man, as some of these chapters show. W. J. Mc Cormack, for instance, argues here in a wide-ranging study that not only do our efforts to recover the 'original', pristine Goldsmith founder on the rocks of a certain kind of historicism, but that our whole notion of the 'Anglo-Irish tradition' into which we try conveniently to assign him is in need of radical re-examination. On the same theme, Bernard Harris suggests that Goldsmith's plays represent the sometimes unhappy attempts of an isolated Irishman to find acceptance in an English culture he both embraces and subverts.

The reader of this volume will quickly discover that these essays do not conform to any single orthodoxy. On the contrary, I have positively welcomed those contributions which disagree one from another, with contrary assumptions and opinions rubbing shoulders. Goldsmith, after all, would not have found such inconsistency about himself surprising, and

nothing seems more damaging to a writer's reputation—
elevated or obscure—than a comfortable, settled orthodoxy of
agreement. Thus, for example, D. W. Jefferson returns to his
own influential essay of some thirty years ago, 'Observations on
The Vicar of Wakefield', and modifies some of the views he
expressed there whilst retaining the essential conviction that we
cannot read the novel as an exercise in irony, as a number of
recent studies would have us believe. However, this is implicitly
challenged by Seamus Deane, who argues that *The Citizen of the
World* is in fact deliberately and carefully ironical on a number
of levels. J. A. Downie, in comparing the satirical verse of
Goldsmith and Swift, reveals both Goldsmith's comparative
failure and the degree of his indebtedness to Swift, whilst
reminding us of the different kinds of satire we ought to expect
in the eighteenth century. Donald Davie, focusing on Goldsmith's political views as expressed in *The Deserted Village* and
The Traveller, forcefully contends that Goldsmith's politics hold
a challenging significance, and that it is *The Traveller* which is
the more provocative of the two poems. John Montague's essay
on *The Deserted Village* turns to Goldsmith's much discussed
'sentimentalism' and finds in the poem a carefully conceived
and highly effective rhetorical procedure, a structural precision
which Pat Rogers also analyses in his study of *The Traveller*.
Graham Parry and John Buxton discuss some relatively
neglected aspects of Goldsmith's work and show the extent of
his reliance on the assumptions and conventions of his age.

If there is one theme running through many of these essays, it
is the problem of originality. Whether we consider Goldsmith as
novelist, poet, dramatist or literary journeyman, we constantly
discover him as plagiarist. Much work has been done to show
that the premium we set on originality is inapplicable to
Goldsmith's age. Given that such notions were in any case
hazy, we are now in a position, surely, to suffer little dis-
comfiture in his popularization of other men's work which,
properly considered, is of a piece with his general conservatism.
T. S. Eliot, in his essay 'Poetry in the Eighteenth Century',
discussed the same problem:

> The originality of Goldsmith consists in his having the old and
> the new in such just proportion that there is not conflict; he is

13

> Augustan and also sentimental and rural without discordance
> . . . their [i.e. Goldsmith's and Johnson's] kind of originality is
> as remarkable as any other: indeed, to be original with the
> *minimum* of alteration is sometimes more distinguished than to
> be original with the *maximum* of alteration.

In his Introduction to *Goldsmith: The Critical Heritage* G. S.
Rousseau attacks these lines as typical of the modern age's
response to Goldsmith: a half-hearted, dutiful appreciation
expressed in 'so many clichés and worn phrases, critical tags
empty of meaning'. This seems to me a quite remarkable
misreading of Eliot in so grossly under-estimating the importance he attached to the *prosaic* quality of Johnson and
Goldsmith: 'We may say positively with Mr. Ezra Pound, that
verse must be at least as well written as prose.' Eliot was not
simply repeating the tired dictum about Johnson's being an
Age of Prose; he was being momentously earnest in proposing
that the first and minimum requirement of good poetry is that
it possess the virtues of good prose. And since the prose of
Goldsmith and his contemporaries itself drew upon the conventions of civilized *conversation*, it is not surprising that
conventional proprieties, the stock-in-trade features of a particular idiom, are carefully observed so that there is an easy
commerce between writer and reader. In style, subject, form,
manner of address, Goldsmith's originality lies not in *uniqueness*,
but in a sometimes perfect arrangement of those elements by
which speaks not an individual voice, but the voice of a
language at a particular phase of its development.

   Rousseau's lugubrious comments on the state of modern
criticism of Goldsmith do not make for sanguine reading,
though he surely overstates his case when he condemns the
'critical heritage' of the past century as 'one that is not much
more inspiring or perceptive than that of the first hundred
years of criticism nor which rescues from near obscurity its
maligned victim'. After the labours of R. S. Crane, Katharine
Balderston and Arthur Friedman, the brief but generous
essays of Henry James, T. S. Eliot, Virginia Woolf, even the
fruitfully provocative use Susanne Langer makes of *The
Deserted Village* in her philosophical treatise *Feeling and Form: A
Theory of Art*—Rousseau's remark, as it stands, hardly bears
examination. And when he goes on to say that, except for the

attentions of cultural historians of the Industrial Revolution, *The Traveller* and *The Deserted Village* have been 'buried forever' and that 'poets most of all, have forgotten them, don't read them, and probably never will again', I can imagine the outraged exclamations of at least two poets represented here (Donald Davie and John Montague) who have elsewhere made clear their own debts—as practising poets—to Goldsmith's achievement in these poems. But however exaggerated, Rousseau's remarks spring from a justifiable concern: that there is a paucity of contemporary evaluation of Goldsmith's literary achievements even as we continue to include his works on school and university curricula. The essays gathered here are an attempt to help remedy that poverty. If the contributors to this volume disagree in their judgements, if they bring radically different criteria to bear, that is only further evidence that literary criticism is not an exact science. Still evading our categories, it is 'poor Poll' himself who, in posterity as only rarely in his life, has the last word.

Editorial Note: quotations are taken from *Collected Works of Oliver Goldsmith*, ed. Arthur Friedman, 5 vols. © Oxford University Press 1966, by permission of Oxford University Press. Acknowledgement is also due to the Board of Trinity College, Dublin, for permission to transcribe and publish an extract from the Rev. John Goldsmith's Deposition of 1643.

John Montague's essay first appeared in *The Dolmen Miscellany of Irish Writing* (Dublin, 1962).

1

The Vicar of Wakefield and Other Prose Writings: A Reconsideration

by D. W. JEFFERSON

In the reassessment of authors that has taken place during the last half century, a process that has enhanced so many reputations, Goldsmith is not among those who have benefited, and the reason is not difficult to discover. His gifts were of the lighter kind. The aspects of eighteenth-century literature that he represents are akin to those associated with Addison, another Augustan who has not gained ground. Both writers had ease, grace, a pleasant humour. The present age attaches more importance to the deeper and weightier qualities of Samuel Johnson, whose work was scandalously underrated by critics in the nineteenth and earlier twentieth centuries, the supreme greatness of his finest prose going virtually unrecognized by generations of literary scholars and presumably of readers. That Johnson should now be receiving some of the praise so long withheld is very much as it should be, and it is not a matter for serious complaint if lighter talents should have suffered a degree of eclipse. But Goldsmith was greatly admired in Johnson's circle and he has been a much loved author for too long to be excluded from the kind of serious critical attention that others have received. Lightness is not the only issue. Sterne might be described as light by Johnsonian

17

standards: Johnson himself could have put it more crushingly, but Sterne's reputation has enjoyed enormous enhancement in recent decades. There is something elusive about the nature of Goldsmith's achievement, and about the merits of *The Vicar of Wakefield*, with which we shall be mainly concerned.

His characteristic qualities, of mind and style, probably need to be seen as limitations before their positive aspects can be appreciated, and a brief glance at some minor works may be of use here. In *The Vicar of Wakefield* he found a medium in which the limitations do not count as such. They become virtues because the effect lies so much in what is not attempted as well as in what is. A limited writer with artistic tact and a sense of the felicitous cannot only produce a masterpiece; he can throw light on the character of other masterpieces which attempt bigger things. The *Enquiry into the Present State of Polite Learning in Europe* (1759) is his earliest work of any importance, and while it provides some examples of his merits as a prose writer it also reveals characteristic weaknesses. The first impression it gives, as the question of cultural decline is broached in the opening pages, is of neatness and ease: 'The publick has been often excited by a false alarm, so that at present the nearer we approach the threatned period of decay, the more our fatal security increases' (I, 257).[1] His habit generally is to introduce topics with pleasantly turned phrases. His enterprise here involves the reduction of an enormously large area of material to a small compass; the course of ancient and modern learning, with reference in the modern period to several countries, is surveyed in about eighty pages. Goldsmith's light touch could have been entirely effective had it been combined with another quality: authority, evidence of solid knowledge, however little detail was to be used. The brief essay on the big subject can be an impressive literary vehicle, and of this there is no better example than Johnson's 'Introduction to the Political State of Great Britain', published three years before in the *Literary Magazine*: a masterly account of two centuries of history in about twenty pages, clear in outline, cool in manner, though with a few strokes of overwhelming moral condemnation of his country's policies. Goldsmith has no such strength. The prevailing attitude in the early chapters of the essay is of a facile Augustanism, an often embarrassing air of confidence in the value of a 'politeness' that can dismiss whole ages of bookishness and scholarly effort. 'Libraries were crammed, but not enriched with . . . works [which] effectually encreased our application, by professing to remove it.' '. . . if Terence could not raise [the reader] to a smile, Evantius was at hand, with a long-winded scholium to encrease his titillation' (I, 265, 266). Of the philosopher in the time of Lucian he says that 'he was chiefly remarkable for his avarice, his impudence, and his beard' (I, 268), one of several sallies that do no more for urbanity than for learning. He makes too frequent use of phrases like 'specious triflers' and 'speculative idlers'. The passage about men who 'carried on a petty traffic in some little creek . . . but never ventured out into the great ocean of knowlege' (I, 268) fails of its effect because Goldsmith himself gives so little evidence of important experience of the great writers or great issues of those ages. Occasionally there is a critical comment that makes eighteenth-century taste look absurdly provincial: '[Dante] addressed a barbarous people in a method suited to their apprehensions; united purgatory and the river Styx, St. Peter and Virgil . . . and shews a strange mixture of good sense and absurdity' (I, 274). But one passage at least may be quoted in which Augustan elegance and agility in phrasing are wedded to acute social observation. He is commenting on the conditions of authorship in France and England:

> The French nobility have certainly a most pleasing way of satisfying the vanity of an author, without indulging his avarice. A man of literary merit, is sure of being caressed by the Great, though seldom enriched. His pension from the crown just supplies half a competence, and the sale of his labours, makes some small addition to his circumstances; thus the author leads a life of splendid poverty, and seldom becomes wealthy or indolent enough, to discontinue an exertion of those abilities, by which he rose. With the English, it is different; our writers of rising merit are generally neglected; while the few of an established reputation, are over paid by a luxurious affluence. The first encounter every hardship which generally attends upon aspiring indigence; the latter, enjoy the vulgar, and, perhaps, the more prudent satisfaction of putting riches in competition with fame. Those are often seen to spend their

19

youth in want and obscurity; these are sometimes found to lead an old age of indolence and avarice. (I, 298–99)

He is at his best in places where his subject can be treated largely as one of social manners. Another example may be found in his rather refreshing comments on the poetic taste of the time. He objects to the current vogue of blank verse, and in general to a 'disgusting solemnity' in poetry. In both verse and prose he prefers the 'agreeable trifling which . . . often deceives us into instruction' (I, 319). In keeping with all this is his review of Gray's Odes (1757), where he laments that 'talents so capable of giving pleasure to all'—presumably in the *Elegy*—are 'exerted in efforts that, at best, can amuse only the few' (I, 112). In general he shows a preference for the literature of the early part of the century, which addressed itself to society and cultivated the virtue of ease, avoiding what he saw as heaviness and pedantry. But on the subject of blank verse one would have liked to know whether he responded to Thomson at his best. With no discussion of examples his comments here, as in most of the *Enquiry*, are somewhat superficial.

His limitations as well as his strengths are evident in his short biographical studies. Characteristically he begins his life of Bolingbroke on a promising note:

> There are some characters that seem formed by nature to take delight in struggling with opposition, and whose most agreeable hours are passed in storms of their own creating. The subject of the present sketch was perhaps of all others the most indefatigable in raising himself enemies, to shew his power in subduing them; and was not less employed in improving his superior talents, than in finding objects on which to exercise their activity. (III, 437)

A 'sketch' of these aspects of Bolingbroke would have been very acceptable; but as Friedman has shown, 'fully four-fifths' of the life were borrowed from the *Biographia Britannica*, and this was not material for the animated and personal account which the reader has been led to expect. Perhaps Goldsmith should not be judged on such obvious hackwork, but the discrepancy here gives an impression of irresponsibility. His life of Richard Nash is a different matter, and Donald A.

Stauffer couples it with Johnson's life of Savage as an example of biography that aims at a close study of the human truth with an attempt to weigh moral strengths and weaknesses. Quoting the preface in which he claims to have described 'the man as he was . . . , a weak man, governing weaker subjects', Stauffer writes that Goldsmith 'deserves the praise accorded to a pioneer'.[2] The formidable comparison with Johnson, which inevitably haunts the study of Goldsmith, was suggested by a contemporary writer in the *Monthly Review*: 'A trivial subject, treated for the most part in a lively, ingenious, and entertaining manner. Mr. Samuel Johnson's admirable Life of Savage seems to have been chosen as the model of this performance' (quoted by Friedman, III, 282–83). The contrast between the two could hardly be steeper. Johnson's theme is tragedy and inordinate failure, relieved by flashes of goodness, with scenes of an underworld of desolation which he himself had experienced. As an exercise of moral realism, magnanimity and compassion, it stands by itself. Goldsmith took as his subject a man whose career is a monument to values or vanities that belong to society at its most artificial. The choice, if it was made with Johnson's work in mind, might almost be an act of self-recognition, showing Goldsmith's awareness of his fitness for surfaces rather than depths. But it shows also his gift, not exhibited everywhere, for cultivating with fine judgement the possibilities of a limited theme. Limited it is, but Nash touched many lives and attracted notice in a great variety of ways; so what might be called his experiment at Bath had consequences which, to a modern reader, is of very considerable sociological and documentary significance. It was a happy instinct that caused Goldsmith to illustrate his biography with such a wealth of anecdotes, letters, public notices and, finally, obituary compositions, items which in other biographies of this time a reader might be tempted to pass over. We can be grateful that a writer of Goldsmith's quality saw it as a task worth performing, and that he made so much of it. An element of paradox is present from the outset in his reference to 'the pains he took in pursuing pleasure, and the solemnity he assumed in adjusting trifles' (III, 288), and in the early part of the life the emphasis is on the more trivial part of his character. After his first successes at Bath, the level of praise is modest: 'But to talk more simply, when we talk at best of trifles. None could possibly conceive a person more fit to fill this employment than *Nash*' (III, 301), and here the reference is to his easy manner with fashionable people and his general vivacity. But gradually the evidence accumulates of his practical ability, the initiative that led to the improvement of accommodation and amenities, and the laws governing behaviour which he put up in the Pump-room. Two of these, one concerning manners, the other morals, may be quoted: '3. That gentlemen of fashion never appearing in a morning before the ladies in gowns and caps, shew breeding and respect. . . . 10. That all whisperers of lies and scandal, be taken for their authors' (III, 303). There were strict hours at which dancing should begin and end, rules relating to the orderly departure of ladies, and he conducted skilful propaganda against the wearing of boots in the rooms. He also introduced measures to prevent duels. In all this, and in many other matters, Nash grows in our estimation as a genuine reformer, shaping the community in accordance with new styles of living, and making his contribution to the development of outlook that we associate with the names of Addison and Steele, though he fell so far short of them in seriousness. As the ups and downs of his character are traced, his lavish generosity along with his vanity and irresponsibility, his substantial share in the establishing of a hospital juxtaposed with his more whimsical acts of charity, his genuine efforts to protect female virtue and save gamesters from ruin against a background of his own wasteful folly and habitual ostentation, we may admire Goldsmith's control of the effect. Extreme old age, relative poverty, failure to change his ways when nature and fortune no longer supplied the means: with these sobering themes the record concludes. On its own level it is as balanced a study as the life of Savage, though of course it lacks the momentous heights and depths and the sombre eloquence.

Goldsmith's style is ideal for the depiction of Bath's social life. Writing of the primitive pleasures of this and other resorts he describes them as

> merely rural, the company splenetic, rustic, and vulgar. . . .
> People of fashion . . . usually spent that season amidst a solitude

22

of country squires, parsons wives, and visiting tenants. . . . To a person, who does not thus calmly trace things to their source, nothing will appear more strange, than how the healthy could ever consent to follow the sick to those places of spleen, and live with those, whose disorders are ever apt to excite a gloom in the spectator. The truth is, the gaming table was properly the salutary font, to which such numbers flocked. (III, 299)

'A solitude of country squires', 'the salutary font' are characteristic turns of phrase. The passages where Nash's character is summed up are full of well-shaped formulations; for example:

He was naturally endued with good sense; but by having been long accustomed to pursue trifles, his mind shrunk to the size of the little objects on which it was employed. His generosity was boundless, because his tenderness and his vanity were in equal proportion; the one impelling him to relieve misery, and the other to make his benefactions known. (III, 378)

What we learn from these works provides some approach to the question of where Goldsmith's gifts lie, and is relevant to our discussion of *The Vicar of Wakefield*; but the latter contains another element. It is a specifically Christian work, it exhibits values and beliefs the treatment of which must raise questions concerning the author's own central attitude to life. Goldsmith seems to have been a man of slender human capacity, and we can welcome the adjustment of his art whereby he succeeded in conveying these convictions without falsity. He chose a form which, as it were, reduces them to an appropriate scale. But there can be no doubt that he intends us to take them seriously. 'The hero of this piece', he writes in his Advertisement, 'unites in himself the three greatest characters upon earth; he is a priest, an husbandman, and the father of a family.' He dissociates himself from those who 'have been taught to deride religion', and who will therefore 'laugh at one whose chief stores of comfort are drawn from futurity'.

In an essay published over thirty years ago I discussed the process whereby the emotional effect of the calamities suffered by the vicar is reduced.[3] The episode of Olivia's abduction was described as 'between the serious and the comic', the account of the fire 'full of words which ought to suggest emotional intensity . . . but quite without emotiveness', the events

23

having all the marks of 'story-book contrivance'. Some components—the autobiographical digressions, for example— were categorized as miniature versions of familiar traditions, while the narrative as a whole was a much modified and attenuated Book of Job. This view still seems to me to be valid in many respects, but my statement of it was over-simplified and I now welcome the opportunity to reconsider it. The passage in which the vicar, who has endured so much pain and affliction but has succeeded in winning the support of his fellow-prisoners, preaches an eloquent sermon to them, now seems to me moving and beautiful. The refined Augustan idiom of the sermon, so unsuitable to the occasion if we imagine the scene realistically, is both elevated and discreet. The use of this convention in the eighteenth century could be regarded as a distancing of religion in the interests of good manners, but Johnson could use this kind of language with breath-taking effect, and Goldsmith's sermon, if rather light-weight compared with the great *Ramblers*, has genuine purity of feeling. No harm results from the fact that in some of the phrases ('To fly through regions unconfined as air, to bask in the sunshine of eternal bliss, to carroll over endless hymns of praise . . .') the vicar loses himself a little in his dreams (such standardized dreams too) of heavenly happiness. There is room for some amusement, but as an Augustan set-piece the episode has nobility.

All students of *The Vicar of Wakefield* should be aware of Robert H. Hopkins's lengthy discussion of the book and its critics.[4] Hopkins argues that the author's intention is satirical at the expense of the vicar, and this view, although I disagree with it, may be regarded as a helpful background against which to develop an alternative one. My belief is that Goldsmith offers us the vicar in the same spirit of com-mendation as the Advertisement would suggest, and that the modifying elements in the portrait which a satirical theory would make use of are not in fact to be interpreted so negatively. The style of character portrayal has kinship with conventions we are familiar with in earlier writers. They are more boldly exploited by Fielding, whose techniques are relevant here. Parson Adams on most occasions uses the challenging and dignified idiom of a man of God to which he is abundantly entitled, though his misjudgement of circumstances often renders his performances comic; but in Chapter 8 of the second book something very surprising happens. It is as if he had been caught with his cassock off. In his very plebeian tale concerning the more mundane side of his existence, his style changes: it rambles, he has become ordinary. Of Sir Thomas he says: 'I have always found his kitchen, and his cellar too, open to me: many a time, after service . . . have I recruited my spirits with a glass of his ale.' And later he speaks of the occasions, 'such as the approach of an election', when he has thrown 'a dash or two' into his sermons, for which Sir Thomas has been grateful. We have no reason to conclude that he has done anything very base, and this remarkable chapter does Adams no harm. But we are reminded that there may be a commonplace side to gospel Christians, and that a poor parson's life had exigencies, which is not surprising. What is more relevant here is that eighteenth-century characters in the comic tradition are creations of artifice and rhetoric, sometimes shifting from one idiom to another, revealing not only a different side of character but also a change of persona. Goldsmith's method is not the same as Fielding's, but the vicar must be seen in terms of the style with which he is endowed as narrator, and this style has a generally formalizing effect. We may begin with an example that raises only very mildly the controversial issues relating to the suggestion of satirical intention. In Chapter VI, after an evening of simple entertainment (with gooseberry wine and old songs), the vicar's family realize that it is too late to send their guest Mr. Burchell to an ale-house; so the younger children vie with each other in offering a share of their beds:

> 'Well done, my good children,' cried I, 'hospitality is one of the first christian duties. The beast retires to its shelter, and the bird flies to its nest; but helpless man can only find refuge from his fellow creature. The greatest stranger in this world, was he that came to save it. He never had an house, as if willing to see what hospitality was left remaining amongst us. Deborah, my dear,' cried I, to my wife, 'give those boys a lump of sugar each, and let Dick's be the largest, because he spoke first.'

Gooseberry wine and lumps of sugar belong to the same level, but it is the mark of Goldsmith's style that the Christian eloquence can be so easily accommodated. The amiable mood of the episode forestalls any suggestion that the vicar is too ready with his moral lesson or that the humble system of rewards is a ridiculous anti-climax. The amiability operates through the style. It is a matter of easy assimilation of one kind of discourse to another.

The easy manner in which the vicar can refer to his more peculiar eccentricities expresses sublime unawareness, and in some kinds of literature such a style could be used satirically; but the easy manner is also Goldsmith's and it invites us to be amused rather than critical. One of the vicar's most egregious peculiarities is his obsession with strict monogamy, which causes him to compose an epitaph for his 'only' wife

> . . . in which I extolled her prudence, œconomy, and obedience till death; and having got it copied fair, with an elegant frame, it was placed over the chimney-piece, where it answered several very useful purposes. It admonished my wife of her duty to me, and my fidelity to her; it inspired her with a passion for fame, and constantly put her in mind of her end. (Ch. II)

We enjoy the neatness of Goldsmith's wit too much to complain of the perverse neatness of the vicar's logic. We do not accept the vicar at his own valuation, obviously; but we accept him, and this means that we accept Goldsmith and the tone of the narration generally. It might be said that both the vicar and his creator appeal to and are in need of our good humour, though for different reasons. The reader soon realizes that acceptance of Goldsmith as a novelist entails tolerance of many devices (such as the rôle of Mr. Burchell) which are inept by normal standards. But in the Advertisement he pleaded that 'a book may be amusing with numerous errors', and readers have found part of their amusement in the exercise of the tolerance he solicits. Goldsmith's tone is such as to induce tolerance of the many episodes in this story of contemporary life which are reduced to a fairy tale primitiveness.

One of the characteristics of this kind of artifice in eighteenth-century fiction is that it does not invite us to translate it into 'reality'. When Joseph Andrews writes very much in the style of a servant to his sister, a fellow servant, and in a later chapter cries out in the exalted rhetoric of the romances in his sickroom delirium, we are not invited to ask questions about his actual range of verbal expression. There is no actuality. But we can trust Fielding to keep his novels so alive that such specifications are unnecessary. A character can be created by these comic means and yet give a sufficient impression of human solidity. A similar principle holds good for the vicar. Such questions as 'How naïve is the vicar?' are not invited.[5] The story demands that in some matters he should appear to be totally lacking in powers of observation and reflection, but partly because it *is* a necessity required by the story (just as Elizabethan dramatic plots may require special credulity in the characters who are to be deceived) we are never in a position to say quite what sort of person he 'really' is. It is not the intention of this kind of fiction that we should ask such questions.

Sometimes the play between the vicar's excellent literary manners and competence as a reporter, and his apparently imperfect recognition of what he is reporting, produces considerable piquancy. For example, he fails to identify Squire Thornhill's dubious guests in the fact of very plain evidence of their true character, which he presents as sharply as we could wish:

> The ladies of the town strove hard to be equally easy [i.e. compared with Olivia], but without success. They swam, sprawled, languished, and frisked; but all would not do: the gazers indeed owned that it was fine; but neighbour Flamborough observed, that Miss Livy's feet seemed as pat to the music as its echo. . . . One of them, I thought, expressed her sentiments upon this occasion in a very coarse manner, when she observed, that by the *living jingo*, she was all of a muck of sweat. Upon our return to the house, we found a very elegant cold supper. . . .

In conversation with the vicar's wife and daughters

> . . . they once or twice mortified us sensibly by slipping out an oath; but that appeared to me as the surest symptom of their distinction, (tho' I am since informed that swearing is perfectly unfashionable.) Their finery, however, threw a veil over any grossness in their conversation. (Ch. IX)

Goldsmith endows the vicar here with a shifting and slightly ambiguous persona, such as humorous writers have adopted to portray absurdities without immediately exploding them. We are accustomed to a shifting persona in *Gulliver's Travels*, though misguided readers in recent times have tried to establish consistency. Two chapters later the proposal is made to find jobs in London for Olivia and Sophia through these ladies' good offices, and the vicar registers not the slightest suspicion. There is no way of accounting for this except by recognizing that here we have a literary joke, which consists in stretching the credulity of a character beyond intelligibility. But *The Vicar of Wakefield* would not be the masterpiece it is if Goldsmith's strategies were not also a vehicle of meaning; though by its very nature the meaning is not to be precisely defined. Eighteenth-century fiction may be an issue of artifices, but ultimately we judge it as an imaginative state-ment about life. In exploring further the treatment of the vicar's relations with Mr. Thornhill we must try to understand what this highly artificial work is achieving.

In the passage where the vicar and his family receive from the landlord of an inn their first information about Mr. Thornhill the vicar's narrative gives Augustan neatness and polish and a flavour of comedy of manners, as well as moral correctness, to his statement:

> This gentleman he described as one who desired to know little more of the world than its pleasures, being particularly remarkable for his attachment to the fair sex. He observed that no virtue was able to resist his arts and assiduity, and that scarce a farmer's daughter within ten miles round but what had found him successful and faithless. Though this account gave me some pain, it had a very different effect upon my daughters, whose features seemed to brighten with the expectation of an approaching triumph, nor was my wife less pleased and confident of their allurements and virtue. (Ch. III)

The sexual response of the female members of the family rather modifies the image of ideal domestic, social and Christian order which, in an equally composed style, he describes in the next chapter:

> The little republic to which I gave laws, was regulated in the following manner: by sun-rise we all assembled in our common

appartment; the fire being previously kindled by the servant. After we had saluted each other with proper ceremony, for I always thought fit to keep up some mechanical forms of good breeding, without which freedom ever destroys friendship, we all bent in gratitude to that Being who gave us another day. (Ch. IV)

The order so felicitously depicted by the vicar is continually subverted by the elementary follies and vanities of wife and daughters in ways that could only occur in literature. Only in literature could the harmony and its disruption co-exist on such easy terms. Contradictions in real life could be much more complex and disturbing.

Sociability between the squire and the vicar's family immediately develops. When Mr. Thornhill makes an offer which amounts to a proposal to take Olivia into 'keeping', the vicar's resentment is on the grounds of honour, of which his family has the nicest sense: 'Honour, sir, is our only possession at present, and of that last treasure we must be particularly careful', as if family honour were the only issue at stake. We must ask ourselves whether the vicar's urbanity as a host, his reluctance to mention sin and damnation on a social occasion, accounts for this response, or whether some Augustan principle of moderation prompts him to withhold the more solemn sanctions when principles drawn from social custom are adequate for the occasion. He goes as far as urbanity could go when he apologizes for speaking so warmly, and Mr. Thornhill goes as far as moral unawareness (or is it insolence?) could go when he says:

> 'I protest nothing was farther from my heart than such a thought. No, by all that's tempting, the virtue that will stand a regular siege was never to my taste; for all my amours are carried by a coup de main.' (Ch. IX)

These words offend the two whores, who then

> began a very discreet and serious dialogue upon virtue: in this my wife, the chaplain, and I, soon joined; and the 'Squire himself was at last brought to confess a sense of sorrow for his former excesses. We talked of the pleasures of temperance, and of the sun-shine in the mind unpolluted with guilt. . . . Mr. Thornhill even went beyond me, and demanded if I had any objection to giving prayers. (Ch. IX)

What are we to make of this; that is, if explanations need to be attempted? One view might be that the vicar's complaisance, respectable in this situation, is exploited by the cynical Thornhill, who then fools him with his assumed piety. But Goldsmith's game is surely more interesting than this. In a society where such mixtures of moral types might occur in company, rôles could change in unexpected ways. It is almost as surprising to find the vicar's wife discoursing on virtue as the London ladies. Can we be sure that the rake, if not genuine in his wish for prayers, is not at least desirous of making a conventionally harmonious gesture? But it must again be stressed that Goldsmith is not depicting his world realistically. His story demands distortions of attitudes and rôles. Yet such passages may tell us more about the eighteenth century, and the chaotic pressures and confusions within a society that liked to see itself in orderly terms, than straight social history. They are not translatable into social history, but they provide us with images of the comic imagination which raise questions about the reality.

These are not the images for which the book is best known, and most of those who have loved it have associated it with less problematic issues. *The Vicar of Wakefield* may be numbered among those late eighteenth-century texts, along with Cowper's *The Task* of nearly two decades later, in which the love of nature and the love of domesticity are pleasantly combined: an unpretentious expression of the English spirit which has become permanent. As in *The Task*, the drinking of tea gives completion to the Englishness:

> At a small distance from the house my predecessor had made a seat, overshaded by an hedge of hawthorn and honeysuckle. Here, when the weather was fine, and our labour soon finished, we usually sate together, to enjoy an extensive landscape, in the calm of the evening. Here too we drank tea. . . . (Ch. V)

Older features of the English popular tradition are also represented with an agreeable explicitness and fullness that remind one of Washington Irving's *Sketch Book*, another work which was endlessly reprinted in the nineteenth century. And, of course, Goldsmith, like Irving, has the viewpoint of a non-English connoisseur of the scene. The Virgilian *O fortunatos . . . agricolas*, another eighteenth-century theme, is in the background of the following passage:

> Remote from the polite, they still retained the primaeval simplicity of manners, and frugal by habit, they scarce knew that temperance was a virtue. They wrought with chearfulness on days of labour; but observed festivals as intervals of idleness and pleasure. They kept up the Christmas carol, sent true love-knots on Valentine morning, eat pancakes on Shrove-tide, shewed their wit on the first of April, and religiously cracked nuts on Michaelmas eve. (Ch. IV)

The style is such that it does not matter in the least whether any such rural perfection still existed, or had ever existed. The truth about any rural community would in any case include more than is suggested here. And there is the most obvious and elementary favourite: the episode of the green spectacles. It may not be a great example of wit, but it has no doubt been the sole representative of the coney-catching *genre* for countless readers. The gullibility of the innocent is one of the most familiar of themes and in this story the combination of the amusing with the innocuous was to be an infallible recommendation in the coming century. But there is more than this. With his genius for simplicity Goldsmith creates something like a fairy tale.

The twentieth century, which looks closely into texts and can even find a satirical intention in this one, may not easily appreciate Goldsmith's success in creating a work which became a legend. One understands only too well why Thackeray, after recoiling from Sterne, should have taken such pleasure in the thought of Goldsmith's 'sweet story'. With a few passages taken out it meets Victorian requirements for domestic literature, but this does not help its reputation today. This aspect of the legend is relevant historically because when the nineteenth century, so concerned with improvement, looked at the past, it was glad to have figures like Addison, Goldsmith and Cowper to represent a century in which other figures were in some respects alien or disquieting. But Goldsmith's more lasting achievement was the creation of a work which conveys quintessentially and with wonderful freshness certain parts of the English scene in an age when the scene

31

was about to change. His instinctive sense of history, his artist's recognition of his rôle in relation to the changing world, is exquisitely manifest in his choice of subject for *The Deserted Village*. This was a poem that had to be written, and his authorship of this very special epitaph would be enough to place Goldsmith among the immortals, if he had done nothing else. *The Vicar of Wakefield* has none of its poignant feeling for worlds lost or about to be lost. And yet it too is a monument. Goldsmith could not have realized in what sense it was to be a monument, because he could not have foreseen the impossibility in the fiction of later periods of the peculiarly Augustan combination of elements present here. As a recapitulation in miniature of so many old fictional *motifs* it is an appropriate product of the decade before the old tradition ceased with the death of Smollett. As a personal achievement, a work of art within the limits of a genius that is at ease with its limits, it stands as a monument to virtues which greater writers of later periods have not always shown.

NOTES

1. All quotations from Goldsmith are given from the text of the *Collected Works of Oliver Goldsmith*, ed. Arthur Friedman, 5 vols. (Oxford, 1966). Volume and page numbers of this edition are cited except for quotations from *The Vicar of Wakefield* which have only chapter numbers.
2. Donald A. Stauffer, *The Art of Biography in Eighteenth-century England* (Princeton and Oxford, 1941), p. 383.
3. D. W. Jefferson, 'Observations on *The Vicar of Wakefield*', *The Cambridge Journal*, 3, No. 10 (1950), pp. 621–28.
4. Robert H. Hopkins, *The True Genius of Oliver Goldsmith* (Baltimore, 1969), pp. 166–230. Sven Bäckman's *This Singular Tale. A Study of 'The Vicar of Wakefield' and its Literary Background* (Lund, 1971), which contributes valuable information and insights on points relating to the vicar and other characters, follows Stuart Tave, with some reservations, in placing the vicar among the 'amiable humorists'.
5. This principle applies to the question 'How witty is he?' Ronald Paulson attributes wit to him, but if he is credited with all of Goldsmith's wit his naïvety becomes difficult to place. See *Satire and the Novel in Eighteenth Century England* (New Haven and London, 1967), p. 271.

2

Goldsmith's *The Citizen of the World*

by SEAMUS DEANE

The one hundred and nineteen Chinese letters, which first appeared in the daily newspaper *The Public Ledger* in late January 1760 and appeared weekly thereafter until 14 August 1761 were collected, with additions, in two volumes, published in 1762 under the title *The Citizen of the World; or Letters from a Chinese Philosopher, Residing in London, to his Friends in the East.* On the 14 October 1762, *The Life of Richard Nash, of Bath, Esq;* appeared. Both works betray an almost parasitic dependence on the writings of others. Yet they manage to achieve a degree of distinction all the more remarkable, given their origin as paid hack-work, done by Goldsmith for the publisher John Newbery. Goldsmith's blatant plagiarizing of his sources (the *Lettres chinoises* of the Marquis d'Argens and John Wood's *Essay towards a Description of Bath* are the best known examples) and his readiness to pad his material (especially evident towards the close of *The Life of Richard Nash*) would seem to disqualify any attempt to consider these works as notable and coherent works of art. However, this is not the case. They have their own internal coherence and they help to reveal the coherence which characterizes Goldsmith's collected writings, most particularly *The Vicar of Wakefield* (1766) and *The Good Natur'd Man* (1768). The treatment of the theme of misplaced benevolence and its embodiment in characters of a suspiciously sweet disposition is an insistent preoccupation in all of these

33

works. By looking at this afresh and by recognizing its connection with the fiction of the foreign, or, more specifically, the Oriental traveller, we may learn to appreciate the subtlety and the power of Goldsmith's irony with renewed enjoyment.

The history of the Oriental tale in eighteenth-century literature is well known and need not be rehearsed in any detail here.[1] Since the publication of Montesquieu's famous *Lettres Persanes* in 1721, a variety of writers, Lord Lyttelton, the Marquis d'Argens and Horace Walpole among them, had established a vogue for the kind of tale in which Oriental travellers, visiting a European country, remarked on its oddities and corruptions in a series of letters home, avowing at all times the degree to which their *faux-naïf* innocence had been shocked by what they had observed and experienced. The difficulties of sustaining the credibility of the traveller's Oriental credentials worried some commentators but never so far as actually to influence the practice of the writers. Goldsmith reviewed a work called *Letters from an Armenian in Ireland, to his Friends at Trebisonde*, for *The Monthly Review* in 1757. He began resoundingly:

> The Writer who would inform, or improve, his countrymen, under the assumed character of an Eastern Traveller, should be careful to let nothing escape him which might betray the imposture. If his aim be satirical, his remarks should be collected from the more striking follies abounding in the country he describes, and from those prevailing absurdities which commonly usurp the softer name of fashions. His accounts should be of such a nature, as we may fancy his Asiatic friend would wish to know,—such as we ourselves would expect from a Correspondent in Asia. (I, 90–1)

It is true that the Armenian in Ireland fails to keep up the mildest pretence of being an Armenian. But, equally, it is true that Goldsmith forgot his own words five years later when he came to write his own Chinese letters. Lien Chi Altangi has many qualities which recommend him to our attention, but being credibly Chinese is not one of them. He pays as close attention to the manners and politics of English society as did the Armenian to those of Irish society. He is in fact an insider who has created a form of freedom for himself by the pretence of being an outsider. The Chinese fiction increases the opportunities for irony. It allows reportage to assume an air of innocence when it is in fact determined by polemical intent. It also helps to bring the whole question of civilization into the centre of the various debates and issues raised in the course of the narrative. For the foreign commentary on native customs has something more than a tonic effect on provinciality. It questions the shared assumptions upon which European civilization rested, all the more forcefully because of the high reputation China then enjoyed as the most civilized of all the Asiatic nations.

Goldsmith paid serious attention to the problem of civilization, its rise and fall in various parts of the world, the features which distinguished it, the symptoms which bespoke its decline. This is not surprising in a century which had consistently shown itself to be fascinated by the apparently exemplary fall of Rome (incomparably analysed by Montesquieu and Gibbon), and by the threatened fall of the British or French states, under the influence of Walpole and Louis XV respectively. For Goldsmith, his age lived in the twilight of the true Augustan period which had come to an end with the accession of George I to the throne and Walpole to power.[2] The writers who lived in 'the illustrious reigns of Queen Anne and Lewis XIV' were, in his opinion, so far superior to his contemporaries that they 'not only did honour to their respective countries, but even to human nature' (I, 291). Since then, however, the decline in the system of patronage, the consequent dependence of the writer upon the bookseller and the degradation of literary standards which resulted, are all marks of the failure of Augustan civilization to sustain itself in eighteenth-century England. In a group of essays written for *The Royal Magazine* in 1759–60, under the title *The Proceedings of Providence vindicated. An Eastern Tale*, Goldsmith wondered at the way in which the states of Asia minor had, after glorious achievements, 'relapsed into more than the pristine barbarity' (III, 83). Of all the Asiatic countries only 'the polite Chinese' (III, 79) seemed to him to have escaped the breakdown which had afflicted the others. The various reasons he adduces for this, including the influence of climate, are not very persuasive. Yet the problem was there, it was felt to be central, it had its contemporary parallels and analogies, and yet it was insoluble. Goldsmith's satire, as that of his contemporaries, might be less easily countered if we could recreate the sense of crisis which he knew and which yet seems so remote from the structure and tone of his wonderfully versatile and serene prose.

Nothing attracted the scorn of the satirist in the age of Walpole more than English society's submission to the demands of fashion. Principles, which they sought to define in universal terms, were abandoned when the vogue for things Gothic or things Chinese held sway. This was more particularly the case when the vogue was associated with certain political attitudes or loyalties. William Mason and Horace Walpole both regarded the taste for the so-called Chinese garden as part of an attempt to undermine those English liberties of which the English garden itself had become, for them, a natural symbol. They regarded it as an essentially Tory fashion, culturally and politically retrograde in its effects. William Chambers, whose three famous works *Designs of Chinese Buildings, Furniture, Dresses, Machines, and Utensils* (1757), *Plans, Elevations, Sections, and Perspective Views of the Gardens and Buildings at Kew in Surry* (1763) and *A Dissertation on Oriental Gardening* (1772) established him as one of the leaders in this fashion for China and its artifacts, bore the brunt of these attacks.[3] But the absurdities to which the fashion led were by no means confined to gardening. Literature, interior decoration, porcelain, furniture were all affected by it. The ludicrous and frequently insipid innovations which it produced were regarded by devout Whigs as symptoms of a decadence which threatened what Burke was later to praise as the 'manly, moral regulated liberty'[4] of the English. The austerity which is part of the Whig aesthetic, itself integral to the English Whig conception of liberty, was by nature opposed to the luxurious tastes and frippery which fashion promoted. It led, it then seemed, to a trivialization of serious matters, deflecting attention away from true worth and placing ephemeral glamour in its stead. It was one of Goldsmith's constant laments that, in the world of letters, the writer of genuine merit had been reduced to the rôle of a hack, competing in the market-place with writers who were as devoid of genius as they were of principle. He would have preferred the retention of the system of patronage, revealing thereby his hostility to the increasing dominance of middle-class commercial values in his society.[5] He clearly saw his own position as victim to that dominance while being at the same time a satirist of its increasingly vulgar success. Thus, his adaptation of the fiction of a Chinese traveller as commentator on English habits and customs, is not simply a means of preserving a satiric perspective on their foibles. The fact that the traveller is Chinese is itself a satiric device.

Although the Oriental tale as such contributed a good deal to Goldsmith's adaptation of this sub-genre for his *The Citizen of the World*, only Montesquieu, among its various practitioners, could be said to have produced, in the *Lettres Persanes*, a work which was analogous to it in any deeper respect. The Voltairian *conte* (*Candide, Micromégas, Zadig*) and Johnson's *Rasselas* are of the same family. Yet in comparison with these, Goldsmith's work seems to be much less organized towards a particular aim or effect. It has the air of a miscellany, mixing together various commentaries on the contemporary London scene with individual comic portraits (like that of Beau Tibbs and his wife), and absurdly far-fetched and sentimental stories, like those of Lien Chi Altangi himself and of the Man in Black. The impression of a uniformity which overrides this apparently infelicitous mixture is given, initially at least, by the style of the work. Perhaps it would be more accurate to speak, not simply of the style, but of the attitude towards writing and the function of the writer to which Goldsmith frequently refers throughout all his works and which, in its conviction, helps to determine the tone of his address to the reader. In this respect, he makes a contrast with Dr. Johnson, as is well-known, but he also enters into and plays an important rôle in an ongoing debate on the function of the writer in an age of increasing specialization. In his Preface to *A General History of the World* (1764), Goldsmith indicates his preference for an account that will be both

> concise and perspicuous, tho' it must be candidly confessed, that we sate down less desirous of making a succinct history than a pleasing one; we sought after elegance alone, but accidentally found conciseness in our pursuit. (V, 285)

His attack upon critics in *An Enquiry into the Present State of Polite Learning in Europe* (1759) and his explanation of the decay of ancient letters are united by the single theme that the separation of learning from 'common sense', effected by the critics, made it 'the proper employment of speculative idlers'. Those who render 'learning unfit for uniting and strengthening civil society' (I, 267) are virtuosos, specialists, who create a professional jargon of their own and batten on the original work of true writers in order to prolong and justify their own trifling endeavours. It is interesting, later in the century, to find that this distinction between specious jargon and writing, which, by being perspicuous and elegant, retains its necessary social function, is transformed into a debate between the solid learning of the English historian and the sprightly, shallow elegance of the French. It is one of those instances in which an admired quality, like the Whig austerity Goldsmith so encouraged, becomes separated from the clear compendious style which was regarded as its necessary literary accompaniment under the pressure of a changing political situation. To be solemn and learned, even given to specialized language, became a virtue in the '90s, although it was widely regarded as a vice in the '60s. The reconciliation between the two attitudes was finally achieved by Gibbon, in his *Decline and Fall of the Roman Empire*, a work famously elegant and appropriately learned.[6] Appropriate too was its subject matter: the concern with the reasons for the decline of ancient civilization. Goldsmith was exercised by this problem, as we have seen, but it had less dramatic relevance during his lifetime than it was to have during Gibbon's, when the spectacle of the French Revolution dominated the European imagination. Nevertheless, Goldsmith's contribution to the debate is valuable in itself and in its clarification of his attitude towards the supremacy of that kind of writing which entertains and instructs the reader. His attitude towards speculation for its own sake is close to that of Burke. It is to both of them a vacuous and dangerous exercise, the product of the age's hunger for compilations, digests, ready-made knowledge. This was fostered by the booksellers who could see that this kind of thing would sell to the increasingly large bourgeois audience. It was also fostered by Goldsmith's own activities, although here again he tried to disclaim his part in the propagation of knowledge and in the fashionable taste for packaged learning and culture. He trod an uneasy path between his desire to strengthen public morality and his fear of being nothing more than a hired hack of the avaricious bookseller. Again in the *Enquiry* we read:

> If the present enquiry were a topick of speculative curiosity, calculated to fill up a few vacant moments in literary indolence, I should think my labour ill bestowed. To rank in the same despicable class with the dissertations, aenigmas, problems, and other periodical compilations with which even idleness is cloyed at present, is by no means my ambition. True learning and true morality are closely connected; to improve the head will insensibly influence the heart, a deficiency of taste and a corruption of manners are sometimes found mutually to produce each other. (I, 259)

Thus, however we may admire the lucidity of Goldsmith's language in *The Citizen of the World*, we do better to think of it in relation to his general theory of writing rather than an illustration of his idiosyncratic gift. For whatever his gifts were, Goldsmith always used them in the service of a corporate ideal of civilization and the necessity of maintaining it on the basis of truth by the articulation of principles. He is recognizably a child of the Enlightenment in his anxieties and beliefs, believing in the necessity of society, in the ultimacy of the distinction between politeness and barbarism, in the utility of knowledge and the writer's function in promoting it in alliance with morality. The achievement of civil society in Europe was something to be improved and defended. He therefore shared the attraction of his contemporaries for the polite society of China, which had, it seemed, persisted in an Asia where all former civilizations had collapsed. Yet he was very far from being a radical thinker, having no appreciation of Rousseau's importance, being hesitant about the main developments in English politics, especially insofar as they seemed to threaten a diminution of the powers of the monarch. His Chinese traveller, seen in the most obliging and positive light, is a member of a polite society who discovers in a European capital, some worrying signs of an incipient barbarism. Most of these are obvious and will bear recital. But among the less obvious but more pervasive signs of this sort are the instabilities of conduct which proceed from the indulgence in various kinds of sentimental philanthropy epitomized directly by the Man in Black and obliquely by Lien Chi Altangi himself.

The vogue for China and the vogue for an excessive form of philanthropic sentimentality are ironically combined with one another in *The Citizen of the World*. Goldsmith does not only exploit the traveller's tale; he exploits the traveller in the tale as much as he exploits the people, or, more accurately, the types with whom the traveller meets. Lien Chi Altangi and the Man in Black have two different kinds of function within the work. One is to comment upon the frailties of others, the defects of society in general. As such, they are no more than mouthpieces. Their other function is less obvious but more subtly intricate. They are representatives of the Man of Reason and of the Man of Feeling, respectively. Lien Chi reasons with his son Hingpo, the only member of his family to escape the wrath of the Chinese emperor who has enslaved Altangi's family, to bear misfortune with stoical endurance, to give up his passion for the beautiful Zelis, to follow, in effect, the example of Confucius and of Altangi himself. Yet Altangi's wisdom seems to become more proverbially confident as the misfortunes of others increase. Insofar as Altangi is 'Chinese', a member of a 'polite' society, he is an egotistic fool given to moral maxims. He embodies rationality untempered by experience or common feeling. As such, he has many counterparts in eighteenth-century literature. His search for happiness through knowledge, his desire to live invulnerable to the vicissitudes of fortune, is absurd. He condemns himself out of his own mouth.

> . . . a man who leaves home to mend himself and others is a philosopher; but he who goes from country to country, guided by the blind impulse of curiosity, is only a vagabond. (II, 41)

Swift's Gulliver, Voltaire's Candide, Johnson's Rasselas and the more obscure heroes of the radical novels of the 1790s, share with Lien Chi Altangi the capacity to be vagabonds and doctrinaire together, almost ineducable in the face of their varied and sometimes shocking, sometimes incredible experiences. In an odd way, this literary type seems to have found later actual embodiment in William Godwin, although it is probably more sensible to envisage Godwin as the epitome of a kind of doctrinaire rationality so common that the literature of the time was doing no more than registering this as one of the new but characteristic aberrations of the modern, innovatory spirit. The persistent connection between the Man of Reason and the foreign traveller survived after Goldsmith's death. As late as 1792, a Mrs. A. M. Mackenzie produced a novel, *Slavery; or, the Times*, in which an African prince, a combination of the Noble Savage and the Man of Reason, comes to England to comment on its numerous irrational and inhumane practices. The Oriental traveller is not far removed in some respects from the Noble Savage, since, although he may have the advantages of being a member of a polite and cultured society, he has also the kind of ignorance and capacity for surprise which we associate with the untutored and un-sophisticated being who sees as odd that which convention has decreed to be normal. Lien Chi Altangi's foreignness is exploited by Goldsmith to expose his own as well as English provinciality. But it also is used to disturb unquestioned assumptions about what constitutes normality in any society. Of its nature, travel literature raised issues of an anthro-pological and sociological kind. It made the idea of culture a subject for speculation and, later, of research.

A good deal of the commentary in *The Citizen of the World* is concerned with the various issues raised by the recent devel-opments in the English social structure. Among these is the increase in the output of books, the consequent replacement of the preacher by the writer as the acknowledged instructor of the masses, the failure of the society to reward the writer sufficiently for the new and important services which he now performs. Letters LVII and LXXV concentrate on these matters. In the latter, we read:

> In proportion as society refines, new books must ever become more necessary. Savage rusticity is reclaimed by oral admonition alone; but the elegant excesses of refinement are best corrected by the still voice of studious enquiry. In a polite age, almost every person becomes a reader, and receives more instruction from the press than the pulpit. The preaching Bonse may instruct the illiterate peasant; but nothing less than the insinuating address of a fine writer can win its way to an heart already relaxed in all the effeminacy of refinement. Books are

41

necessary to correct the vices of the polite, but those vices are
ever changing, and the antidote should be changed accordingly;
should still be new. (II, 311–12)

In the same letter, Altangi goes on to assert that the country
where the writer has gained pre-eminence over the preacher is
more enlightened, less given to 'ignorance, superstition, and
hopeless slavery' (II, 313). This is interesting sociological
information, especially as we are later informed that even the
hack-writers, the dunces of the trade, have a useful function to
perform in England (if not in France). Of course, the question
of the reliability of this report is unavoidable. Given that the
facts may themselves be sufficiently accurate, the viewpoint
may still be tendentious, directed towards Altangi in an ironic
spirit or indulged by Goldsmith as one of his own idio-
syncratically obsessive themes. In other words, the commentary on social changes and practices would seem to be
threatened at all times by the ironic undercurrents which the
narrative form sets in motion, or its importance would seem to
run the risk of being diminished by the strong element of
special pleading which Goldsmith might bring to any particular issue or cause. Yet, in this letter, and in the whole work,
the possibility of relief from the instabilities of the narrative
method is left open. The last paragraph reads

> Thus even dunces, my friend, may make themselves useful. But
> there are others whom nature has blest with talents above the
> rest of mankind; men capable of thinking with precision, and
> impressing their thought with rapidity. Beings who diffuse
> those regards upon mankind, which others contract and settle
> upon themselves. These deserve every honour from that com-
> munity of which they are more peculiarly the children, to such I
> would give my heart, since to them I am indebted for its
> humanity! (II, 314)

Although this idealized portrait is given by a narrator whom
we have learned to suspect, it is nevertheless one which we can
accept at face value. For the appeal to a corporate ideal, to the
idea of humanity, is never seriously undermined by Goldsmith
in this or any other of his writings. The uniformity of human
nature, the universality of great literature, the affective
function of such writing—these were all convictions which he

shared with most of his important contemporaries and which underlay his whole conception of civilization itself.

There is, therefore, ground for confidence in believing that *The Citizen of the World* does establish a norm by virtue of which we can measure the various and often acute angles of ironic refraction which otherwise complicate its surface. Much of the comedy supplied by figures like Beau Tibbs is heightened by the descriptive precision of the set pieces in which he and his ilk are displayed. Letter LXXI, the account of the evening spent at Vauxhall Gardens, almost entirely dispenses with Altangi as narrator-traveller, while the succeeding letter, in which the Marriage Act of 1753 is censured, restores him to his central position as commentator on the oddities of the country's laws. Letter LXXIII reintroduces Altangi at the height of his moral bent—'Age', we are told in the opening sentence, 'that lessens the enjoyment of life encreases our desire of living' (II, 303). Such *sententiae* have their own independent force, but it is obliquely rendered in this instance by being cast as Altangi's opinion. These variations in emphasis are not so extreme as to leave the reader in any confusion. On the other hand, the weight of each sentence has to be carefully assayed for the ironic ingredient which it may contain. The story is not retarded by the ironic procedure, but the reader's reception of it is almost always restrained by the tonal ambiguity of the writing. A similar, if more intense example of this is to be found in Jane Austen's novels. As in them, criteria of worth exist and are applied; but the degree to which any single figure embodies those criteria is always questionable.

This may not seem to be the case with the Man in Black. Two attitudes have dominated the audience's reception of him since he first appeared in the pages of *The Public Ledger*. One, more common in Victorian times than now, was to regard him in an altogether favourable light as an example of true feeling abashed by its own irresistible force and by the contrast it made with the more selfish and cooler feelings of the world he affected to imitate.[7] The other, more common in recent years, has been to regard him as a pathological case, given to displays of idiotic generosity for reasons which are neurotically rather than rationally produced.[8] It is certainly the case that

43

some of Goldsmith's best-known creations—the Vicar, Honeywood in *The Good Natur'd Man*, Beau Nash and the Man in Black—all practise benevolence with effects which are disastrous. The Man in Black is indeed a version of the Man of Feeling, that lachrymose philanthropist whose very foolishness is endearing. From Squire Allworthy in Fielding to the terrifyingly sincere preachers of Bage's and Holcroft's novels in the '90s, this figure appears even more frequently than did his counterpart, the Man of Reason. Sterne's loving parody of Yorick's endless capacity for exaggerated sensibility in the *Sentimental Journey* is a gentler treatment than Goldsmith's portraits. The straightforwardly didactic versions of the sentimental hero, given in novels like Henry Brooke's *The Fool of Quality* (1766–70) and Henry Mackenzie's *The Man of Feeling* (1771), itself deeply influenced by *The Vicar of Wakefield*, entirely lack that nefarious sweetness of disposition which make Goldsmith's characters so ambiguously attractive. The lack of common prudence in their conduct is emphasized time and again.[9] Letter XXVII, in which we are given the inset story of the Man in Black (with its strong redolence of Goldsmith's own childhood and his own imprudently benevolent father), opens in such a manner as to leave the note of acerbity distinctly audible:

> As there appeared something reluctantly good in the character of my companion, I must own it surprized me what could be his motives for thus concealing virtues which others take such pains to display. I was unable to repress my desire of knowing the history of a man who thus seemed to act under continual restraint, and whose benevolence was rather the effect of appetite than reason. (II, 112)

Once more, as we remind ourselves that the speaker is Lien Chi Altangi, that monument to calm rationality in the midst of distress, we cannot but hesitate on the final word 'reason'. Yet the story which follows is a cautionary tale which demonstrates the dangers and the futility of this kind of impulsive and uncontrolled philanthropy, especially when it is seen to be a form of appetite which neither reason nor affected cynicism can effectively quell. Goldsmith's most penetrating analysis of the strong element of egoism involved in the desire to be, and to be known to be, philanthropic is found in his account of the career of Richard Nash. In that short account, we are constantly faced with two versions of Nash's career. One version emphasizes its pathos, the other its triviality. When they converge, they do so to ponder the phenomenon of this petty King of Bath and the degree to which he was a symptom of the age's outstanding characteristics:

> Whatever might have been Mr. *Nash's* other excellencies, there was one in which few exceeded him; I mean his extensive humanity. None felt pity more strongly, and none made greater efforts to relieve distress. If I were to name any reigning and fashionable virtue in the present age, I think it should be charity. The numberless benefactions privately given, the various public solicitations for charity, and the success they meet with, serve to prove, that tho' we may fall short of our ancestors in other respects, yet in this instance we greatly excel them. I know not whether it may not be spreading the influence of Mr. *Nash* too widely to say, that he was one of the principal causes of introducing this noble emulation among the rich; but certain it is, no private man ever relieved the distresses of so many as he did. (III, 333)

As in the story of the Man in Black, the history of Nash illustrates the dangers and the foolishness of improvidence and emphasizes to what degree it was, in his case, a fashionable, rather than a moral, phenomenon.

The apparent opposition between the inert rationality of the Chinese traveller and the impulsive generosity of the Man in Black is rather absurdly reconciled at the level of the sentimental story when Altangi's son, Hingpo, marries the beautiful Christian captive Zelis, who is discovered to be the niece of the Man in Black. This happy-ever-after ending is perhaps nothing more than a desperate attempt on Goldsmith's part to have done with the Chinese letters, even if it meant catering to the sickly sentimental taste which he had so insistently satirized. On the other hand, the marriage, laughable as it is, domesticates the foreign traveller and his family. It shows plainly what a patent fiction the Chinese traveller is, for, in the end, he is nothing more than one aspect of the English mentality wedded finally to its counterpart. The marriage of the children is less significant than the marriage it represents between the parents. Reason and Feeling, Stoicism and Sentimentality are united in circumstances which indicate how distant these great abstractions are from the practical exigencies of daily existence. The children receive from the Man in Black

> a small estate in the country, which added to what I was able to bestow, will be capable of supplying all the real but not the fictitious demands of happiness. (II, 476)

The parents now combine to spend the remainder of their lives in visiting different countries, a pair of vagabond doctrinaires whose orotund wisdom seems to be dependent entirely on their status as onlookers rather than participants.

Even this reconciliation is not so neat a conclusion to the story of mighty opposites as it might seem to be. Lien Chi Altangi had, after all, begun to demonstrate some of the qualities of a Man of Feeling even before the concluding marriage took place. In Letter CXVII, the famous city night-piece, his peroration is exclamatory in the approved sentimental manner:

> Why was this heart of mine formed with so much sensibility! or why was not my fortune adapted to its impulse! Tenderness, without a capacity of relieving, only makes the man who feels it more wretched than the object which sues for assistance. (II, 454)

What has been called 'the cult of distress'[10] is visible here in the outpourings of one whose anguish derives almost entirely from his position as a spectator, as one who cannot relieve suffering but whose sensibility is aroused by the sight of it to the point where it becomes nothing more noble than self-pity. Suffering is the occasion for feeling, but feeling is the treasured thing, that which gives savour to existence. In this light, the story of Lien Chi Altangi takes on another aspect. A rational man, monotonously Confucian, is educated by his English experience into becoming a *dévot* of feeling. Yet he remains a traveller. Like the Man in Black he will remain an observer, an outsider, enjoying the idea of the pursuit of happiness but having nothing more than travelling more and more as his goal. Goldsmith does not sentimentalize the close of *The Citizen of the World*. Instead, the title assumes a heavier shade of irony.

The world, as Altangi puts it, 'being but one city to me' (II, 476) loses its universal connotation and becomes instead the setting for this vagabond's inexhaustible and futile curiosity. His sententious wisdom, allied now to the cult of feeling, is nothing more than a sublime form of egoism.

Yet it would obviously be unwise to assume that everything in *The Citizen of the World* is determined by the unreliable character of this foreign witness. Many of the letters are instances of local satire, directed against the various abuses which disfigured English society. The various accounts of the republic of letters, with all the attendant corruptions, jealousies and injustices which proliferate there, the portraits of the absurdities and the ruthless competitive spirit which informs the middle and upper levels of English commercial, political and social life, the detailed survey of popular taste in drama, clothes, furnishings, the rituals of marriage, funerals, religious services, the excesses of Methodism, the comic epidemic of fear over mad dogs, of trust in medical quacks, of prejudice against the French and all the other ills to which England was then prone, are not revelations of Altangi's personality (since he has none) but comic exploitations of his traditional position as wondering foreigner.

But it is still true that the mixture of satire and sentimental romance in this work seems anomalous. Goldsmith was in fact attempting to blend together two different traditions of Orientally-inspired literature. Ever since Antoine Galland's French translation of the *Thousand and One Nights* (1704–17), Europe had been much taken with the Oriental vogue in literature. Montesquieu diverted that vogue from romance towards satire, but the elements of romance remained and were to reappear more powerfully than ever after the turn of the century. In English literature, Johnson's *Rasselas* preserved some of the elements of romance, although the moral imperative of that work kept the romance strictly under control. William Beckford's *Vathek* (1786) extended the Oriental romance into the region of terror and helped to initiate a kind of fiction which is remote indeed from anything Goldsmith or earlier practitioners attempted. However, the peculiar combination of satiric elements with those of romance, however uneasily achieved in *The Citizen of the World*, is perfectly realized in *The Vicar of Wakefield*. There the spirit of philanthropic goodness, of endearing foolishness, embodied in Dr. Primrose, and of 'something reluctantly good' in the character of Burchell (alias Sir William Thornhill), have both been taken so readily as unreservedly sponsored by Goldsmith, that the novel has been sentimentalized by its readers more thoroughly than it ever was by its author. *The Citizen of the World*, if read with attention, would put the reader on guard and help to reveal that the fusion of the satire and the romance was characteristic of much of Goldsmith's work and recognizably part of the tradition of the Oriental tale in eighteenth-century Europe.

Thus the sojourn of Lien Chi Altangi in England is an instance of Goldsmith's exploitation of a well-established tradition. Irony subverts sentimentality, sentimentality softens irony. But the dominant concern here, as in the works of so many satirists in this century, is with the fate of civilization. The thin line which divides polite society from barbarism is one which Goldsmith wished to draw as clearly and distinctly as possible, even though at times the complexity of the evidence he accumulated did not allow for any simple demarcation. Yet Goldsmith was at one with Johnson, Burke, Reynolds, and other conservative thinkers in his conviction that speculative inquiry led man too far from the realities of practical existence. Morality was a tradition, not a personal possession or invention. Civilization finally depended for its preservation on the widom of the past. Everything else, however brilliant or original, tended to produce waywardness in conduct and to gratify nothing more than egoism. In his *The Life of Henry St. John, Lord Viscount Bolingbroke* (1770), he announced:

> Wisdom, in morals, like every other art or science, is an accumulation that numbers have contributed to increase; and it is not for one single man to pretend, that he can add more to the heap, than the thousands that have gone before him. Such innovators more frequently retard, than promote knowledge; their maxims are more agreeable to the reader, by having the gloss of novelty to recommend them, than those which are trite, only because they are true. Such men are therefore followed at first with avidity, nor is it till some time that their disciples begin to find their error. They often, though too late, perceive, that they have been following a speculative enquiry, while they

have been leaving a practical good; and while they have been practising the arts of doubting, they have been losing all firmness of principle. (III, 472–73)

Such a comment is salutary when we read Goldsmith's more famous works. The originality of thought, for which Bolingbroke strove, was to Goldsmith as futile as the originality of feeling for which the sentimentalists of his own day ached. In each case, a harmful egoism replaced traditional wisdom. If we read *The Citizen of the World* as a work in which civilization is defended on the basis of traditional wisdom and firm principle against the extremities of fashion, rationality, feeling, and egoism in all its protean forms, we will appreciate more keenly the spirit in which Goldsmith's ironic portrayal of the Chinese sage in England was intended.

NOTES

All references to Goldsmith's works are from the *Collected Works of Oliver Goldsmith*, ed. Arthur Friedman, 5 vols. (Oxford, 1966). The volume number and page are given in brackets after each quotation.

1. See H. J. Smith, *Oliver Goldsmith's The Citizen of the World: A Study* (New Haven, 1926); Martha P. Conant, *The Oriental Tale in England in the Eighteenth Century* (New York, 1908); Cecil A. Moore, *Backgrounds of English Literature, 1700–1760* (Minneapolis, 1953); A. L. Sells, *Les Sources Françaises de Goldsmith* (Paris, 1924).
2. James W. Johnson, 'The Meaning of Augustan', *Journal of the History of Ideas*, 19 (1958), 507–22.
3. See *The Genius of the Place: The English Landscape Garden, 1620–1820*, ed. J. D. Hunt and P. Willis (London, 1975), especially pp. 283–88, 308–22.
4. *Reflections on the Revolution in France*, ed. C. C. O'Brien (London, 1966), p. 146.
5. Levin L. Schucking, *The Sociology of Literary Taste* (New York, 1944), pp. 13–15; Arnold Hauser, *The Social History of Art*, 4 vols. (New York, 1960), III, 52, 66.
6. A. Momigliano, 'Gibbon's Contribution to Historical Method', *Historia*, 2 (1954), 450–63.
7. See John Forster, *The Life and Times of Oliver Goldsmith*, 2 vols. (London, 1854), I, 261.
8. Robert H. Hopkins, *The True Genius of Oliver Goldsmith* (Baltimore, 1969), pp. 124–37.

9. See R. S. Crane, 'Suggestions toward a Genealogy of the "Man of Feeling" ', *The Idea of the Humanities*, 2. vols. (Chicago, 1967), I, 188–213; George Sherburn, 'The Periodicals and Oliver Goldsmith', in *A Literary History of England*, ed. A. C. Baugh (New York, 1948), pp. 1057–58; W. F. Galloway, 'The Sentimentalism of Goldsmith', *PMLA*, 48 (1933), 1167–181; E. L. McAdam, 'Goldsmith the Goodnatured Man', in *The Age of Johnson*, ed. F. W. Hilles (London, 1964), pp. 41–7; John Dussinger, 'Oliver Goldsmith, citizen of the world', *Studies in Voltaire and the Eighteenth Century*, 55 (1967), 445–61.

10. Henry Mackenzie, *The Man of Feeling*, ed. Brian Vickers (London, 1967), p. x.

3

'Animated Nature': Goldsmith's View of Creation

by GRAHAM PARRY

Goldsmith wrote *An History of the Earth and Animated Nature* as a commercial venture for a London publisher during the final crowded years of his life when he was also engaged on several other popular compilations, yet in spite of the unfavourable circumstances of composition, the finished work has a vivacity and a universality of appeal that saw it through some twenty editions in the hundred years following its first publication in 1774. In his rather ingenuous preface, where he disparages modern investigators of nature for their excessively systematic and scientific approach, he claims that his true inspiration and model has been Pliny's *Natural History*, a statement that immediately alerts the reader to what he might expect: a panoramic survey of the natural creation undertaken from a broadly humanist viewpoint rather than from a specifically scientific angle, and copiously illustrated with a variety of remarkable and instructive detail. Not the least consequence of imitating Pliny's engaging selection of detail is a tendency towards anecdote, and a lively sense of wonder at the marvels of creation. Goldsmith makes no bones about his own genial involvement with his subject: 'Let us dignify natural history never so much with the grave appelation of *an useful* science, yet still we must confess that it is the occupation of the idle and the speculative.' Unquestionably he writes to please, hoping to make agreeably available to a wide public the present state of knowledge concerning the animal creation as it stands after an epoch of exploration and research.

In keeping with these far from exacting intentions, Goldsmith contented himself to a large extent with the transmission of received opinion, in particular the opinion of the French naturalist Buffon, whose *Histoire Naturelle* began publication in 1749 and was still in progress when *Animated Nature* was being compiled.[1] From Buffon Goldsmith lifted whole tracts of material that he translated and assimilated into his own fluent manner, sometimes with acknowledgement and more often without; plagiarism would be a graceless accusation, considering the lax standards in these matters in the eighteenth century, and one might better describe Goldsmith's working habits as a kind of elegant modification of original material. Nevertheless, in spite of the second-hand nature of much of the descriptions, the scope of the book and the fact that it professes to offer a coherent and comprehensive survey of the natural world oblige Goldsmith to express his beliefs about the large issues of purpose and intelligence in the creation, issues that he was not inclined to confront in the main body of his writings, which are primarily social in character. A certain philosophic resolution must underlie a large scale natural history, and one can learn a good deal about Goldsmith's intellectual assumptions from this work. They are for the most part assumptions common to the thoughtful people of the age, and it is precisely their representative quality that makes them a valuable index of the complacent optimism of late Augustan society.

God is a power infrequently mentioned in *Animated Nature*; a century of deism had reduced him from omnipresent creator to a discreet first cause, far removed from direct human experience. As Goldsmith observes at the opening of the work:

> Modern philosophy has taught us to believe, that, when the great Author of Nature began the work of creation, he chose to operate by second causes; and that, suspending the constant exertion of his power, he endued matter with a quality, by which the universal economy of nature might be continued without his immediate assistance.[2]

This quality is called *attraction,* by which Goldsmith means gravity, and it is counterbalanced by *impulsion,* 'a progressive force which each planet received when it was impelled forward by the Divine Architect upon its first formation'. Having thus satisfactorily accounted for the grand motion of the planetary system, and observing with a calm delight the discipline of the cosmic dance, 'We see nothing but uniformity, beauty and precision. The heavens present us with a plan, which, though inexpressibly magnificent, is regular beyond the power of invention.' The order of the macrocosm assures the philosophic enquirer that the microcosm has been created with a similar perfection, so that all apparent defects in the natural world are the result of our inadequate perspective ('' 'Tis but a part we see and not the Whole'), because we stand too close to see the large connections and benevolent intersections that sustain the economy of the earth. Everywhere the understanding eye perceives the 'wisdom and omnipotence' of the creator; Nature in fact is God revealing himself through natural laws. Goldsmith belongs essentially in the Physico-Theology tradition deriving from John Ray and William Derham.[3] Ray's *Wisdom of God in the Creation* (1691), as its title suggests, proposes a universe which, from the movement of the stars in their courses down to the provident activity of the ants, is informed by a benevolent intelligence that displays its power in the infinite variety of created forms. The world of nature exists to serve man as the lord of creation, but it also exists as an expression of the essential attributes of the Deity: his infinite wisdom, power and goodness. As a zoologist and botanist, Ray had been able to demonstrate the perfect interlocking of all the elements of the animal and vegetable worlds, the necessary interdependence of all forms of life, the wonderful adaptation of all organisms to their function in the natural world. Ray represents the scientist who finds his faith in a wise and purposeful creator amply supported by his observations and investigations of organic nature. This harmony between science and theology was consolidated in Derham's *Physico-Theology* (1713), a book with a very wide circulation in the eighteenth century, which offered a reassuring account of a world governed by general laws that promote the maximum well-being of all species compatible with the minimum amount of distress. There is no concern with sin or with the fall of man in Derham, nor is there any mention of Christ or concern with eschatology—what might be considered evil or imperfect in the ordinance of the world is the fault of our understanding of the divine plan. The closeness of these attitudes to Leibnitz's 'best of all possible worlds' philosophy is apparent, although the English Physico-Theology school lacked the intellectual rigour of Leibnitz's system. Goldsmith refers on a number of occasions to Derham, and his basic presuppositions in general reflect the optimistic deism of which Derham's work is representative. Nature affords all creatures pleasures relative to their kind, and although man may not readily identify these pleasures, the reflective observer will soon recognize that each animal enjoys its own peculiar happiness. The subterranean mole leads a life of dark felicity, and even the sloth, by many described as 'the meanest and most ill-formed' of all creatures, knows inscrutable satisfactions:

> If we measure their happiness by our sensations, nothing, it is certain, can be more miserable; but it is probable, considered with regard to themselves, they have some stores of comfort unknown to us . . . if a part of their life be exposed to pain and labour, it is compensated by a larger portion of plenty, indolence and safety. In fact, they are formed very differently from all other quadrupeds, and, it is probable, they have different enjoyments.[4]

Compensation is an important principle in Goldsmith's view of the world. All disadvantages are offset by corresponding advantages, because all things are adapted to their state of life. Happiness proper to the kind, though not necessarily to the individual, prevails throughout the creation.

Animated Nature begins: 'The world may be considered as one vast mansion, where man has been admitted to enjoy, to admire, and to be grateful', and the preliminary survey of the terraqueous globe concludes with a noble peroration, the tone of which guarantees that the author will range the vast expanses of his subject in a spirit of unqualified admiration and delight:

> When, therefore, we survey Nature on this side, nothing can be more splendid, more correct, or amazing. We there behold a

Deity residing in the midst of an universe, infinitely extended every way, animating all, and cheering the vacuity with his presence! We behold an immense and shapeless mass of matter, formed into worlds by his power, and dispersed at intervals, to which even the imagination cannot travel! In this great theatre of his glory, a thousand suns, like our own, animate their respective systems, appearing and vanishing at Divine command. We behold our own bright luminary fixed in the centre of its system, wheeling its planets in times proportioned to their distances, and at once dispensing light, heat, and action. The earth also is seen with its two-fold motion; producing, by the one, the change of seasons; and, by the other, the grateful vicissitudes of day and night. With what silent magnificence is all this performed! with what seeming ease! . . .

But not only provisions of heat and light are thus supplied, but its whole surface is covered with a transparent atmosphere, that turns with its motion, and guards it from external injury. . . . Waters also are supplied in healthful abundance, to support life, and assist vegetation. Mountains arise, to diversify the prospect, and give a current to the stream. Seas extend from one continent to the other, replenished with animals, that may be turned to human support; and also serving to enrich the earth with a sufficiency of vapour. Breezes fly along the surface of the fields, to promote health and vegetation. The coolness of the evening invites to rest; and the freshness of the morning renews for labour.[5]

Goldsmith admits that the world may be full of terrors, but all these oppositions to man are intended to draw forth our resilience and exercise our abilities to overcome adversity.

A world thus furnished with advantages on one side, and inconveniences on the other, is the proper abode of Reason; is the fittest to exercise the industry of a free and a thinking creature. These evils, which Art can remedy, and Prescience guard against, are a proper call for the exertion of his faculties; and they tend still more to assimilate him to his Creator. Gold beholds, with pleasure, that being which he has made, converting the wretchedness of his natural situation into a theatre of triumph; bringing all the headlong tribes of Nature into subjection to his will; and producing that order and uniformity upon earth, of which [h]is own heavenly fabric is so bright an example.[6]

Prose of this order suggests that the author does not propose any very searching enquiry into the arcana of natural history.

This is the prose of a good-natured man, smooth, contented and unruffled. Its tone is almost too agreeable for its purpose, in that it conveys an air of uncritical approbation on its subject matter, as if the creation need only be admired, not investigated with any rigour. Its satisfied generalizations reveal a mind not inclined to strike out any independent line of speculation. 'Safe in the hand of one disposing Power' might be the apt epigraph of this section of the book. Goldsmith is not anxious to think for himself in any sustained fashion—that is the debilitating result of being a compiler and presenter of information from other men's books. For example, he offers a résumé of the principal theories of creation currently available, from Burnet to Buffon, without any serious attempt at discrimination. 'Too much speculation in natural history is certainly wrong', he remarks, and the pursuit of truth to its obscurer recesses is not a very profitable exercise in his view.

> Instead of knowledge, we must be content with admiration. To be well acquainted with the appearances of Nature, even though we are ignorant of their causes, often constitutes the most useful wisdom.[7]

A particular instance of Goldsmith's excessive complacency appears in his consideration of the optimum conditions for human life to flourish. The earth is providentially placed at a sufficient distance from the sun to ensure a favourable habitation for mankind, and on the globe itself the location ideally suited to encourage the fullest development is the region mid-way between the extremes of heat and cold—Europe, in fact. Within Europe, the most desirable situation (when one considers the mild aspect of nature, the temperate climate, the recurring variety of the seasons and the excellent ventilation) is unquestionably England.

> Happy England! where the sea furnishes an abundant and luxurious repast, and the fresh waters an innocent and harmless pastime; where the angler, in cheerful solitude, strolls by the edge of the stream, and fears neither the coiled snake, nor the lurking crocodile; where he can retire at night, with his few trouts, to borrow the pretty description of old Walton, to some friendly cottage, where the landlady is good, and the daughter innocent and beautiful; where the room is cleanly, with

lavender in the sheets, and twenty ballads stuck about the wall! There he can enjoy the company of a talkative brother sportsman, have his trouts dressed for supper, tell tales, sing old tunes, or make a catch! There he can talk of the wonders of Nature with learned admiration, or find some harmless sport to content him, and pass away a little time, without offence to God, or injury to man![8]

There is the felicity to which the whole creation tends! Quite what passages like this are doing in a natural history is difficult to say. They reveal the sentimental essayist who hides behind the historian and who emerges not infrequently in *Animated Nature* to admire an unusual prospect or to reflect upon the human condition. Being a sociable man, Goldsmith seems to hint that amid all the endless paths of nature there should be some spot where his affections can recognize a home; the strain of unremitting 'observation with extensive view' causes him to break down from time to time and seek the reassurance of familiar scenes. We find here the sentimental patriotism of *The Traveller* elevated to the cosmic plane.

Goldsmith pities those unfortunate races who live beyond the European shores. He has no doubt that it is primarily climate that has caused the remarkable development of the 'polite nations', and foresees no probable alteration in the relative conditions of humanity. His survey of the different races makes interesting reading these days as an example of eighteenth-century anthropology and ethnology. With the lofty confidence of one of 'the lords of human kind', rotating the globe for his pleasure and instruction, Goldsmith distinguishes some six varieties of fellow creature—although he is not anxious to acknowledge their fellowship too closely. The Laplanders comprise all those peoples living in the sub-arctic regions, and who are literally nasty, brutish and short:

> These nations not only resemble each other in their deformity, their dwarfishness, the colour of their hair and eyes, but they have, in a great measure, the same inclinations, and the same manners, being all equally rude, superstitious, and stupid.[9]

Having no scientific principles that will guide him in a disciplined analysis of racial characteristics, Goldsmith immediately flounders into a morass of picturesque detail that makes him seem closer to Mandeville than to the savants of the Enlightenment.

> The Danish Laplanders have a large black cat, to which they communicate their secrets, and consult in all their affairs. Among the Swedish Laplanders there is in every family a drum for consulting the devil; and although these nations are robust and nimble, yet they are so cowardly that they never can be brought into the field.[10]

For all their degraded condition, Goldsmith recognizes in them the universal traits of self-esteem:

> Wretched and ignorant as the[y] are, yet they do not want pride; they set themselves far above the rest of mankind; . . . They are obliged, indeed, to yield [to Europeans] the pre-eminence in understanding and mechanic arts; but they do not know how to set any value upon these. They therefore count themselves the only civilized and well-bred people in the world.[11]

Then comes the Tartar group of peoples that we today would call Mongolian, who exhibit a variety of unpleasing characteristics. In this group, Goldsmith includes the Chinese and Japanese, about whom he has very little to say, except to assure us that they owe their civilization wholly to the mildness of the climate in which they reside, and to the peculiar fertility of the soil. Indians compose another group, but they are entirely debilitated by their climate, which renders them 'slothful, submissive, and luxurious'. Goldsmith spaciously dismisses them with a finality worthy of Podsnap himself:

> On the whole, therefore, they may be considered as a feeble race of sensualists, too dull to find rapture in any pleasures, and too indolent to turn their gravity into wisdom.

The Negroes of Africa are even more unfortunate. 'This gloomy race of mankind is found to blacken all the southern parts of Africa.' Their lack of personal beauty distresses Goldsmith, and he can scarcely bring himself to talk about their morals, only hinting that they are 'in general, found to be stupid, indolent and mischievous'. They verge on the monstrous:

> The women's breasts, after bearing one child, hang down below the navel, and it is customary with them to suckle the child at their backs, by throwing the breast over the shoulder.

The Indians of North America come off lightly. The worst that can be said of them is that 'they all have a serious air, although they seldom think.'

After this judicious estimate of mankind, it is with some relief that the Citizen of the World turns to Europe, where harmony and proportion reign, and the perfection of manners and morals adorns the rational being with every grace. Even the colour of a European's skin is cause for congratulation:

> Of all the colours by which mankind is diversified, it is easy to perceive, that ours is not only the most beautiful to the eye, but the most advantageous. The fair complexion seems, if I may so express it, as a transparent covering to the soul; all the variations of the passions, every expression of joy or sorrow, flows to the cheek, and, without language, marks the mind.[12]

Goldsmith will not be drawn into the question of the origin of the different races: that is one of the remoter issues where enquiry is unprofitable. He will admit, however, that 'man is naturally white', and all the deviations from that colour are the result of latitudes unfavourable to the full growth of the human faculties.

> Thus, taking our standard from the whitest race of people, and beginning with our own country, which, I believe, bids fairest for the pre-eminence, we shall find the French, who are more southern, a slight shade deeper than we; going farther down, the Spaniards are browner than the French; [etc.][13]

At this point Sir Thomas Browne is called in for an opinion and, given his own whimsical tendencies, seems a very appropriate consultant in these circumstances.

It seems worth while to highlight the preposterous complacency of Goldsmith's notions in order to expose what one could get away with in intelligent circles in the 1770s. *Animated Nature* was widely admired and much reprinted. The endemic habit of generalizing, the confidence engendered by an assertive and authoritative prose style, coupled with the need to make firm statements that instructional books like *Animated Nature* required, all these factors tend to show up Goldsmith's intellectual weakness when he is not relying on some dependable source. One begins to appreciate the force of Johnson's criticism:

> He had, indeed, been at no pains to fill his mind with know-
> ledge. He transplanted it from one place to another; and it did
> not settle in his mind; so he could not tell what was in his own
> books.

In the awkward intervals between his transplantings, when he
was on his own, as it were, there was a strong danger of falling
into pompous nonsense.

   Goldsmith does have one principle of organization to sustain
him through his survey of the vast extent of creation; he
believes firmly in the truth of the 'Chain of Being' concept,
and *Animated Nature* is effectively the fullest exposition of this
principle in English in the eighteenth century.[14] Although
several of his principal sources for the book were 'Great Chain'
men, notably Buffon, Pluche and Pennant, Goldsmith himself
seems committed to the idea and to have reflected on its
implications, so that one has the impression that it is not a
borrowed notion so much as a settled conviction. The significant propositions of this thesis were plenitude or fullness,
'that the universe is a *plenum formarum* in which the range of
conceivable diversity of *kinds* of living things is exhaustively
exemplified',[15] and that all the spaces of creation are filled
with some form of life. Among these forms there is an endless
continuity and gradation from kind to kind:

> Far as creation's ample range extends,
> The scale of sensual, mental pow'rs ascends:
> Mark how it mounts, to man's imperial race,
> From the green myriads in the peopled grass.[16]

Nor must there ever be a gap in the chain, for 'one step
broken, the great scale's destroyed'. *Animated Nature* extends
from man down to the polypus, at which point the animal
world merges into the vegetable. Man heads the chain by
virtue of his reason, and because of his anatomical complexity,
which is a clear sign of his superior organization. Goldsmith
explains his beliefs on this matter at the beginning of the
section on the birds:

> As in mechanics the most curious instruments are generally the
> most complicated, so it is in anatomy. The body of man
> presents the greatest variety upon dissection; quadrupeds, less
> perfectly formed, discover their defects in the simplicity of their

conformation; the mechanism of birds is still less complex; fishes are furnished with fewer organs still; while insects, more imperfect than all, seem to fill up the chasm that separates animal from vegetable nature.[17]

On the whole, the larger the creature, the higher its place in its particular part of the chain (and, incidentally, the larger the creature is within its kind, the more likely Goldsmith is to describe it as noble, generous, sagacious, etc., while the inferior creatures are abused as puny, abject or vile). Goldsmith is particularly attentive to those creatures that act as links between one class and another; so, for example, the ostrich unites the quadrupeds and birds, the humming bird shares certain properties with the insects, the manatee 'terminates the boundary between quadrupeds and fishes', and the polypus links animate with inanimate nature. Within the different classes, the hog kind 'serves to fill up that chasm which is found between the carnivorous kinds and those that live upon grass', and similarly the crane kind is of a middle nature between landbirds and water fowl. Goldsmith states one of the cardinal principles of the chain of being concept when he writes 'The progressions of Nature from one class of beings to another, are always by slow and almost imperceptible degrees.' It is for this reason that he is unwilling to accept the idea of separate and distinct species, for he sees no clear dividing lines anywhere, and therefore he disagrees with naturalists such as Linnaeus or Ray who categorized living forms by genus in the way that became the basis of modern zoology.[18]

The most interesting case of a link creature concerns the orang-outang, the ape whose similarity to mankind raised critical questions about man's origins and status. During the 1760s Lord Monboddo had been circulating his views about the creature as the key to the understanding of man's relationship with the primitive world, and in 1773 he published the *Origin and Progress of Language* to give full expression to his views.[19] Monboddo had been a subject of discussion and ridicule in the Johnson circle during the years when *Animated Nature* was being written, so Goldsmith must have been aware of the arguments in favour of and against man's connection with the higher primates. His own treatment of the issue will allow us to see where he stands on the question of man's uniqueness or his kinship with the animal creation. Monboddo had proposed that the orang-outang (under which name he included both the chimpanzee and the great ape of Borneo) belonged to the same species as man, but for reasons yet unknown had not developed; it remained therefore an invaluable indication of what the primitive condition of mankind had been. Even the orang-outang does not represent man's aboriginal state, which Monboddo conceived to be that of a 'solitary wild beast', but had developed certain social characteristics:

> they live in society and have some arts of life: for they build huts, and use an artificial weapon for attack and defence, viz. a stick; which no animal merely brute is known to do. . . . They appear likewise to have some civility among them, and to practise certain rites, such as burying the dead. It is from these facts that we are able to judge whether or not the orang-outang belongs to our species. Mr. Buffon has decided that he does not.[20]

Monboddo disagrees with Buffon, and instances the ape's intelligence, 'as much as can be expected in an animal living without civility and the arts', his affections and modest temperament. Anatomically the ape closely resembles a human being, a sure indication of its close kinship. It lacks the use of language, but then Monboddo argues in his book that mankind originally had no power of speech, but gradually acquired it as he evolved from a primitive state. For Monboddo, man's development has been a slow progress from savagery, on which journey the orang-outang marks an early stage; there was no fall from a primitive perfection, but a long emergence from rudimentary origins. Monboddo was one of the first evolutionists, claiming that what distinguished mankind from the rest of creation was his capacity for perfectibility, a trait that the orang-outang shared in a limited degree. The implications of his theory were far-reaching. There had been no special divine creation of man, human nature had not been constant throughout history, humans are not uniquely in possession of a soul, species are capable of change and transformation, and there is no gap between man and the animal world. With Monboddo we have entered into a rational and secular view of the creation. Buffon had believed that intelligence and language constituted a permanent and unbridgeable distinction between man and the rest of the primates. What was Goldsmith's position? Conservatism prevails. Drawing his material chiefly from Buffon, with additions from the anatomist Edward Tyson's *Orang-Outang, sive homo sylvestris* (1699), he acknowledges the remarkable similarities between man and ape, and the ape's amazing powers of imitation, of which he gives many striking examples (including what may be the first description of a chimpanzee's tea party); for all their remarkable abilities, he cannot credit them with any share of human faculties. Their imitation of human behaviour is the result of training, and bears no relation to their true nature.

> I have never seen one of these long-instructed animals that did not, by their melancholy air, appear sensible of the wretchedness of their situation. Its marks of seeming sagacity were merely relative to us and not to the animal; and all its boasted wisdom was merely of our own making.[21]

Although he describes its advanced social organization in its natural state in considerable detail (the illustration even shows it carrying its stick like a gentleman's cane, and the huts it was reputed to construct can be seen in the background) and exclaims over its anatomical development, yet Goldsmith cannot bring himself to reject the common wisdom of the centuries and make the imaginative leap of recognizing that man may be the product of natural, not supernatural, forces. The logic of the chain of being theory requires a constant gradation of forms, and could well accommodate the idea that the highest of the apes shares some of the properties of humanity, but Goldsmith turns his back on the evidence he has heaped up, and retreats to the safety of traditional conviction, quoting Buffon to the effect that

> no disposition of matter will give mind, and that the body, how nicely soever formed, is formed in vain, when there is not infused a soul to direct its operations.[22]

As a work of science, *Animated Nature* has its limitations, the chief of which is a lack of first-hand observation of so many of the creatures discussed.[23] But, after all, it was avowedly a work of popularization, the product of one of the leading literary men of the day, and one must recognize that its literary attractiveness and its sheer readability must have been responsible for keeping it in print for so long, even after Darwin had given its contents a thoroughly superannuated air. In spite of the many different sources used, Goldsmith has impressed an agreeable uniformity of style over all, presenting his material in a manner that is sociable, assured and intelligent. Throughout a very long book Goldsmith's style retains its freshness and buoyancy and consistently communicates a sense of pleasure and discovery; he is an excellent guide to the natural world because his delight in the subject never tires, and his fluency renders all difficulties slight. The steady flow of opinions, and the frequent statements of general observations that relate the details of a particular subject to larger principles, give the reader the pleasing sense of insight and understanding. Another factor makes a notable contribution to the tone of the book; because of the remoteness of the author from his primary material, a mood of fiction easily sets in. Goldsmith has seen few of the creatures he describes, yet he has read an abundance of travellers' narratives that stress the wonderful and the extraordinary, and he is prepared to believe most of what he reads. In any case, natural history abounds in curiosities, and Goldsmith is not one to forego the intrinsic advantages of his subject. As a result, there are many scenes of an almost fabulous nature. Of the reindeer, for example, we learn that:

> The bears now and then make depredations upon the herd; but of all their persecutors, the creature called the *glutton* is the most dangerous and the most successful. The war between these is carried on not less in Lapland than in North America, where the rein-deer is called the *carribou*, and the *glutton* the *carcajou*. This animal, which is not above the size of a badger, waits whole weeks together for its prey, hid in the branches of some spreading tree; and when the wild rein-deer passes underneath, it instantly drops down upon it, fixing its teeth and claws into the neck, just behind the horns.[24]

Goldsmith's eye for picturesque detail helps to give the book its distinctive character. The migration of squirrels is memorably described:

When these animals, in their progress, meet with broad rivers, or extensive lakes, which abound in Lapland, they take a very extraordinary method of crossing them. Upon approaching the banks, and perceiving the breadth of the water, they return, as if by common consent, into the neighbouring forest, each in quest of a piece of bark, which answers all the purposes of boats for wafting them over. When the whole company are fitted in this manner, they boldly commit their little fleet to the waves; every squirrel sitting on its own piece of bark, and fanning the air with its tail, to drive the vessel to its desired port.[25]

The polar bear also has enterprising means of transport:

It often happens, that when a Greenlander and his wife are paddling out at sea, by coming too near an ice-float, a white bear unexpectedly jumps into their boat, and if he does not overset it, sits calmly where he first came down, and, like a passenger, suffers himself to be rowed along. It is probable the poor little Greenlander is not very fond of his new guest; however he makes a virtue of necessity, and hospitably rows him to shore.[26]

The lemming is guaranteed to cause amazement:

Several millions in a troop deluge the whole plain with their numbers. They move, for the most part, in a square, marching forward by night, and lying still by day. . . . Their march is always directed from the north-west to the south-east, and regularly conducted from the beginning. Wherever their motions are turned, nothing can stop them; they go directly forward, impelled by some strange power; . . . If a lake or a river happens to interrupt their progress, they all together take the water and swim over it; a fire, a deep well, or a torrent, does not turn them out of their straight lined direction; they boldly plunge into the flames, or leap down the well, and are sometimes seen climbing up on the other side. If they are interrupted by a boat across a river while they are swimming, they never attempt to swim round it, but mount directly up its sides; and the boatmen, who know how vain resistance in such a case would be, calmly suffer the living torrent to pass over, which it does without further damage.[27]

The picturesque may be considered as the basic literary mode of *Animated Nature*. Goldsmith does not take up the opportunities for sublime description offered by the great phenomena such as volcanoes, earthquakes, hurricanes, etc., being more inclined to recount incidents of an affecting kind that have occurred in conjunction with these phenomena: explorers lost in unfathomable caves, families buried by snow, the dog—'this poor philosophical martyr'—employed to demonstrate the effect of poisonous exhalations near Naples, travellers making for a town that is swallowed up before their eyes by a sudden earthquake. Then, too, Goldsmith is apt to paint verbal pictures to evoke the remote scenes that are the habitat of his obscurer creatures. These scenes tend to be picturesque landscapes, full of appeal to the imagination, and endowed with a rich emotional atmosphere. The deserts of Arabia represent one extreme which may pleasantly dismay the comfortable English reader of *Animated Nature*:

> Nothing can be more dreary than the aspect of these sandy plains, that seem entirely forsaken of life and vegetation: wherever the eye turns, nothing is presented but a steril [*sic*] and dusty soil, sometimes torn up by the winds, and moving in great waves along, which when viewed from an eminence, resemble less the earth than the ocean; here and there a few shrubs appear, that only teach us to wish for the grove that reminds us of the shade in these sultry climates, without affording its refreshment; the return of morning, which, in other places, carries an idea of cheerfulness, here serves only to enlighten the endless and dreary waste, and to present the traveller with an unfinished prospect of his forlorn situation.[28]

The monsoon season as painted by Goldsmith could serve as an inspiration for one of Turner's elemental fantasies:

> Upon the approach of the winter months, as they are called, under the line, which usually begin about May, the sky, from a fiery brightness, begins to be overcast, and the whole horizon seems wrapt in a muddy cloud. Mists and vapours still continue to rise; and the air, which so lately before was clear and elastic, now becomes humid, obscure, and stifling: the fogs become so thick, that the light of the sun seems, in a manner, excluded; nor would its presence be known, but for the intense and suffocating heat of its beams, which dart through the gloom, and, instead of dissipating, only serve to increase the mist. After this preparation, there follows an almost continual succession of thunder, rain, and tempests. During this dreadful season, the

streets of cities flow like rivers; and the whole country wears the
appearance of an ocean. . . . the whole sky seems illuminated
with unremitted flashes of lightning; every part of the air seems
productive of its own thunders; and every cloud produces its
own shock. The strokes come so thick that the inhabitants can
scarce mark the intervals; but all is one unremitted roar of
elementary confusion. . . . The intense beams of the sun,
darting upon stagnant waters, that generally cover the surface
of the country, raise vapours of various kinds. Floating bodies of
fire, which assume different names, rather from their accidental
forms, than from any real difference between them, are seen
without surprise. The *draco volans*, or flying dragon, as it is
called; the *ignis fatuus*, or wandering fire; the *fires of St. Helmo*, or
the mariner's light, are every where frequent.[29]

When Johnson predicted that *Animated Nature* would be 'as
entertaining as a Persian tale', he had a shrewd idea of
Goldsmith's manner of proceeding. The book combines in
itself the attractions of several popular types of literature: the
adventurous narrative of travel, reports of outlandish societies,
and the encyclopaedic history, all brought together to enhance
a reasoned account of the whole economy of the natural world.
'Entertainment to the imagination' is essential to his plan; a
long educational work addressed to a 'polite' readership is
obliged to ingratiate itself with its audience, and the picturesque mode is admirably adapted to that end. The pro-
tracted success of *Animated Nature* proves how well Goldsmith
judged the taste of that leisured class of reader who sought the
painless route to self-improvement.

NOTES

Since there are so many editions of *Animated Nature*, references are made to
part, book and chapter rather than to individual pages. Goldsmith's chapters
are short. The quotations given here are taken from the 1804 edition (York)
in 4 vols.

1. The principal sources for *Animated Nature* are Buffon's *Histoire Naturelle*,
   the Abbé Pluche's *La Spectacle de la Nature* (1757; translated as *Nature
   Displayed*—Goldsmith used the English version), Francis Willoughby's

Ornithology (1678), John Ray's *Synopsis Methodica* (1693), Jan Swammerdam's *Historia Insectorum Generalis* (1685) and the reports contained in the periodical *Philosophic Transactions*.

2. Pt. I, Bk. I, Ch. I. 'A Sketch of the Universe.'
3. For a succinct discussion of this Physico-Theological tradition, see Basil Willey, *The Eighteenth Century Background* (London, 1940), Ch. II.
4. Pt. II, Bk. VII, Ch. XX. 'Of the Sloth.'
5. Pt. I, Bk. I, Ch. XXII. 'The Conclusion.'
6. Ibid.
7. Pt. I, Bk. I, Ch. XXI. 'Of Meteors.'
8. Pt. IV, Bk. III, Ch. II. 'Of Spinous Fishes in General.'
9. Pt. I, Bk. II, Ch. XI. 'Of the Varieties in the Human Race.'
10. Ibid.
11. Ibid.
12. Ibid.
13. Ibid.
14. The historian of this idea, Arthur O. Lovejoy, does not examine Goldsmith's work in *The Great Chain of Being* (Cambridge, Mass., 1936), where he gives it only a passing mention.
15. Lovejoy, op. cit., p. 52.
16. Pope, *Essay on Man*, I, ll. 207–10
17. Pt. III, Bk. I, Ch. I. 'Introduction.'
18. Although Buffon, the greatest single influence on *Animated Nature*, adhered to the concept of the chain of being, yet Goldsmith found that the *Histoire Naturelle* 'has almost entirely rejected method in classing quadrupeds. . . . He describes his animals almost in the order they happen to come before him' (Preface). Goldsmith decided to employ the criterion of utility in his scheme, and animals of any given kind are described in the order in which they are useful to man. This is a fairly arbitrary system too, but it suits Goldsmith's literary approach, and it harmonizes with his tendency to discuss animals anthropomorphically.
19. I am indebted in this paragraph to A. O. Lovejoy's article 'Monboddo and Rousseau', in *Essays in the History of Ideas* (New York, 1960), pp. 38–62.
20. *Origin and Progress of Language* (1773), pp. 289–90. Quoted in Lovejoy's article.
21. Pt. II, Bk. VII, Ch. I. 'The Oran-Outang.'
22. Ibid.
23. For example, Goldsmith devotes a chapter to the dodo without realizing that it has been extinct for a hundred years (see Pt. III, Bk. I, Ch. VII).
24. Pt. II, Bk. II, Ch. V. 'The Rein-Deer.'
25. Pt. II, Bk. V, Ch. I. 'The Squirrel.'
26. Pt. II, Bk. VII, Ch. IX. 'The Bear.'
27. Pt. II, Bk. VI, Ch. I. 'The Leming.'
28. Pt. II, Bk. VII, Ch. VI. 'The Camel and the Dromedary.'
29. Pt. I, Bk. I, Ch. XXI. 'Of Meteors.'

4

Goldsmith's Classicism

by JOHN BUXTON

On the afternoon of 30 April 1773, Boswell was dining at Topham Beauclerk's with Dr. Johnson, Joshua Reynolds and other members of The Club; the ballot for his admission was to be held that evening. Somebody mentioned Goldsmith's name and, after remarking 'how little Goldsmith knows',[1] Dr. Johnson went on, a little paradoxically, to praise him as an historian. This was too much for Boswell: 'An historian! My dear Sir, you surely will not rank his compilation of the Roman History with the works of other historians of this age?' But Johnson was unabashed:

> it is the great excellence of a writer to put into his book as much as his book will hold. Goldsmith has done this in his *History*. . . . Goldsmith tells you shortly all you want to know.[2]

The Roman History had been published four years earlier, and in the preface Goldsmith had said that his 'aim was to supply a concise, plain, and unaffected narrative of the rise and decline of a well known empire', because (he said), 'we had no history of this splendid period in our language, but was either too voluminous for common use, or too meanly written to please.'[3] He was rightly confident that he could avoid this fault.

For this book—like Boswell, Goldsmith referred to it as a 'compilation'—he received 250 guineas. In 1773 he wrote *The Grecian History*, for which he received £250; Johnson's opinion is unrecorded, but it would almost certainly have been favourable. Both books went through many editions in the fifty years after publication and were translated into French and German; the *Grecian History* appeared also in Italian and Spanish versions, which perhaps suggests that it had the greater reputation. In these histories Goldsmith made no pretence to original scholarship. One day, while he was writing his *Grecian History*, Gibbon called, and Goldsmith sought his help. 'Tell me,' he said, 'what was the name of that Indian king who fought Alexander?' 'Montezuma', was Gibbon's immediate reply. But when he saw Goldsmith writing down the name, he relented. 'But stay,' he said, 'I mistake. 'Twas not Montezuma. 'Twas Porus.'[4] Goldsmith's histories have scarcely more claims to our attention now than other pot-boilers two centuries old; yet they may supplement our understanding of his response to the civilizations of the classical past. The range and accuracy of Goldsmith's knowledge of ancient history concerns us less than his personal comment.

The later history of Western Europe derives much of its political and legal organization and much of its linguistic inheritance from the centuries of Roman domination, and those parts which were never brought within the Empire have remained comparatively barbarous and troublesome. But however great the debt of Western civilization to Rome, its more fundamental, intellectual sources are Greek, and were determined at Marathon.

> Upon the event of this battle depended the complexion which the manners of the West were hereafter to assume; whether they were to adopt Asiatic customs with their conquerors, or to go on in modelling themselves upon Grecian refinements, as was afterwards the case.[5]

Goldsmith leaves us in no doubt that his preference was for the literature and culture of Greece. In the unlikely event of his being present at a dinner of the Society of Dilettanti he would have raised his glass to the toast of the Grecian Taste more eagerly than to that of the Roman Spirit. In the final pages of his *Grecian History* he states his creed unequivocally.

> It is certain that Greece was the country which enlightened, exalted, and adorned the rest of Europe, and set an example of whatever is beautiful and great to the nations. . . . As the light

of Greece illuminated her Macedonian, so it spread over her Roman conquerors.[6]

I have argued elsewhere that the customary view of Goldsmith as an Augustan cannot withstand examination; and Goldsmith himself, in his *Account of the Augustan Age of England*, considers it from outside, not from within. It was an age in which he had had no part to play but which was now past, and which he must regard with the objectivity of an historian. Such an attitude was coming rapidly into fashion. In the year in which Goldsmith published his *Roman History* David Hume observed that History had become the Favourite Reading with the majority,[7] and a year later Goldsmith himself, as if seeking to explain Hume's general assertion, claimed that 'Experience every day convinces us, that no part of learning affords us so much wisdom upon such easy terms as history' (V, 277). Contemporary publishers shared this opinion; that is why they invited Goldsmith to write compilations not only on ancient history, but on the *History of England from the Earliest Times to the Death of George II* and on the *History of the Earth and Animated Nature*. And a group of London publishers commissioned a *Universal History* of which the modern part appeared between 1759 and 1766 in forty-four volumes: the appetite for such things was apparently insatiable. History, no longer the drama and not yet the novel, was the dominant form which aspiring authors were likely to attempt. Some, like Bolingbroke and Robertson, were real historians, and it is no accident that the greatest prose work of the century, *The Decline and Fall of the Roman Empire*, was a historical work. Goldsmith's dismissal of Byzantine History as suitable only for the virtuoso (I, 270), which was belied by the success of Gibbon, perhaps confirms Boswell's scepticism, and certainly nowadays his reputation is that of poet, playwright, novelist and essay-writer. This is extensive enough, and if we add Johnson's praise, that he 'was a man, who, whatever he wrote, did it better than any other man could do',[8] it could hardly be excelled.

Nevertheless, much of what Goldsmith wrote, especially in his early days, has some historical method or perspective: *An Enquiry into the Present State of Polite Learning in Europe*, which was his first independent piece, published early in 1759; the *Account of the Augustan Age of England*, which followed later in the same year; and *The Traveller*, which, though not published until 1764, had been begun in Switzerland in 1755. This was the poem which, Johnson said, laid the foundation of his reputation. It had at first been entitled *A Prospect of Society* (which was retained as the sub-title) and in it Goldsmith recounts his vain search for a happy state of human society while travelling through Italy, Switzerland, France, Holland and Britain. Here, in spite of the scepticism with which he had referred to Montesquieu's *L'Esprit des Lois* in *An Enquiry*, Goldsmith was clearly adopting Montesquieu's comparative method, and suitably enough for he had there judged him to be 'more a poet than a philosopher' (I, 301). And elsewhere he quoted Montesquieu's commendation of Plutarch's *Lives*, of which he himself published an abridgement in 1762.

In his preface to this work Goldsmith wrote,

> Biography has, ever since the days of *Plutarch*, been considered as the most useful manner of writing, not only from the pleasure it affords the imagination, but from the instruction it artfully and unexpectedly conveys to the understanding. (V, 226)

His own principal essay in this form was his Life of *Richard Nash* (1762) but he contributed biographical studies to *The Bee* and other periodicals; there are biographical sketches of a satirical kind in *Retaliation*, and there are elegiac portraits in *The Deserted Village*. Dr. Johnson, on that April afternoon when he had dismayed Boswell by praising Goldsmith as an historian, also said, 'Take him as a poet, his *Traveller* is a very fine performance; ay, and so is his *Deserted Village*, were it not sometimes too much the echo of his *Traveller*.'[9] The later poem is so much the better known nowadays that most of us would be more likely to regard *The Traveller* as a preliminary sketch for *The Deserted Village*: the principal theme of rural depopulation had there been briefly treated. Goldsmith dedicated *The Traveller* to his brother Henry, who had 'retired early to happiness and obscurity, with an income of forty pounds a year'.[10] Henry died in May 1768, about the time when Goldsmith began writing *The Deserted Village*, and this loss must have contributed to the elegiac tone of the whole poem, in addition to prompting the fifty lines of tribute to the idealized Village Preacher who was the central figure in the life of the pastoral community depicted: charitable, compassionate, comforting.

When reviewing Langhorne's translation of Bion's *Death of Adonis* for *The Critical Review* in 1759 Goldsmith had made the surprising judgement that 'Of all the different kinds of poetry, elegy has been least cultivated since the revival of letters' (I, 162). Spenser's *Astrophel*, Milton's *Lycidas* and Dryden's odes in memory of Anne Killigrew and Henry Purcell, to mention but the most obvious challenges to such a judgement, should have led to its revision. But Goldsmith's praise of the Village Preacher (modelled, no doubt, on his lately deceased brother Henry) owes little to classical models, since his praise was for essentially Christian virtues, which would not have evoked the praise of pagan authors. Bion's pastoral lament for Adonis followed in the tradition established by Theocritus with the lament for Daphnis in his first idyll—the tradition which would be followed by Spenser, Milton, Shelley and Arnold in the most celebrated elegies in the English language. It was regarded as especially suitable for mourning someone who had died prematurely, as Sidney and Edward King, Keats and Arthur Clough, and also Henry Goldsmith died.

In *The Citizen of the World*, a few years before, Goldsmith had parodied the affectations of pastoral elegies on the dead. 'There are', says Lien Chi Altangi,

> several ways of being poetically sorrowful on such occasions. . . .
> But the most usual manner is this: Damon meets Menalcas, who
> has got a most gloomy countenance. The shepherd asks his
> friend, whence that look of distress? to which the other replies,
> that Pollio is no more. If that be the case then, cries Damon, let us
> retire to yonder bower at some distance off, where the cypress
> and the jessamine add fragrance to the breeze; and let us weep
> alternately for Pollio, the friend of shepherds, and the patron of
> every muse. Ah! returns his fellow shepherd, what think you
> rather of that grotto by the fountain side; the murmuring stream
> will help to assist our complaints, and a nightingale on a
> neighbouring tree will join her voice to the concert. (II, 413)

But the death of a beloved brother would turn his mind to serious pastoral elegy.

That Goldsmith in *The Deserted Village* had Theocritus's first idyll in mind can hardly be denied. Fondness for the repetition of a word was a characteristic that, in Hazlitt's opinion, gave a 'peculiar felicity'[11] to his style (but which Dr. Johnson expunged from *The Traveller* as un-Augustan), and Theocritus also made use of the device. In *The Deserted Village* the insistent repetition of the epithet 'sweet'

> Sweet AUBURN, lovliest village of the plain . . .
> Sweet smiling village, loveliest of the lawn . . .
> Sweet AUBURN! parent of the blissful hour . . .

and

> Sweet was the sound when oft at evening's close,
> Up yonder hill the village murmur rose;

would be insipid and tiresome were it not that this recalls the similar repetition of the same epithet 'hadus' ('sweet') in Theocritus's first idyll:

> Hadu ti to psithurisma kai ha pitus, aipole, Iēna,
> Ha poti tais pagaisi, melisdetai, hadu de kai tu surigdes . . .
> Hadion, O poimēn, to teon melos ē to kataches
> Tēn apo tas petras kataleibetai hipsothen hudōr.[12]

This passage perhaps suggested 'the plashy spring' of Goldsmith's ideal village. And certainly the lines had such appeal for Spenser that in *The Return from Parnassus* this image was taken to characterize him; he was the poet who especially delighted in the sound of falling water.[13] Milton in *Lycidas*, also echoes Theocritus's lament for Daphnis, the poem which had been the foundation of all such pastoral elegy, as Goldsmith would have known. We may see further evidence of the lack of embarrassment in repetition of an epithet which, but for its Theocritean associations, would have seemed trivial, in the revision at l. 123 of the reading 'soft' of the first three editions (perhaps because he had 'softened' at l. 116) to 'sweet', although that had been the emphatic first word of the whole paragraph. Theocritean precedent could justify such a change, as it could justify the frequent use in pastoral elegy of such a colourless epithet, the epithet which Milton had placed last in the diminuendo of compliment with which Adam addressed Eve after the Fall: 'Holy, divine, good, amiable or sweet'.[14] But

Theocritus had used 'hadus' eight times in his first idyll.

Goldsmith's classicism is thus to be found in his manner rather than in his matter. He did not, like the Augustans, seek to imitate Theocritus or Virgil, as Pope did in his Pastorals; he did not transpose models found in Horace or Juvenal into the political context of eighteenth-century England; nor would he treat the heroic couplet as a substitute for the Latin elegiac couplet. Nowhere is this more clearly illustrated than in the contrast between the Augustan lines which Johnson inserted in *The Traveller* and *The Deserted Village* and Goldsmith's verse in the body of both poems. Goldsmith's couplet,

> The pensive exile, bending with his woe,
> And faintly fainter, fainter seems to go,

with its characteristic repetition of a word, was unacceptable to any Augustan. Johnson revised it to read (ll. 419–20),

> The pensive exile, bending with his woe,
> To stop too fearful, and too faint to go . . .

This has a heavy caesura, which Goldsmith's lines seldom have, a chiasmic arrangement of the two halves of the line, and a typically Augustan antithesis which the figure emphasizes. No one with any sensitivity to Goldsmith's manner could mistake Johnson's lines for his. But the rejection of the Augustan manner resulted in a shift to a different manner, which is most appropriately designated 'Grecian' since this was the word used in the eighteenth century by those who were consciously adopting it. This was less insistent, more unobtrusive than the manner of the writers of Queen Anne's reign: in prose, the style of Xenophon rather than of Cicero. 'What historian can render virtue so amiable as Xenophon?' (V, 297) Goldsmith asked, and perhaps no ancient writer could better exhibit Goldsmith's ideal of writing naturally rather than finely.

Goldsmith considered that to 'have read the Ancients with indefatigable industry' (III, 423) was essential to any aspiring writer, and his preference for the Greeks is always apparent. Doubtless he knew Horace's advice:

> Make the Greek Authors your supreme Delight;
> Read them by Day, and study them by Night.[15]

When George Primrose attempted to persuade the Principal of the University of Louvain to accept him as a teacher of Greek, he convinced him of his knowledge by offering to translate any passage into Latin; but this was a practice of which Goldsmith disapproved.

> We should . . . imitate such as first revived Greek learning in the West; who, without translations, instructed those that afterwards became so eminent for their skill in this enchanting language. (I, 129)

In *The Vicar of Wakefield* Mr. Burchell no doubt expresses his creator's view when he condemns Gay and Ovid alike for introducing 'a false taste into their respective countries, by loading all their lines with epithet' and compares modern English poetry to that in the later Roman Empire, 'nothing . . . but a combination of luxuriant images, without plot or connexion' (Ch. VIII). Even Gray's *Elegy written in a Country Church Yard* did not escape similar censure, 'a very fine poem, but overloaded with epithet'. And Goldsmith was prepared to prove the point 'by leaving out an idle word in every line'— the omitted words being 'parting', 'slowly' and 'weary' in the first stanza. By such means would he demonstrate what he meant by 'writing naturally' (V, 320, and fn. 2). He abjured the connotative richness of epithet which is a quality of so much English writing, whether in verse or prose, and though there is no evidence that he had read any of Winckelmann's work (whose epoch-making essay, the *Gedanken*, was published in the year in which he visited Italy), he would surely have agreed with his dictum that

> Beauty should be like the best kind of water, drawn from the spring itself; the less taste it has, the more healthful it is considered, because free from all foreign admixture.[16]

Lien Chi Altangi claims that 'a cool, phlegmatic method of writing prevails' in China with 'metaphors almost wholly unknown' (II, 145–46). As usual, he is recommending what Goldsmith preferred.

Theocritean precedent may make certain stylistic devices acceptable, but in *The Deserted Village* Goldsmith reveals no intimate understanding of the lives of his rustic peasants. He observed them kindly but condescendingly, from a different class in society. He would have agreed with Dr. Johnson that

> the state of a man confined to the employments and pleasures of the country, is so little diversified, and exposed to so few of those accidents which produce perplexities, terrors, and surprises, in more complicated transactions, that he can be shown but seldom in such circumstances as attract curiosity.[17]

He regrets the destruction of his imagined Arcadia and is moved to sympathy with its inhabitants, but never to anger, like Crabbe or Wordsworth. He sees them not as they are, as Thomas Hardy would, but through a haze of sentiment. Sweet Auburn is very far distant from Egdon Heath, and Reynolds's portrayal of the character in Goldsmith's poem which he entitled *Resignation* would have been inadequate as a portrait of Wordsworth's *Michael*.

Yet Goldsmith's characters, such as the Village Preacher and the Village Schoolmaster, are not lacking in individuality, perhaps because the Augustan tradition of satire gave sharpness to his observation. The parody of pastoral elegy in *The Citizen of the World* made him look more closely at the figure of his brother when he wished to write serious elegy, and this same quality is to be found in his study of the Schoolmaster, though we need not deduce from this that he was attempting a portrait of someone known in his youth. It is an ideal portrait sharpened by satire (ll. 207–12):

> The village all declared how much he knew;
> 'Twas certain he could write, and cypher too;
> Lands he could measure, terms and tides presage,
> And even the story ran that he could gauge.
> In arguing too, the parson owned his skill,
> For even tho' vanquished, he could argue still. . . .

Here the matter is Augustan, not far removed from *Imitations of Horace*, but the manner of the verse is Goldsmith's not Pope's or Johnson's.

'Goldsmith', said Dr. Johnson, 'has the art of compiling and of saying every thing he has to say in a pleasing manner.'[18] From that judgement few would dissent, even though his modern audience have not had the training in the ancient languages that his earliest audience enjoyed. But the effect remains, and, as Bradley said, it is 'only when you put the book down [that you] become aware that your mind has been moving with perpetual ease and grace'.[19] This is pleasing; it is also flattering.

NOTES

1. James Boswell, *Life of Samuel Johnson, LL.D.*, ed. R. W. Chapman, corrected by J. D. Fleeman (Oxford, 1970), p. 527.
2. Ibid., p. 528.
3. *Collected Works of Oliver Goldsmith*, ed. Arthur Friedman, 5 vols. (Oxford, 1966), V, 333. Subsequent citations in the text refer to vol. and page nos.
4. Quoted by G. M. Young, *Gibbon* (London, 1948), p. 108.
5. *History of Greece* (London, 1821), I, 100.
6. Ibid., II, 354.
7. Letter to Rev. Hugh Blair, 28 March 1769. *Letters of David Hume*, ed. J. Y. T. Greig (Oxford, 1932), II, 196; cf. II, 230.
8. Boswell, *Life*, p. 918.
9. Ibid., p. 527.
10. *The Poems of Gray, Collins and Goldsmith*, ed. Roger Lonsdale (London, 1969), p. 629.
11. 'Lectures on the English Poets, VI, 1818', in *Complete Works*, ed. P. P. Howe (London, 1930), V, 119.
12. 'Sweet is the whispering music of yonder pine that sings
    Over the water-brooks, and sweet the melody of your pipe,
    Dear goatherd . . .
    Sweeter, O shepherd, is your song than the melodious fall
    Of yonder stream that from on high gushes down the rock.'
    (Theocritus, *Idyll* I (ll. 1–3; 7–8), trans. R. C. Trevelyan, 1927.)
13. *The Return from Parnassus*, I. ii, in *The Three Parnassus Plays*, ed. J. B. Leishman (London, 1949), p. 237.
14. *Paradise Lost*, IX, l. 899.
15. Horace, *Ars Poetica*, ll. 268–69, trans. Philip Francis, *The Epistles and Art of Poetry* (1746).
16. *History of Ancient Art*, IV. ii. 23, trans. G. H. Lodge (1881).
17. *Rambler*, 36.
18. Boswell, *Life*, p. 528.
19. A. C. Bradley, *A Miscellany* (London, 1929), p. 147.

5

Notes on Goldsmith's Politics

by DONALD DAVIE

There are many things for which we go back to Horace
Walpole; but we certainly don't look to him for any just estimate
of who among his contemporaries achieved immortality in
literature. All the same we must surely be startled when
Walpole in his *Memoirs*, writing of the year 1768 and undertaking 'to say a few words on the state of literature during the
period I have been describing', remarks: 'Two other poets of
great merit arose, who meddled not with politics; Dr.
Goldsmith, the correct author of *The Traveller*; and Mr. Anstey,
who produced as original a poem as *Hudibras* itself, the *New
Bath-guide*.'[1] In one whose chief correspondent about poetry was
the Reverend William Mason, the rating of Goldsmith on a
level with Christopher Anstey is not really surprising. (And of
Goldsmith Walpole says no more, but of Anstey a great deal:
'the most genuine humour, the most inoffensive satire, the
happiest parodies . . . the most harmonious melody. . . .')
What is startling, surely, is to have it said of the author of *The
Traveller* that he 'meddled not with politics'. What did Walpole
think that Goldsmith *was* meddling with, when he wrote such
lines as these? (ll. 379–92):

> Calm is my soul, nor apt to rise in arms,
> Except when fast approaching danger warms:
> But when contending chiefs blockade the throne,
> Contracting regal power to stretch their own,

When I behold a factious band agree
To call it freedom, when themselves are free;
Each wanton judge new penal statutes draw,
Laws grind the poor, and rich men rule the law;
The wealth of climes, where savage nations roam,
Pillag'd from slaves, to purchase slaves at home;
Fear, pity, justice, indignation start,
Tear off reserve, and bare my swelling heart;
'Till half a patriot, half a coward grown,
I fly from petty tyrants to the throne.

What did Walpole think these lines were about, if not about politics? The answer must be that Walpole, that fierce though fluctuating Whig, understood by 'politics' precisely the contentions of the 'contending chiefs', the matter of who was in and who was out of favour and of power, Pelhamites today, Rockingham Whigs tomorrow; just that level of politics which in *Retaliation* Goldsmith was to treat with contempt in his searing lines on Burke (ll. 31–4):

Who, born for the Universe, narrow'd his mind,
And to party gave up, what was meant for mankind.
Tho' fraught with all learning, kept straining his throat,
To persuade Tommy Townsend to lend him a vote; . . .

Which of them do we agree with when we ask ourselves what we mean by 'politics', more particularly when we ask if politics is a proper concern for earnest and impassioned poetry? The answer surely is not far to seek: it is Walpole, we think, who is speaking of *practical* politics, the day-by-day hurlyburly in Westminster; and politics is a practical matter, 'the art of the possible'; accordingly, Goldsmith's loftier view of it is futile. And so we are likely to conclude that politics is what poetry should not stoop to. When it does so stoop, as in *The Traveller*, we tut-tut indulgently and look elsewhere in the poem for whatever it is we admire it for. And is not that indeed how *The Traveller* has been read in every generation, including our own? Because we thus conspire to suppress from our attention and our recollection those passages where the poem is political, and indeed politically *tendentious*, we are more than halfway to agreeing with Walpole that Goldsmith 'meddled not with politics'.

80

Moreover, if we narrow our sights to the politics of Westminster in Goldsmith's day, and consult those who have made that their special study, we find them in effect vindicating Horace Walpole. For we are nowadays invited by political historians to see the politics of that time as a *system*, and a system that worked. It worked, and *could* work, only because of those elements in it that were denounced, then and later, as 'faction' and as 'corruption'. We must, we are told, tough-mindedly recognize such denunciations for what they were taken to be at the time—a rhetorical ritual expected of politicians out of office; just as we must equally dismiss, as rhetorical smoke-screens, all those accounts of Britain in the 1760s which see Liberty, in the person of John Wilkes, threatened by Autocracy, in the person of George III. Accordingly, when we re-read *The Traveller* and find Goldsmith making play with all these notions—'corruption' and (especially) 'faction', and 'freedom' in relation to 'the throne'—we are presented with a straight choice: either this is an instance of the smoke-screen, and Goldsmith is being disingenuous; or else he has been deluded by the rhetoric, and is being naïve.

And here at last we are on solid ground. For all the contemporary accounts agree: Golsmith was ingenuous, a naïf. Walpole again is as good a witness as any: time and again, in Walpole's letters, Goldsmith crops up—and always as *a silly*. In several of the anecdotes about him, not just from the poisoned pen of Boswell, we see Goldsmith attempting to 'put on airs' or 'make an impression', and ludicrously failing—when he wanted to be disingenuous, he couldn't, effectively. Thus there can be no question: if indeed Goldsmith in *The Traveller* deceives us about what was at issue in the England of the 1760s, he deceived himself first. He meant what he said; he was not writing in code.

But in that case, what are we to make of the contention that no one at the time was deceived by fulminations about faction, and corruption, and freedoms endangered? Goldsmith may have been naïve, but surely he wasn't uniquely so. And of course the evidence is overwhelming that he was not. However readily the fulminations and protestations may have been discounted by people in the know such as Burke and Walpole, up and down the country patriotic citizens took them at face-value, finding in their own experience much to bear them out. The political system may not in fact have reached a crisis in the 1760s, but plenty of thoughtful people thought it had. And Goldsmith was one of them.

Thus when he says that he will 'tear off reserve, and bare my swelling heart', we may as well believe him. And where does his swelling heart impel him? To 'the throne' (ll. 393–412):

> Yes, brother, curse with me that baleful hour
> When first ambition struck at regal power;
> And thus, polluting honour in its source,
> Gave wealth to sway the mind with double force.
> Have we not seen, round Britain's peopled shore,
> Her useful sons exchang'd for useless ore?
> Seen all her triumphs but destruction haste,
> Like flaring tapers brightening as they waste;
> Seen opulence, her grandeur to maintain,
> Lead stern depopulation in her train,
> And over fields, where scatter'd hamlets rose,
> In barren solitary pomp repose?
> Have we not seen, at pleasure's lordly call,
> The smiling long-frequented village fall?
> Beheld the duteous son, the sire decay'd,
> The modest matron, and the blushing maid,
> Forc'd from their homes, a melancholy train,
> To traverse climes beyond the western main;
> Where wild Oswego spreads her swamps around,
> And Niagara stuns with thund'ring sound?

This is of course a passage that everyone remembers, because it contains in embryo what was to become *The Deserted Village*. But if that later treatment surpasses this one, as of course it does, we ought to recognize a price that is paid: *The Deserted Village* is in crucial ways a great deal less specific. Nothing in *The Deserted Village* is so uncompromising as 'Her useful sons exchang'd for useless ore . . .'. Indeed, as is notorious, in the later poem the reason for the expropriation of the villagers is left notably unclear—a vagueness that permits of the time-honoured and still inconclusive debate about whether the village is in Ireland (Lissoy) or in England. The debate to be sure is misconceived, for the poetic imagination surely often transforms disparate experiences by amalgamating and compounding them, and so to the question, 'Ireland or England?' the most plausible answer is no doubt: 'A bit of both'. All the same the pressures on rural Ireland in the 1760s were, surely, significantly different from those that bore in on rural England; and our inability to specify which kingdom is meant shows how far the poem is from specifying the cause of the calamity. In both poems the interests which expropriate the villagers are mercantile, but in reading *The Deserted Village* we have to be attentive, to notice this. If in that poem we identify 'the man of wealth and pride' who throws out the villagers as a *nouveau-riche*, possibly a 'nabob' returned from the East or West Indies, who wants a country-seat without any manorial obligations, this is no more than a plausible conjecture on our part; the poem itself doesn't identify him in that way, nor in any other. And we can't help but wonder if it isn't precisely this lack of specificity which (along with other features, to be sure) has always made *The Deserted Village* the more appealing poem. It enunciates sentiments to which, we might say, every bosom returns an echo:

> But a bold peasantry, their country's pride,
> When once destroyed, can never be supplied.

Who would not agree? Who would be inconvenienced or put out of countenance, except the perhaps fictitious nabob himself? But in *The Traveller*, where the expropriation is emphatically presented as a direct consequence of commercial imperialism, the sentiment would be embarrassing to any one who practised, or profited by, the import of raw material ('ore') from overseas.

Moreover *The Deserted Village* prescribes no remedy for the state of affairs it deplores, and therefore puts no reader under any obligation to do anything about it. *The Traveller* however *does* prescribe a remedy: enhanced power for George III. How very unappealing that has been, for readers through the generations and still today! It flies in the face of the Whig Interpretation of History—an interpretation which, though we have recognized and diagnosed its partiality, most of us are still bound by more than we realize. It is one thing to exculpate George III from the charges hurled at him by Tom

Paine; it is something else to believe, as Goldsmith wants us to, that in the contention between the King and demagogues like Paine or Wilkes the right (and also the *freedom*) was with the King. For that is certainly what Goldsmith means when he calls on his brother to join him in cursing the inroads made on 'regal power'. *The Traveller* is a fervent apologia for the monarchical form of government, taking the time-honoured ground that, since the unprivileged need a power to appeal to above the power of local privilege, the only such power conceivable is the power of the Monarch, elevated above all sectional interests.

It is astonishing that the British, who live to this day under a monarchical government and have shown their readiness to fight and die for it, still refuse to give a hearing to this most cogent argument in its favour. Among Americans, on the other hand, such reluctance is not astonishing at all. And this reflection is not gratuitous. For 'Auburn' names a city or a settlement in no less than fifteen states of the Union; and whereas Auburn, California, is almost certainly named after Auburn, Massachusetts, or Auburn, Maine, the Auburns in the eastern states must surely have been named by readers of *The Deserted Village*. After all, by 1816 Goldsmith's *Political Works* as well as *The Vicar of Wakefield* had been published in a city as far from the Atlantic sea-board as Pittsburgh.[2] Certainly Auburn University, in Auburn, Alabama, proudly declares its allegiance by calling its campus newspaper, 'The Plainsman'. (And 'Plains' or 'The Plains' crops up as a place-name in Georgia, Kansas, Montana, Ohio and Texas.) 'Sweet Auburn, loveliest village of the plain' would hardly have sired so many communities in republican America, if American readers of *The Deserted Village* had also read *The Traveller*, and had recognized that Goldsmith's Auburn originally looked for its security to powers that would be clawed back by George III from his Parliament. It is a telling instance of how much more palatable and inoffensive *The Deserted Village* is than *The Traveller*.

Nothing has yet been quoted from *The Traveller* which, simply as an exploitation of the resources of English, deserves much more than the tepid commendation of Horace Walpole: 'correct'. But much more can and must be claimed for an earlier passage, where Goldsmith makes a smooth and yet momentous transition from considering the Netherlands to considering Great Britain (ll. 313–34):

> Heavens! how unlike their Belgic sires of old!
> Rough, poor, content, ungovernably bold;
> War in each breast, and freedom on each brow;
> How much unlike the sons of Britain now!
> Fir'd at the sound, my genius spreads her wing,
> And flies where Britain courts the western spring;
> Where lawns extend that scorn Arcadian pride,
> And brighter streams than fam'd Hydaspis glide,
> There all around the gentlest breezes stray,
> There gentle music melts on every spray;
> Creation's mildest charms are there combin'd,
> Extremes are only in the master's mind;
> Stern o'er each bosom reason holds her state.
> With daring aims, irregularly great,
> Pride in their port, defiance in their eye,
> I see the lords of human kind pass by
> Intent on high designs, a thoughtful band,
> By forms unfashion'd, fresh from Nature's hand;
> Fierce in their native hardiness of soul,
> True to imagin'd right above controul,
> While even the peasant boasts these rights to scan,
> And learns to venerate himself as man.

Goldsmith never wrote better than this. And there could be no better example of how a stilted convention can, in certain circumstances and in the right hands, achieve effects more suave and economical than are available to more 'natural' idioms. The panegyric is keyed so high, and the diction so fulsome ('courts the western spring' . . . 'Arcadian pride' . . . 'fam'd Hydaspis' . . . 'gentlest/gentle'), precisely so that the sentiment it conveys can be undermined so soon, and so insidiously. The effect is that when this florid oratorical voice begins to drop into its discourse words like 'extremes' and 'irregularly' and 'pride', our first reaction is to ask ourselves: 'Does he understand what he is *saying?*' We begin to think that he does, when we reach 'the lords of human kind', but we are not wholly sure of it until 'True to imagin'd right above controul'. For the claims to be advanced, acceded to, and then denied, all inside twenty lines, is masterly.

And the verses that bite and drive most fiercely are yet to come (ll. 339–48):

> That independence Britons prize too high,
> Keeps man from man, and breaks the social tie;
> The self dependent lordlings stand alone,
> All claims that bind and sweeten life unknown;
> Here by the bonds of nature feebly held,
> Minds combat minds, repelling and repell'd;
> Ferments arise, imprison'd factions roar,
> Represt ambition struggles round her shore,
> Till over-wrought, the general system feels
> Its motions stopt, or phrenzy fire the wheels.

The metaphors that blaze in the last two couplets—from chemistry, from medicine, from mechanics—seem 'mixed' only because in a Shakespearean way the imagination is whirling so rapidly from one analogy to the next. And 'factions' here means something more inclusive than power-blocs vying and shouldering at court, in parliament, or in Whitehall offices. It is *minds* that are factious, and more than minds; personalities or sensibilities, human beings, are locked into this prison of unending combat, 'repelling and repell'd'. What we have in fact is what may be the earliest and is certainly to my mind the most caustic indictment of the world of 'free enterprise', unstructured and unrestricted competitiveness, the morality of the market—in ideas, in status, and in feelings, as well as commodities. Why is the passage seldom remembered and extolled? Because for most of us the indictment is launched from the wrong end of what we conceive of as the political spectrum. Such sentiments and insights are thought to be the privileged monopoly of the liberal Left, and we refuse to acknowledge them when they are uttered by a Tory monarchist like Goldsmith or like Johnson.

Already we must suppose it was this prejudice, or something like it, that prevented the Whig Walpole from recognizing in such a passage anything to do with politics. Yet at least once more, before he submerged his analysis in the indulgent haze of *The Deserted Village*, Goldsmith re-stated it. This was in Chapter XIX of *The Vicar of Wakefield* (1766):

> 'I wish,' cried I, 'that such intruding advisers were fixed in the pillory. It should be the duty of honest men to assist the

weaker side of our constitution, that sacred power that has for some years been every day declining, and losing its due share of influence in the state. But these ignorants still continue the cry of liberty, and if they have any weight basely throw it into the subsiding scale.'

Thus Dr. Primrose, who subsequently warms to his subject:

> Now, Sir, for my own part, as I naturally hate the face of a tyrant, the farther off he is removed from me, the better pleased am I. The generality of mankind also are of my way of thinking, and have unanimously created one king, whose election at once diminishes the number of tyrants, and puts tyranny at the greatest distance from the greatest number of people. Now the great who were tyrants themselves before the election of one tyrant, are naturally averse to a power raised over them, and whose weight must ever lean heaviest on the subordinate orders. It is the interest of the great, therefore, to diminish kingly power as much as possible; because whatever they take from that is naturally restored to themselves; and all they have to do in the state, is to undermine the single tyrant, by which they resume their primaeval authority.

Since wealth is power (thus the argument develops), and since 'an accumulation of wealth . . . must necessarily be the consequence, when as at present more riches flow in from external commerce, than arise from internal industry', it follows that in proportion as fortunes are made by international trading more and more attempts will be made to abridge the power of the Monarch. The speaker, whom we may as well call Goldsmith as Primrose, accordingly declares his allegiance to 'people without the sphere of the opulent man's influence', a 'middle order of mankind' in whom 'are generally to be found all the arts, wisdom, and virtues of society'. Indeed, he does not scruple to say, 'This order alone is known to be the true preserver of freedom, and may be called the People.' If the historical circumstances are such as he has described, what is in the interest of this middle order? And he replies:

> to preserve the prerogative and privileges of the one principal governor with the most sacred circumspection. For he divides the power of the rich, and calls off the great from falling with tenfold weight on the middle order placed beneath them.

This sustained disquisition in Goldsmith's prose is inferior both in scope and in passion to the passage from *The Traveller*; but it teases out in detail, for those who need the demonstration, the logical coherence of his anti-commercialism and anti-imperialism (why not say, his anti-capitalism?) with his monarchism. And must we not concede that out of the terms of his argument we could contrive an at least plausible explanation of how Whiggism behaved in the next century, how it made way for Liberalism, and how both Whigs and Liberals were able to make accommodations with the Radicals, including some who were overtly or implicitly republican?

There is no doubt in my mind that the arguments and sentiments in Chapter XIX of *The Vicar of Wakefield* are those of Goldsmith himself. And I'm sure Donald Greene was right in *The Politics of Samuel Johnson* (p. 185) to quote from the chapter in that spirit, calling it 'the view of Goldsmith . . . one of the most vigorous rebuttals of the Whig contention that what was good for Russells and Cavendishes was good for England.' But alas, for those who want to overlook or circumvent the case that Goldsmith makes, there is always available the figure of Dr. Primrose. And Dr. Primrose is, like his creator, a silly, 'too good for this world', lovable. Thus we are allowed to think that we should not take seriously sentiments put in his mouth. This is unfortunate, and a bad miscalculation on Goldsmith's part. For when Addison had created his lovable old Tory, Sir Roger de Coverley, he had done so as a Whig, adroitly letting the reader's heart go out to Sir Roger even as his head approved the Whig, Sir Andrew Freeport. Goldsmith by contrast was very maladroit indeed, when he put sentiments that mattered to him into the mouth of a speaker who can be discounted so easily.

Cowper told Lady Hesketh in 1785:

> I have read Goldsmith's Traveller and his Deserted Village, and am highly pleased with them both, as well for the manner in which they are executed, as for their tendency, and the lessons that they inculcate.[3]

Not many readers have, like Cowper, taken seriously the 'tendency' of Goldsmith's two poems, let alone 'the lessons that they inculcate'. And it is true that the tendency of *The Deserted Village* can easily be missed unless that poem is read along with *The Traveller*. No one will deny that in the later poem Goldsmith tapped new resources, and found new ways to move us, ways more specifically 'poetic'. But there is more clarity in *The Traveller*, and more urgency. It is the earlier poem that is challenging.

NOTES

1. *Horace Walpole: Memoirs and Portraits*, ed. Matthew Hodgart (London, 1963), p. 188. Quotations from Goldsmith are given from the text of the *Collected Works of Oliver Goldsmith*, ed. Arthur Friedman, 5 vols. (Oxford, 1966).
2. Louis B. Wright, *Culture on the Moving Frontier* (Bloomington, Ill., 1955 and 1961), p. 83. I have ignored 'Auburndale' (Wisconsin, Florida) and 'Auburntown' (Tennessee).
3. *Letters and Prose Writings of William Cowper*, ed. J. King and C. Ryskamp (Oxford, 1981), II, 407.

6

The Sentimental Prophecy: A Study of *The Deserted Village*

by JOHN MONTAGUE

> On a summer midnight, you can hear the music
> Of the weak pipe and the little drum
> And see them dancing around the bonfire . . .
> Rustically solemn or in rustic laughter
> Lifting heavy feet in clumsy shoes,
> Earth feet, loam feet, lifted in country mirth
> Mirth of those long since under earth
> Nourishing the corn. Keeping time,
> Keeping the rhythm in their dancing
> As in their living in the living seasons. . . .
>
> T. S. Eliot, *East Coker*

The Deserted Village, like *The Vicar of Wakefield* and *She Stoops to Conquer*, is one of Goldsmith's acknowledged masterpieces, probably the most distinguished long poem by an Irishman. And yet, one is surprised, despite its popularity and apparent simplicity, by the general confusion of views concerning it: enough, indeed, to suggest something curious about the poem. The description of the village, in particular, has proved a stumbling block; according to Macaulay, 'It is made up of incongruous parts.'

> The village in its happy days is a true English village. The village in its decay is an Irish village. The felicity and the

90

misery which Goldsmith has brought close together belong to different countries, and to two different stages in the progress of society . . . by joining the two he has produced something which never was and never will be seen in any part of the world.

For the Irish literary nationalist, of course, the question is simple: the village is Lissoy, as sketched by Newell (Goldsmith's *Poetical Works*, 1811) and signposted by the Irish Tourist Board with familiar couplets. The Rev. Annesley Strean, who succeeded Goldsmith's brother in the curacy of Kilkenny West, has related the incident upon which the poem is supposedly based:

> The poem of *The Deserted Village* took its origin from the circumstance of General Robert Napper . . . having purchased an extensive tract of the country surrounding Lissoy or *Auburn*; in consequence of which many families, here called cottiers, were removed, to make room for the intended improvements of what was now to become the wide domain of a rich man. . . .[1]

This is valuable information, tracing the development of the theme from the poet's boyhood, but it does not prove that Lissoy is Auburn, and that *The Deserted Village* is a specifically Irish poem, although it is much loved and quoted in Ireland, even by Ministers of Agriculture. More subtly, Yeats saw Goldsmith as part of the Anglo-Irish tradition: 'Goldsmith and the Dean, Berkeley and Burke have travelled' on his winding stair. But his picture of *The Deserted Village* in 'The Seven Sages' is curiously selective; he seems to regard it as a vision of the ills of Ireland before the rise of nationalism.

> Oliver Goldsmith sang what he had seen,
> Roads full of beggars, cattle in the fields,
> But never saw the trefoil stained with blood,
> The avenging leaf those fields raised up against it.

Robert Graves, who also regards himself as an Anglo-Irish poet, gives the most forceful expression of this point of view in *The Crowning Privilege*, relating the poem to the Gaelic Aislings or Vision poems of the eighteenth century:

> . . . *The Deserted Village*, despite its aim of formality, is a true poem, because, like Swift, Goldsmith was in earnest. He was

offering, disguised as an essay on the break-up of English village society, a lament for the ills of Ireland, modelled on contemporary Irish minstrel songs—walk, description, meditation, moral vision, invocation of the Goddess; even the distressful crone is there, and the damsel who tears out her hair in handfuls. Auburn really lies in County Roscommon; the poem is full of personal recollections, and glows with sorrowful anger.[2]

Against this, of course, there is the fact that the poem is specifically about 'England's griefs'; that the whole argument is a development of the vision of England in decay in lines 393–412 of *The Traveller*; that the Dedication speaks (like a correspondent in the *Public Advertiser* of 29 September 1780[3]) of what Goldsmith had seen in the English countryside, 'for the four or five years past'. On this, and the evidence of Goldsmith's remarkable early essay 'The Revolution in Low Life', R. S. Crane, one of the most intelligent of Goldsmith's academic critics, concludes:

> . . . that the immediate social background of that poem must be sought in England, not in Ireland, and that, historically the lament over the ruin of Auburn must be regarded as simply the most memorable of a long series of pamphlets called forth in the sixties and seventies of the eighteenth century by the English agricultural revolution.[4]

But even at that level, there is a certain confusion, for as some critics have pointed out, Goldsmith seems less concerned with the agricultural revolution than with the growth of a commercial aristocracy, the 'Nabob' class described also in Samuel Foote's plays and Langhorne's *The Country Justice*. In *The Traveller*, such men, enriched with the gains of empire, threaten the liberties of England; their purchase of estates is part of their movement towards position and power. In England, says Dorothy George, 'it was a general ambition to own land, the chief source of social consideration and political influence.'[5] It is 'the man of wealth and pride' in *The Deserted Village* who 'takes up a space that many poor supplied'. This process is somewhat different from the desire for agricultural improvement which gave rise to the Enclosure Acts, of which there were over a thousand in the period 1760–80 alone, as opposed to a hundred in the first half of the century. But at least some of the 'Nabobs' were improving farmers; the result, in any case, tended to be the dispossession of the small holder, and the beginnings of the flight from the land; the better conditions of the earlier part of the century when the rural population had increased, became by contrast an Arcadia, a Golden Age. Here again, the nationalist element cannot be discounted, for it may well have been Goldsmith's early experiences in what one commentator has called 'the rural slum' of Ireland which created his bias against landlordism. The agrarian problem has been one of the major subjects of Irish poetry in English from Goldsmith's near neighbour and contemporary, Lawrence Whyte, a Westmeath schoolmaster,[6] to Allingham's *Laurence Bloomfield*; perhaps even to Patrick Kavanagh's *The Great Hunger*, which is, like Crabbe's *The Village*, a repudiation of the traditional rustic idyll, a sort of anti-Goldsmith.

We have said enough, I think, to suggest that the simplicity of *The Deserted Village* is rather deceptive. A song of exile from Lissoy, a protest against the Enclosure Acts and/or the new commercial oligarchy, a vision of the ills of Ireland: the poem does indeed answer partly to each of these descriptions. But it is also something more, something which includes and transcends all these things; seen in the context of Oliver Goldsmith's career it has the force of a final statement, the culminating vision of that decay in his own time, which haunted him from his earliest essay, *An Enquiry into the Present State of Polite Learning* (1759), onwards. Whether Auburn is an Irish or an English village is, from this point of view, irrelevant; it is a composite picture, deliberately striving beyond detail to a general view. Whether the weight of meaning Goldsmith places upon the poem does not, in fact, have an effect other than he intended is something we can only discover from a closer examination. In dealing with it we are in the unusual position of possessing something very near a first prose draft in 'The Revolution in Low Life', published in *Lloyd's Magazine* eight years earlier, on 14–16 January 1762.

The Deserted Village stands in a very close relationship to *The Traveller*; it might be described as a sequel, although the later poem is much the better known. There are indications in the picture of Italy where 'nought remain'd of all that riches gave,/ But towns unman'd, and lords without a slave', but the obvious source is the passage 397–412, including

> Have we not seen, at pleasure's lordly call,
> The smiling long-frequented village fall?[7]

The Deserted Village is, in fact, an expansion of these lines, and for a specific purpose: to dramatize the ravages of opulence in Britain by its effect upon the most vulnerable part of society, rural life. In *The Traveller*, the moral is cumulative, leading to a rhetorical appeal: whatever autobiographical involvement there is is mainly in the analysis of 'the traveller'. In *The Deserted Village*, the autobiographical and the didactic meet: the result is an emotional appeal calculated to wring the withers of the reader. What form it takes we shall soon begin to see.

> Sweet AUBURN, lovliest village of the plain,
> Where health and plenty cheared the labouring swain,
> Where smiling spring its earliest visit paid,
> And parting summer's lingering blooms delayed,
> Dear lovely bowers of innocence and ease. . . .

What one notices in this passage, I think, is its delicate conventionality. Although Goldsmith was a countryman, there are surprisingly few fresh 'images of external nature' (to use Wordsworth's phrase[8]) in the poem; much less, for instance, than in *An History of the Earth and Animated Nature*, where the descriptions often combine great beauty and exactness. One does not expect close natural observation in eighteenth-century poetry—though there is a good deal in Thomson's *Seasons*—but here, one feels, the pastoral clichés of eighteenth-century poetry are being used to a very definite artistic purpose, the evocation of a 'Golden Age' of rural life. Auburn is not a particular, but a universal village, the loveliest of the plain, a pastoral Eden evoking the essence of every Virgilian eclogue and Horatian retreat; it even has special climatic privileges. Notice the enumeration of 'every charm', with its appropriate adjective (ll. 10–11):

> The sheltered cot, the cultivated farm,
> The never failing brook, the busy mill . . .

leading to the ritual of pleasures, 'in sweet succession' (ll. 23–4):

> And still as each repeated pleasure tired,
> Succeeding sports the mirthful band inspired . . .

What is being described here is Goldsmith's ideal society, a local culture based upon ritual and frugal content, as seen in *The Vicar of Wakefield* (particularly the opening of Chapter IV) and in the opening of 'The Revolution in Low Life'.

> I spent part of the last summer in a little village, distant about fifty miles from town, consisting of near an hundred houses. It lay entirely out of the road of commerce, and was inhabited by a race of men who followed the primeval profession of agriculture for several generations. Though strangers to opulence, they were unacquainted with distress; few of them were known either to acquire a fortune or to die in indigence. By a long intercourse and frequent intermarriages they were all become in a manner one family; and, when the work of the day was done, spent the night agreeably in visits at each other's houses. Upon those occasions the poor traveller and stranger were always welcome; and they kept up the stated days of festivity with the strictest observance. (III, 195)

If one remembers that the impulse behind generalization in eighteenth-century literature was often a vision of the universe as divine order—the work of 'the Great Disposer' of *Animated Nature*—then here we have an example of poetic diction being specifically used to recall a section of that order. The relevant comparison is not with Thomson or Wordsworth, but with the passage of *East Coker* quoted at the beginning of this essay.

After this accumulation of images of rural content—the opening is, with the ending paragraph, the longest in the poem—the final half-line has a deliberate curt brutality: 'But all these charms are fled.' Having involved us in his 'smiling plain' (a Virgilian phrase), Goldsmith now—abruptly and dramatically—shows its complete ruin, and it is typical of his talent that this should be one of the most powerful and closely observed passages in the poem (ll. 41–4).

> No more thy glassy brook reflects the day,
> But choked with sedges, works its weedy way.
> Along thy glades, a solitary guest,
> The hollow sounding bittern guards its nest. . . .

From the sentimental to the pathetic: after these two paragraphs, we are ready for a solemn statement of the thesis of the poem (ll. 51–2).

> Ill fares the land, to hastening ills a prey,
> Where wealth accumulates, and men decay. . . .

What strikes in this section of the poem (ll. 51–74) is its directness and simplicity: an immediate and very explicit underlining of the moral behind the destruction of Auburn. What is less obvious is the slurring of the time sequence, so that the rural paradise of Auburn exists both in the immediate past—'But times are altered'—and in the fairy-tale never-never—'A time there was'. Goldsmith's technique in *The Deserted Village* is to carry his thesis by the emotional effect of his skilful alternation between images of original innocence and malignant destruction; the relatively few didactic passages are made as simple and clear as possible. It is not that his argument is unimportant—it is rather so important to him, so much a part of his total vision, that he is prepared to use all the poetic means in his power to invade the reader on its behalf. That is why we cannot, like Alice, read *The Deserted Village* just for its pictures, because its pictures are part of a calculated attack upon our sympathies.

The imaginary walk through a deserted Auburn (ll. 73–135) gives the game away; it is pure 'Mother Machree', the lament of the returned exile who finds nettles growing across the doorstep.[9] One of the more impressive aspects of *The Traveller* is the way the narrator admits the permanence of his exile. Although his wish is often 'to find/ Some spot to real happiness consign'd', he recognizes his fate: 'not destin'd such delights to share'. But the exiled narrator of *The Deserted Village* does return, and his personal lament for the transience of things mortal adds to the emotional bias of the poem. The destruction of the village is not only the destruction of the narrator's childhood, but also of his dream of an ideal retreat and escape (ll. 97–102):

> O blest retirement, friend to life's decline,
> Retreats from care that never must be mine,
> How happy he who crowns in shades like these,
> A youth of labour with an age of ease;

> Who quits a world where strong temptations try,
> And, since 'tis hard to combat, learns to fly.

An interesting example of this poetic 'whitewashing' is the way lines of 'Description of an Author's Bed Chamber', from Letter XXX of *The Citizen of the World*, change on their assimilation into *The Deserted Village*. The original, with its humorously sordid details, has great vivacity, like Swift's 'A Description of the Morning' or Eliot's 'Preludes'; it shows that Goldsmith was capable of energetic, realistic observation.

> Where the Red Lion flaring o'er the way,
> Invites each passing stranger that can pay;
> Where Calvert's butt, and Parson's black champaign,
> Regale the drabs and bloods of Drury-Lane. . . .

But when the room reappears in *The Deserted Village*, 'The humid wall with paltry pictures spread' becomes 'The pictures placed for ornament and use'; 'the twelve rules the royal martyr drew' change to 'the twelve good rules'; 'The rusty grate unconscious of a fire' becomes 'the hearth . . ./ With aspen boughs, and flowers, and fennel gay' and the 'five crack'd tea-cups' reappear as 'broken tea-cups, wisely kept for shew'. The reasons for the change are obvious but there seems to me a thwarting of the original motive behind the lines which is most revealing.

The portraits which follow (ll. 237–50) are the most praised part of *The Deserted Village*: 'a skill and concision seldom equalled since Chaucer', as Eliot says in his essay on 'Johnson as Critic and Poet'. The comparison, we can see, has a deeper relevance, for it is a medieval, i.e. Chaucerian social order Goldsmith is evoking. But with a difference, because Chaucer's portraits contain a good deal of subtle irony and criticism, which Goldsmith, as special pleader, cannot allow. The only relief from unadulterated virtue is humour, 'And even the story ran that he could gauge'; 'And news much older than their ale went round' which hardly compares with the delicate implications in Chaucer's portrait of the Prioress:

> There was also a Nonne, a Prioresse,
> That of hir smylyng was ful symple and coy;
> Hire gretteste ooth was by Seinte Loy;
> And she was cleped Madame Eglentyne.

Ful weel she soong the service dyvyne,
Entuned in hir nose ful semely. . . .

Chaucer's people are human, too human often, he seems to suggest, for their callings. Goldsmith's portraits tend to the ideal, and are saved only by their humour and homely detail. Again, this is not to be attributed entirely to the conventionality of eighteenth-century poetry. Compare the way, for instance, irony plays around the central character in *The Vicar of Wakefield*, or the more bitter portrait of a parson father in The Man in Black's tale in *The Citizen of the World*; nothing of this appears in *The Deserted Village*. The 'sweet oblivion' of the village inn seems far from Goldsmith's very unIrish attack on alehouses in 'Upon Political Frugality': 'Alehouses are ever an occasion of debauchery and excess, and either in a religious or political light, it would be our highest interest to have the greatest part of them suppressed' (I, 441). That Goldsmith was capable of more balanced portraiture in poetry we know from *Retaliation*; I am not objecting to the procedure, only defining its calculated appeal.

A very curious thing happens in the next, and openly didactic, section of the poem (ll. 250–300). One notices the implications Goldsmith makes in passing from 'the woodman's ballad' to 'the midnight masquerade'; from the natural order of 'spontaneous joys' to the unnatural 'freaks of wanton wealth'. There is great rhetorical power in his picture of trade (ll. 269–70),

Proud swells the tide with loads of freighted ore,
And shouting Folly hails them from her shore . . .

where the personifications (as Donald Davie has pointed out of Augustan poetry generally) are energized by the verbs, and joined in a minor dramatic situation or 'plot', like the ocean and rampart in the description of Holland in *The Traveller*. This sweeping vision of energy, however, is broken by the peremptory abruptness of the half-line—'Yet count our gains'—and then reversed in painting the other side of the picture, the usurpations of the commercial magnate (ll. 279–80):

The robe that wraps his limbs in silken sloth,
Has robbed the neighbouring fields of half their growth. . . .

Here the robe becomes a reptile, its strangling presence dramatized in the hissing end of one line, which defeats our expectations ('sloth' instead of 'cloth'), and the dragging length of the next. The rich man's estate 'spurns the cottage from the green'; again the transference of personification works through an active verb. But it is the last couplet in the paragraph to which I especially wish to draw attention, the epic simile which arises from it (ll. 287–308), and their implication in the whole context of the poem.

Here the landscape is compared—one can hardly escape the meaning—to an ageing woman in the hands of a seducer (ll. 285–86):

> . . . adorned for pleasure all
> In barren splendour [she] feebly waits the fall.

One would hesitate to insist on the sexual implication of 'fall' and 'barren' if they were not so consistently carried through in the following paragraph (ll. 291–95):

> But when those charms are past, for charms are frail,
> When time advances, and when *lovers* fail,
> She then shines forth *sollicitous* to bless,
> In all the glaring *impotence* of dress.
> Thus fares the land, by luxury *betrayed*. . . .

At least some of the 'triumphant felicity' Donald Davie attributes to the phrase 'the glaring impotence of dress'—a more striking version of 'barren splendour'—comes from its sexual connotations, its summary of the pathetic drama in which the rake (luxury) betrays the 'fair female' (land), who can now only hope to appeal through artifical skills.[10] The only trouble is the basic confusion in the comparison which leaves the land both waiting for 'the fall' and 'betrayed'; if I make heavy weather of the point, it is because I feel that Goldsmith's excessive involvement with his theme manifests itself in such sleights of word.

Donald Davie has analysed the effects in the rest of this paragraph: 'the startling force given to "smiling land" when it is seen to smile with heartless indifference on the ruined peasant'; the way the cant of the landscape gardener—his 'striking vistas' and 'surprised views'—is used with ironical intent (I am not quite so sure of the way the peasant 'scourged by famine from the smiling land' sinks—presumably in the sea—'without one arm to save'). What has not been commented on, I think, is the contrast between this picture of the landscaped countryside and the picture of desolation presented in the second paragraph of the poem, where 'the long grass o'ertops the mouldering wall'. One could argue that this is not Auburn, but the land around it; yet in both the same drama is taking place, and the peasant is in flight 'from the spoiler's hand'. Goldsmith is presumably presenting the two kinds of rural usurpation, the one of the improving farmer where 'half a tillage stints thy smiling plain' and the other where the land is redesigned as a private garden. It might seem another example of Goldsmith's determination to carry his argument, but it is also justified in view of the fuller picture it gives of the problem. The village, the countryside, and even the 'common's fenceless limits' (l. 305) are all divided by 'the sons of wealth'.[11] Auburn is as symbolically representative a village in its downfall, as in its original order.

The next section (ll. 309–84) deals with the Flight from the Land, and it is the climax of Goldsmith's emotional treatment of his theme. All the clichés are there, the ruined maid (the palpable realization, so to speak, of the parallel between the 'ruined' land and the fallen woman), the family, from 'the good old sire' to 'his lovely daughter, lovelier in her tears', exiled to the 'horrid shore'. And yet, one is not really shocked by it, partly because of its position in the whole movement of the poem; it represents a last emotional appeal before the prophetic vision of the closing paragraphs. Besides, there are passages of considerable power; the picture of urban desolation, for instance, has a Johnsonian vigour and loathing in its contrasts: not quite what one expects in Goldsmith (ll. 315–22).

> Here, while the courtier glitters in brocade,
> There the pale artist plies the sickly trade;
> Here, while the proud their long drawn pomps display,
> There the black gibbet glooms beside the way.
> The dome where pleasure holds her midnight reign,
> Here richly deckt admits the gorgeous train,
> Tumultuous grandeur crowds the blazing square,
> The rattling chariots clash, the torches glare. . . .

This, together with the glimpses of the outcast prostitute, might be said to anticipate aspects of Blake, or even Baudelaire, in 'Le Crépuscule du Soir':

> A travers les lueurs que tourmente le vent
> La Prostitution s'allume dans les rues . . .
> On entend çà et là les cuisines siffler,
> Les théâtre glapir, les orchestres ronfler. . . .

The 'gorgeous train', of course, contrasts with another, very different, the train of poor people driven from Auburn; in one phrase ('thy fair tribes', l. 338) Goldsmith seems to link their fate with that of the Jews. They go (ll. 341–42)

> . . . To distant climes, a dreary scene,
> Where half the convex world intrudes between. . . .

The unusual but geographically correct adjective (their destination is America) and the active verb ('intrudes', like an unfriendly stranger) dramatize the distance separating them from all they have known. The picture of North America that follows is unreal, but dramatically so, one feels: a land enlarged by the exile's anticipation and fear of the unknown. Even the sentimentality of the group portrait can be justified: it is a family which is being driven away; the traditional and sacred unit of society is being violated (ll. 371–73).[12]

> The good old sire, the first prepared to go
> To new found worlds, and wept for others woe . . .
> His lovely daughter, lovelier in her tears,
> The fond companion of his helpless years,
> Silent went next, neglectful of her charms,
> And left a lover's for a father's arms. . . .

The punning irony of 'new-found worlds'—glamorous to explorers and traders but not to them—is saving and bitter, while the lovers, separated by luxury's baleful influence, remind us of Pound's Canto XLV:

> Usura slayeth the child in the womb
> It stayeth the young man's courting
> It hath brought palsy to bed, lyeth
> Between the young bride and her bridegroom.
> CONTRA NATURAM

The ending, of course, is powerful; the rhetorical outbreak in the short second-last paragraph, the long sadness of the close. Now the real motive force of the poem appears; it is not merely that villages, like Auburn, are being dispossessed, but that this dispossession is part of a whole pattern of economic greed which will, in time, destroy society. 'Those who constitute the basis of the great fabric of society should be particularly regarded; for in policy, as in architecture, ruin is most fatal when it begins from the bottom' (III, 151). Goldsmith's comment in his essay on the English clergy might well be applied to the argument of *The Deserted Village*. It is this vision of decay consequent upon imperial expansion and excessive trade, which haunted Goldsmith throughout his career; like the Roman Empire, like the commercial oligarchies of Venice and Holland, Britain will sink into obscurity, destroyed by her 'rage of gain'. Just as Goldsmith has described in Auburn a medieval order, so his rebuke is based upon the medieval analogy between the human body and society[13]; he even invokes, like Pound, the religious sanction against usury, as CONTRA NATURAM (ll. 385–94).

> O luxury! Thou curst by heaven's decree,
> How ill exchanged are things like these for thee!
> How do thy potions with insidious joy,
> Diffuse their pleasures only to destroy!
> Kingdoms by thee, to sickly greatness grown,
> Boast of a florid vigour not their own.
> At every draught more large and large they grow,
> A bloated mass of rank unwieldy woe;
> Till sapped their strength, and every part unsound,
> Down, down they sink, and spread a ruin round.

This paragraph occurs at exactly the same point in the poem as the magnificent outbreak in *The Traveller*, 'But when contending chiefs blockade the throne . . .'; it is an indication of Goldsmith's almost mathematical planning of his effects. The ending sequence of the earlier poem—a vision of destruction and waste, a scene of mournful exile, with a global invocation, leading to a final moral—is triumphantly repeated in *The Deserted Village*; Goldsmith is a master of the melancholy diapason (ll. 395–98):

> Even now the devastation is begun,
> And half the business of destruction done;
> Even now, methinks, as pondering here I stand,
> I see the rural virtues leave the land.

The 'rural virtues', for Goldsmith, as for the Agrarians in Ireland or America, are actually the root virtues of the good society. And since literary and political health are interconnected, poetry joins them in exile; the prophecy at the end of the *Enquiry* is fulfilled, and the Muse is heard weeping 'her own decline' (ll. 407–16).

> And thou, sweet Poetry, thou loveliest maid,
> Still first to fly where sensual joys invade;
> Unfit in these degenerate times of shame,
> To catch the heart, or strike for honest fame;
> Dear charming nymph, neglected and decried,
> My shame in crowds, my solitary pride . . .
> Thou nurse of every virtue, fare thee well.

Imperceptibly, therefore, the destruction of Auburn has come to signify the destruction of many things: the narrator's childhood and his dreams of escape and peaceful retirement (with which the reader presumably identifies), 'rural virtues', 'all the connexions of kindred' in the family unit, 'spontaneous joys' as opposed to unnatural artifice, virginal innocence, and, finally, poetry itself, even perhaps religion (l. 405): 'And piety with wishes placed above. . . .' Auburn, in fact, is identified with the good of society and of England, and *The Deserted Village* is one of the first statements of a great modern theme: the erosion of traditional values and natural rhythms in a commercial society; the fall of Auburn is the fall of a whole social order. It looks forward to Wordsworth, even, as we can see, to Lawrence and to Pound, and to Faulkner's protest against the destruction of the Big Woods. One's attitude towards the poem, therefore, partly depends on one's attitude towards modern history; one cannot help feeling, for instance, that Eliot's admiration for *The Deserted Village* may be partly due to the fact that it represents an anticipation of certain aspects of his own work: a sort of rural *Waste Land*. That Goldsmith deduced so much from what he has seen of the Agricultural Revolution may appear, according to one's viewpoint, misguided or miraculously prophetic. Whether the symbol of Auburn can support the tremendous burden of meaning the poem places on it is another matter; if sentimentality is a display of emotion in excess of the given facts, then *The Deserted Village* might justly be called a sentimental prophecy. And that may be the most Irish thing about it; as 'sad historian of the pensive plain', Goldsmith has a good deal in common with the emotional exaggeration of the Irish bards, described in his essay on Carolan, the harper. For although the idea of an Irish literature in English was outside his experience, *The Deserted Village* rehearses one of the most Irish themes of all, a forecast of the downfall of Britain through imperial greed. He produced the first anti-imperialistic poem in the period of England's greatest imperial expansion. We have, perhaps, a special claim on the poem: but so, I think, has the whole tradition of modern literature, from my own *Rough Field* to the Polish *antentyzm* which claims Goldsmith as ancestor.

NOTES

1. Rev. Edward Mangin, M.A., *Essay on Light Reading*, 1808; quoted also in Newell's edition of the *Poetical Works* (London, 1811).
2. Lecture 2, 'The Age of Obsequiousness' (London, 1955). Lissoy, of course, is not in Roscommon, and there is no damsel in the poem 'who tears out her hair in handfuls'. These vigorous errors in detail do not detract from the element of truth in Graves's feeling about the poem, any more than the supposed 'cattle in the fields' does from Yeats's.
3. 'In one of his country excursions he resided near the house of a great West Indian, in the neighbourhood of which several cottages were destroyed, in order to enlarge, or rather to polish, the prospect.'
4. *New Essays by Oliver Goldsmith*, ed. R. S. Crane (Chicago, 1927), Introduction, p. xl and 'The Revolution in Low Life', ibid., pp. 116–24. See also *Collected Works of Oliver Goldsmith*, ed. Arthur Friedman (Oxford, 1966), III, 195–98. References in the text are to Friedman. A review of *The Oxford Book of Irish Verse* in *Poetry* (July 1959) stresses that 'it is an Anglican village that Goldsmith is writing about, where the pastor is shepherd to all', which would hardly be the case in Catholic Ireland. 'Only perhaps in the poet's description of that "horrid shore" to which the poor are driven in exile is there something of a recognisably Irish exaggeration.'

5. *England in Transition* (London, 1931). Dr. George is opposed to the idea—promulgated by Goldsmith and others—of a Golden Age of British agriculture; while the changes may have struck the yeoman or freeholder harder than any other class, the result was a rise in the overall standard of living. Most modern social historians are so eager to accept this view that one suspects a certain bias.

6. Whether Goldsmith knew Whyte's *Original Poems on Various Subjects, Serious and Diverting* (it was published in Dublin in 1740 and again in 1742, and was presumably easily available to a Trinity student) is problematical, but despite the difference in literary quality, there are sufficient resemblances to indicate that the experience behind *The Deserted Village* was initially Irish:

> Their native soil were forced to quit,
> So Irish landlords thought it fit
> Who without evening or rout,
> For their improvements turned them out. . . .
> How many villages they razed
> How many parishes laid waste . . .
> Whole colonies, to shun the fate
> Of being oppress'd at such a rate,
> By tyrants who still raise this rent,
> Sail'd to the Western Continent.

7. In *A Prospect of Society*, the early version of *The Traveller*, the lines appear as:

> Have we not seen, at pleasure's lordly call
> An hundred villages in ruin fall?

which—with 'The Revolution in Low Life'—shows Goldsmith's quite extraordinarily early awareness of the significance of the Agricultural Revolution.

8. Essay supplementary to the Preface to the *Lyrical Ballads* (2nd edn., 1815). 'Now it is remarkable that, excepting the Nocturnal Reverie of Lady Winchelsea, and a passage or two in the Windsor Forest of Pope, the poetry of the period intervening between the publication of Paradise Lost and The Seasons does not contain a single new image of external nature. . . .' This is sheer pamphleteering, of course, because an image like 'sweet as the primrose peeps beneath the thorn' is botanically exact as anything in Wordsworth.

9. One is not surprised to read in Newell's edition of the *Poetical Works*, of the local belief 'that "the Poet" as he is usually called there, after his pedestrian tour upon the Continent of Europe, returned to and resided in the village some time. . . . It is moreover believed that the havock which had been made in his absence among those favourite scenes of his youth, affected his mind so deeply, that he actually composed a great part of *The Deserted Village* at Lissoy.' There seems little doubt that Goldsmith never returned to Ireland, but he often expressed his acute sense of change. Cf. Friedman, III, 67: 'To grow old in the same fields where we once were young; to be capable of every moment beholding objects that recal our early pleasures . . .' 'Happy could so charming an

105

illusion still continue,' as he says in the second issue of *The Bee* (I, 385).

10. The parallel is repeated in Crabbe's *The Village*, ll. 79–84. See Donald Davie, *Purity of Diction in English Verse* (London, 1952; re-issued 1967), and his edition of *The Late Augustans* (London, 1958) for some of the most valuable discussion of Goldsmith.

11. 'In almost every part of the kingdom the laborious husbandman has been reduced, and the lands are now either occupied by some general undertaker, or turned into enclosures destined for the purposes of amusement or luxury.' 'A Revolution in Low Life' (III, 197).

12. Cf. the corresponding passage in 'The Revolution in Low Life': 'The modest matron followed her husband in tears, and often looked back at the little mansion where she had passed her life in innocence, and to which she was never more to return; while the beautiful daughter parted for ever from her Lover, who was now become too poor to maintain her as his wife. *All the connexions of kindred were now irreparably broken . . .*' (III, 196) (my italics).

13. This analogy is also used in the parable of 'The Kingdom of Lao' in Letter XXV of *The Citizen of the World*: 'Their commerce with their neighbours was totally destroyed; and that with their colonies was every day naturally and necessarily declining . . . In short, the state resembled one of those bodies bloated with disease, whose bulk is only a symptom of its wretchedness' (II, 107). See also Tawney's *Religion and the Rise of Capitalism*, Chapter I, especially, 'The Medieval Background'.

7

The Dialectic of
The Traveller

by PAT ROGERS

In a story by Jorge Luis Borges, called 'El Aleph', the narrator alludes to the manifestations of the topographic urge in literature. He observes that he once had occasion to examine the fifteen thousand Alexandrines ('dodecasílabos') which constitute Drayton's *Poly Olbion*. He terms the poem a considerable, if limited, achievement, and describes it as a less wearisome undertaking than an allied venture by Carlos Argentino:

> He had it in mind to versify the whole wide world. . . . By 1941, he had already dispatched a few hectares of the state of Queensland, rather more than a kilometre of the course of the Ob, a gasometer in the north of Veracruz, the principal business houses in the parish of Concepción, the mansion of Moriana Cambaceres de Alvear in September the Eleventh Street in Belgrano, and one of the Turkish baths not far from the celebrated aquarium in Brighton.[1]

The passage is characteristic of Borges in its apparent literalness, its precision, and its muffled irony. One could say that the joke lies in confronting grandiose literary ambition, to provide a 'comprehensive' reflection of the world, with the minuscule coverage which is all that any writer can achieve. Nevertheless, Drayton comes off relatively well, if not altogether unscathed. The absurdity of *Poly Olbion* is there on the surface, in the fifteen thousand lumbering hexameters. For

107

its time, we feel, it was a noble enterprise; but the modern world has become too complex for any such vaunting designs, so that nowadays the absurdity invades the content.

Oliver Goldsmith stood halfway between Drayton and Carlos Argentino. He wrote at a juncture when it was possible to see the inapplicability of Drayton, and yet when writers had not given up the desire to make sense of the totality of the world they inhabited. In order to survey mankind from China to Peru, it was increasingly felt as necessary that some kind of schema should be imposed on the disparate material. Indeed, the mere 'survey' as such was ceasing to fulfil its task adequately. Understanding appeared to demand an argumentative structure and not just a descriptive basis. From French ideologues, above all, mid-century writers learnt to construct their anatomies of the world in terms of comparison, often in the precise guise of a dialectical system. There are the beginnings of this in James Thomson's *Liberty*; but, as I shall try to show, it is in *The Traveller* that Goldsmith evolved a fully-fledged geographical dialectic.

The main verbal activity plays around ideas which centre on *hard* and *soft*: to that extent, the poem can be related to so-called 'hard' and 'soft' primitivism, as those have been differentiated within the eighteenth century. The opposed notions cover many direct antitheses:

These rocks, by custom, turn to beds of down. (l. 86)

With secret course, which no loud storms annoy,
Glides the smooth current of domestic joy. (ll. 433–34)

These ideas fan out to a wider contrast, between peace, ease, opulence, plenty, as against tumult, penury, deprivation. It is important that social or economic conditions as well as bare geographic or climatic facts may be involved. Indeed, part of the rhetoric of *The Traveller* is designed to equate, or at least align, these different senses of hard and soft.

But there are at least two significant complications, which are related to contemporary sensibility. First, the argumentative structure is overlaid by traditional ideas of cultural differentiation, and specifically by the new overtones of an old dichotomy—that between north and south. Secondly, the stock attributes of the seasons are hinted at, in the central sections of the poem, thus enabling Goldsmith to reinforce national stereotypes with contrasts drawn from the natural order (and thus to make them stick more firmly).

1

The distinction between the hard north and the soft south is very old and very widely spread. As far as Europe goes, it is clearly apparent in the implied contrast Tacitus draws between the virtuous Germanic tribes and the effete Romans.[2] In many uses, the line is drawn around the Alps, with the show of limp effeminacy opening in Venice. The precise placing of the line might vary, but this broad categorization survived for centuries. It was, however, in the wake of the Enlightenment that the values of the 'primitive' north could be most strategically opposed to those of the 'degenerate' south; the rise of Saxon scholarship, the new interest in Nordic folklore, the emphasis on remote embattled bards (far from the Mediterranean seed-bed of high European culture), all came to the support of this strategy. For Goethe and Madame de Staël, the journey to Italy is symbolic of a shift in feeling. Mme. de Staël in Germany picks up the internal north/south distinction which is drawn in most European countries, but even southern Germany is not really 'southern' in the cultural sense:

> L'Allemagne offre encore quelques traces d'une nature non habitée. Depuis les Alpes jusqu'à la mer, entre le Rhin et le Danube, vous voyez un pays couvert de chênes et de sapins, traversé par des fleuves d'une imposante beauté, et coupé par des montagnes dont l'aspect est très pittoresque; mais de vastes bruyères, des sables, des routes souvent négligées, un climat sévère, remplissent d'abord l'âme de tristesse; et ce n'est qu'à la longue qu'on découvre ce qui peut attacher à ce séjour.
>
> Le midi de l'allemagne est très bien cultivé; cependant il y a toujours dans les plus belles contrées de ce pays quelque chose de sérieux, qui fait plutôt penser au travail qu'aux plaisirs, aux vertus des habitants qu'aux charmes de la nature.[3]

When Goldsmith wrote, the precise literary implications which Mme. de Staël had in mind were not yet abroad in

English culture. Nonetheless, *The Traveller* is an important stage in, as it were, unspecifying the cultural meaning of north and south, and thus making the distinction available as part of a general critique.

Modern geopolitics has reasserted the Biblical potency of east and west. But for many centuries it was north and south which seemed the central divide. When an image of absolute contrariety was needed, it was frequently to this notion that writers turned: witness Richard, Duke of York, to the Queen in *3 Henry VI*:

> Thou art as opposite to every good
> As the Antipodes are unto us,
> Or as the south to the septentrion. (I. iv. 136)

The epithets associated with these points of the compass, signifying 'characteristic of the north [south]' came to have definite associations, which may be tracked down in *O.E.D.* citations. Thus Pope in the *Essay on Criticism*:

> Which not alone the *Southern Wit* sublimes,
> But ripens Spirits in cold *Northern Climes*.

Indeed, without any direct mention of climatic factors, the terms brought with them strong implications, so that 'northern' by itself might suggest the 'cold Septentrion blasts' of *Paradise Regained*. Moreover, as interest in the Gothic developed, both in the area of political theory and of linguistic inquiry, the associations of 'northern' acquired a new penumbra, as (by implied absence) did those of its antonym. Many of these tendencies, already hinted at in a writer like Sir William Temple, become acutely present in Montesquieu, notably Book I of *L'Esprit des Lois*, Chapters XIV–XVII. Chapter XIV asserts some of the commonplaces passed down to the Enlightenment: 'people of the North are less capable of [pain] than the delicate fibre of the inhabitants of warm countries. . . . You must flay a Muscovite alive to make him feel.'[4] A Muscovite, note, is culturally a northerner; the term connotes a climatic region and a cultural grouping, not a precise geographic area.

The second standard system which is exploited in *The Traveller* is related in some ways. This is the lore of the seasons, as transmitted through poetry, painting and music. Each season had acquired its own set of attributes, which were commonly employed to define and characterize the particular stage in a yearly cycle. In recent English poetry, two works which contributed powerfully to the tradition were Pope's *Pastorals* and Thomson's *Seasons*; both had given the traditional motifs a new imaginative direction.[5] Today an even more familiar creation produced in this line of artistic thought is the set of concerti by Vivaldi, known collectively as *Le Stagione*; each of the individual items has a sonnet describing the setting and events in terms of the stock seasonal associations. Some of these properties, I shall argue, were borrowed by Goldsmith to enforce his rhetoric of modal contrast and psychological differentiation.

We do not know as much as we might wish about the intellectual genesis of the poem. The dedication to Oliver's brother Henry contains one brief paragraph of some interest, on the fortunes of the different art-forms as civilization expands; but otherwise this is a document of moderate value. The poet's scanty collection of letters does not provide a single reference to *The Traveller* (a single apparent exception occurs in a letter now shown to have been a forgery). The sale catalogue of Goldsmith's library, conveniently reprinted in the Mansell series, does at least permit one to confine one's guesswork regarding influences within a decently measurable span.[6] But of course mere possession of a volume can never by itself be taken to prove familiarity or even bare acquaintance. Nevertheless, this is one of the areas of evidence I shall be drawing on in my account of the poem, along with a slightly less dangerous source—that is, the books cited or alluded to in Goldsmith's published writings (principally, of course, those written prior to *The Traveller*). The parallels noted by previous editors—Dobson, Friedman, Dixon, Lonsdale and others— are incorporated where they bear directly on my case.[7] In checking the contemporary meaning of key terms in Johnson's *Dictionary*, one occasionally encounters illustrative passages which help to draw the intellectual boundaries of Goldsmith's undertaking. These, then, are some of the main aids to my inquiry.

A word should be perhaps added on the previous readings

of this poem, and the relation of my essay to them. The critical heritage is disappointingly thin. G. S. Rousseau's collection shows that a fair amount of attention was devoted to the work in the century following its composition. Indeed, this particular volume of the Critical Heritage series opens with Johnson's famous assessment in the *Critical Review* for December 1764. Nothing else reproduced by Rousseau is much more help than Johnson's account, brief and generalized though it is. John Langhorne in the *Monthly Review* is fuller but scarcely more detailed in his commentary. Among the later items, Dr. John Aikin provides a fairly intelligent paraphrase, whilst Leigh Hunt has some provocative thoughts on the 'metrical weakness' of the poem: 'GOLDSMITH in his *Traveller* is feeble in misplaced emphasis; for his words are of sufficient length and sound to be pompous in a better situation: he slides now and then into a kind of hurried halt, which is as lame as the feebleness of monosyllables.' But the most important contribution is certainly that of the biographer Prior, who offers much more concrete and substantive analysis. He suggests Addison's *Letter from Italy* as a model; he conducts a detailed investigation into Goldsmith's revisions of the text; and, most important, he provides what is still the best comparison with *Childe Harold*, surely a genuine historical conjuncture rather than an arbitrary collision momentarily engineered by dreams of intertextualism.[8]

Later criticism has likewise owed a good deal to biographers. William Black's volume in the English Men of Letters series (1878) devotes a not very illuminating chapter to the poem. But Austin Dobson in his study (1888) is, predictably, more lively and historically aware, whilst John Forster's life of Goldsmith (1848), although drawing heavily on Prior, makes a significant independent contribution (I do not altogether share Rousseau's estimate of the relative merit of these biographies).[9] In the twentieth century Ralph M. Wardle has written much the best of the lives, and his comments on *The Traveller*, if tending towards faint praise, contain some useful information. The recent critics who have engaged most fully with the poem are Robert H. Hopkins and Ricardo Quintana. The latter gives what seems to me a valuable perspective; he mentions not just Addison but also *Cooper's Hill* and *Windsor Forest*. His conclusion is this:

The Traveller is prospect poetry literally and figuratively; it is a series of verse *characters*, by means of which the different national cultures of the west are compared; it is a patriotic poem, though the patriotism is of a different order from the uncritical nationalism of Addison's *Letter*; it is an estimate of contemporary conditions, condemning much but finding consolation in the thought that nature and reason afford mankind a moral mean between deplorable extremities.

Hopkins sees in the poem an 'antithesis of centripetal and centrifugal patterns', more widely a conflict between action and motion.[10] I shall not be pursuing these notions, but Quinatana's phrase regarding 'verse characters' is pertinent to my theme (as is a good deal of Lonsdale's introductory comment). The question is: *how* does Goldsmith characterize the different cultures, and what modes of typing (social, political, psychological) are utilized in the effort?[11]

2

In Chapter XIII of his *Enquiry into the Present State of Polite Learning in Europe*, Goldsmith touched on an important matter of presentation:

> COUNTRIES wear very different appearances to travellers of different circumstances. A man who is whirled through Europe in a post chaise, and the pilgrim who walks the grand tour on foot, will form very different conclusions.
> *Haud inexpertus loquor.* (I, 331)

The implications of this statement for literary travellers were being explored at this very juncture by Sterne, and soon Smollett was also to face them. As far as Goldsmith's poem is concerned, he takes the bold step of dispensing with the ordinary 'progress' framework altogether. By placing his narrator on his aerial vantage point, the poet eliminates the need to mimic a physical journey from one country to another. The observer, set 'on high above the storm's career' (l. 33), possesses a kind of simultaneous visual and moral grasp of all Europe, unaffected by local accidents of weather. The advantage is that his perceptual and conceptual view can seem a panorama achieved at a glance. The necessary transitions

involve merely a 'turn' of the gaze (l. 165), not a perambula-
tion of the body. As a result, his judgements seem less
subjective, less dependent on the mode of entry. His outlook is
spatial, de-temporalized; in McLuhan's terms, one might
almost say, the narrator achieves the instantaneous reception
of messages found in electronic rather than printed means of
communication. Putting the matter in more guarded historical
terms, one could say that Goldsmith is clinging on to the
quasi-impersonality of the epic formula at a time when most of
the newer tendencies in literature—in the novel, above all—
were working in the opposite direction.

What this means, when we come to the review of the
individual countries, is that the traveller escapes just those
rigours of passage which constitute so much of the ordinary
fare of eighteenth-century travel writing. He is, so to speak,
disembodied. Although the opening of the poem tells us of his
aimless journeys about the globe, and of his disconsolate
verdict that he can call 'no spot of all the world [his] own'
(l. 30), once he achieves his eyrie above the Alps, his posture is
static. He is *sitting*, we must always remember, throughout his
survey of Europe. As distinct from the traditional vagabond,
he sees most when he stops still. Unlike Cain, or the
Wandering Jew, or the Ancient Mariner, or the Flying
Dutchman, this traveller is allowed, if not to rest, at least to
escape his curse long enough to take stock of the places he has
visited. His 'pensive hour' is spent not in analysing his own
experiences, but in reaching fresh conclusions. The poem
represents a release from obsession, as 'The Ancient Mariner'
does not. This is all very different from, for example, Savage's
poem *The Wanderer* (1729), a possible distant model for
Goldsmith. Savage describes his poem as 'a vision', and
indeed his narrator achieves only glimpses of insight. Despite
his invocation of

> CONTEMPLATION, whose unbounded Gaze,
> Swift in a Glance, the Course of Things, surveys;
> Who in *Thy-self* the various View can'st find
> Of Sea, Land, Air, and Heav'n, and human Kind. . . .[12]

Savage does not attain any stable perspective on events. There
appears to be some arcane, perhaps Masonic, message; the

ultimate drift of the poem is closer to that of *The Magic Flute* than that of any other work which comes to mind. And Savage's wanderer does wander: that is to say, his movements are jerky, charted only imprecisely, seemingly unplanned. On the other hand, Goldsmith's traveller carries out a logical, almost abstract survey of major western countries. There is no attempt to dramatize the sheer *confusion* which is so often the lot of the traveller on the ground. Why should there be? He is, explicitly and intentionally, not 'on the ground'.

What has happened, crucially, is that the philosophic traveller has done more than travel; he has studied philosophy. It is at this point that Goldsmith's reading becomes relevant. By this I mean not so much his stock of orthodox travel books, to which the sale catalogue unsurprisingly testifies. Rather, we should look to the works on social, political and constitutional theory; the historical tomes which dealt with such matters as the fall of empires; the treatments of large cultural debates such as the *querelle* of Ancients and Moderns. In the library catalogue, we do indeed find represented authors such as Puffendorf; Charles Rollin; Bossuet; Vertot; Père d'Orleans; Fontenelle; Sir William Temple (four volumes), and so on. The dates of the editions are not always cited, but all those named could have been in Goldsmith's possession in 1760. That comment does not apply to other items, which herald the arrival of the Enlightenment: Diderot's *Oeuvres*, in five volumes, or Helvétius *De l'Homme*. The only Rousseau represented is a collection of 1734 which obviously derives from the poet Jean-Baptiste. More intriguing is the set of Voltaire in nineteen odd volumes: when they were acquired it is impossible to guess, though the *Memoirs of M. de Voltaire* indicate that Goldsmith might have had a need for such a thing by 1759.[13] Almost equally intriguing is item 7 among the octavos, 'Voyage par Winckelman'. But these are speculative connections, and it is more appropriate to consider one firm link.

This concerns Montesquieu, who appears twice in the sale catalogue. Item 4 among the smaller books is 'Lettres de Montesquieu'; item 89 is 'Montesquieu on the Roman Empire, 1759'. There can be no doubt about the latter entry: it concerns *Considérations sur les causes de la grandeur des Romains et*

115

de leur décadence (1734). This was translated as *Reflections* . . .
in the same year, and an edition appeared in London in
1759. There is, naturally, no guarantee that Goldsmith
actually obtained it in that year: but it is altogether
probable. As for the other item, that must surely refer to the
Lettres Persanes, though in which of the numerous editions it
is impossible to say. A further piece of evidence is found
among John Newbery's papers, as cited by Forster. These
show that Goldsmith borrowed a number of books in
November 1762, for compilation purposes: these included
'*Encyclopediae* [*sic*], 8 vols., French; *Chinese Letters*, French;
Persian Do'.[14] We also know that in August 1757 Goldsmith
had written for the *Monthly Review* an essay on Voltaire,
ending with a brief discussion of Montesquieu which alludes
to both the works listed in the sale catalogue. There is also
an article on Montesquieu in the *Critical Review* in 1759,
ascribed by Forster to Goldsmith, but not accepted into the
canon by Friedman.[15]

The glaring omission, of course, is *L'Esprit des Lois*. The 1757
article just mentioned does briefly allude to the work: but a
fuller reference occurs in the *Enquiry into the Present State of Polite
Learning*:

> MONTESQUIEU, a name equally deserving fame with the former
> [Voltaire]. The Spirit of Laws is an instance, how much genius
> is able to lead learning. His system has been adopted by the
> literati; and yet is it not possible for opinions equally plausible
> to be formed upon opposite principles, if a genius like his, could
> be found to attempt such an undertaking? He seems more a
> poet than a philosopher. (I, 301)

Those familiar with Goldsmith's habits as a compiler will not
be surprised to hear that this reserved judgement goes along
with unacknowledged borrowings elsewhere. The importance
of Montesquieu lay in something Goldsmith may not have
consciously perceived. He had made the different characteristics of nations an object of philosophic survey rather than
of geographical description.[16]

This sense of abstraction is immediately apparent when, at
line 63, Goldsmith begins to establish his antithetical terms
(ll. 63–72):

But where to find that happiest spot below,
Who can direct, when all pretend to know?
The shudd'ring tenant of the frigid zone
Boldly proclaims that happiest spot his own,
Extols the treasures of his stormy seas,
And his long nights of revelry and ease;
The naked Negro, panting at the line,
Boasts of his golden sands and palmy wine,
Basks in the glare, or stems the tepid wave,
And thanks his Gods for all the good they gave.

The opposition of the 'frigid zone' and equatorial regions is a
traditional way of viewing the range of human existence. Here,
the climatic contrast is enforced by prominent items of diction,
whose conventionality prevents us from lingering too insistently
on their literal import—*shudd'ring*; *basks*; *tepid* (a word given
new energy by Thomson). The contrast is drawn in less
sweeping, that is more specific, terms a little later (ll. 83–6):

With food as well the peasant is supply'd
On Idra's cliffs as Arno's shelvy side;
And though the rocky crested summits frown,
These rocks, by custom, turn to beds of down.

The hint of oxymoron which hovers around much of the text
comes almost to the surface at such junctures. The copulative
'turn' functions as not much more than an equal sign; much of
the work, semantically, is thrust on the concentrated phrase
'by custom' (Lonsdale is the only editor I have seen who notes
the parallel with *Othello* I. iii. 230–32). Behind both passages
lies a body of writing which reviews human life as it is lived in
extreme conditions. *The Seasons* was, of course, a classic
treatment of both tropics and arctic regions; and as McKillop
has shown in his own classic treatment, some well-thumbed
sources regularly provide the material for Thomson. One of
the important sources was the widely popular *Spectacle de la
Nature*, by the Abbé Pluche, which extended physicotheology
into speculations in the field of geology, climatology and
meteorology. It has been shown that Goldsmith used Pluche
in compiling his *Animated Nature*. Here I wish only to add that
among the items in the sale catalogue is no. 18, 'Nature
Displayed, 7 vol. 1757'. This can be identified as a translation

of *La Spectacle de la Nature* which went through several editions in the middle of the century.[17]

There follows a passage meditating on such abstractions as art, 'Wealth, commerce, honour, liberty, content', all typical elements in the cultural debate in which Montesquieu is such a seminal figure. However, it is when we reach the direct application to Italy that Goldsmith's language most insistently plays around the physical and moral terminology used in this debate. Italy, needless to say, is connected with 'soft' values. We must recall that until the Hellenistic revival of the Romantic era, British attitudes towards Mediterranean countries tended to carry many double-edged associations. Goldsmith never uses the simple word 'luxury', that is the noun (although 'luxuriance' and 'luxurious' occur); never-theless, the central unstated subject could be expressed by that word. And underlying the passage is the belief that ancient Rome had endured harsher winters than modern Italy, with a consequent effect on the nature of the inhabitants. This view is expressed in an essay ascribed to Goldsmith by R. S. Crane, which appeared in May 1760 under the title 'The Effect which Climates have upon Man'. The writer describes the climatic shift, and continues: 'Need we then be at such a loss to account for the different manners of the ancient Romans and modern Italians? a warm country ever producing an effeminacy of manners among the inhabitants' (III, 112). *Effeminacy* is a rich concept, historically; its main thrust here is in the direction of the spineless and effete Latins, but the idea of self-indulgence includes a possible notion of sexual over-activity (hetero-sexual, in fact: a strange lexical component as the word is used today).

The vocabulary expressing this view of Italy is built around terms such as *bounty, blooms, torrid, blossom, smiling*. It is, indeed, the precise lexicon appropriated to summer in the standard seasonal division. Several of the key words actually turn up in Thomson's *Summer* (*blooms, torrid, luxurious, bliss, gelid, grove, bright, smiling*, etc.).[18] One might even say that Goldsmith has simply made explicit the political meanings inherent in Thomson's natural order, where 'all-conquering Heat' and 'the powerful King of Day' suggest a potency extending beyond generative force into a sort of absolutism and tyranny.

118

Inevitably, some of the parallels recall other parts of
Thomson's poem: 'the varied year' (l. 116) suggests the
opening line of *Winter*. However, the congruence is far more
pervasive and marked in the case of *Summer*. Italy is the
traditional south, that is a profuse and glaring landscape,
inducing laziness and lack of moral fibre. It is equally summer
transformed into a socio-political phenomenon.[19]

Goldsmith then makes a full turn (the verbal gesture
indicating a geographical shift, but also a switch in poetic
attitude); his next subject is defined thus (ll. 165–68):

> . . . turn we to survey
> Where rougher climes a nobler race display,
> Where the bleak Swiss their stormy mansions tread,
> And force a churlish soil for scanty bread. . . .

'Bleak' as applied to the Swiss might be taken as a transferred
epithet, referring primarily to the setting in which their lives
are lived out. However, it is impossible to be positive on such a
point, since the technique blurs any notion of transference.
The people themselves partake of the quality of their landscape (ll. 169–70):

> No product here the barren hills afford,
> But man and steel, the soldier and his sword.

Again, there are close affinities to the language used by
Thomson in *The Seasons*. But this time *Winter* is the relevant
section, even though Thomson does not have much to say
about the Alps as such. (His treatment of Savoy describes the
effect on 'the happy *Grisons*' when an avalanche destroys their
settlements.) Both poems relate 'the Rigours of the Year'
(*Winter*, l. 424) to deprivation, barren wastes, scanty living.
Words common to the vocabulary of the two poets include
storm, *gloom*, *chill*, *torrent*, *roar* (of wind and sea), *want* (noun),
struggle, *scanty*, *humble*, *calm*, *bleak*, *keen*, and so on—sternness
and severity are imputed to both climate and personality.[20]
Thomson writes explicitly about the northern landscapes;
Goldsmith borrows some of the standard terms to characterize
the Swiss.

In addition, this is one of the places in *The Traveller* where
the connection with Montesquieu becomes quite explicit.

Goldsmith describes the 'level life' of the hardy Swiss mountain people, 'unfit for raptures', and sets out in sharply schematic terms the 'coarseness' of their moral being (ll. 227–38):

> But not their joys alone thus coarsly flow:
> Their morals, like their pleasures, are but low.
> For, as refinement stops, from sire to son
> Unalter'd, unimprov'd the manners run,
> And love and friendship's finely pointed dart
> Fall blunted from each indurated heart.
> Some sterner virtues o'er the mountain's breast
> May sit, like falcons cow'ring on the nest;
> But all the gentler morals, such as play
> Through life's more cultur'd walks, and charm the way,
> These far dispers'd, on timorous pinions fly,
> To sport and flutter in a kinder sky.

There is some individuality in the expression here, as with the simile of the falcons. But the root concepts can all be traced in *L'Esprit des Lois*, notably in Book XIV; I cite the contemporary translation by Thomas Nugent, which Goldsmith is exceedingly likely to have known, although the modern version by Melvin Richter sometimes approaches more closely to the poet's vocabulary.

> In cold countries they have very little sensibility for pleasure. . . . The large bodies and coarse fibres of the people of the North are less capable of laceration than the delicate fibres of the inhabitants of warm countries. . . . In northern regions a machine robust and heavy finds pleasure in whatever is apt to throw the spirits into motion, such as hunting, travelling, war, and wine. If we travel towards the North, we meet with people who have few vices, many virtues, and a great share of frankness and sincerity.[21]

The wants of the Swiss are 'few', their 'barren' state is devoid of any 'pleasing science'. Their course of life is 'unfann'd by strong desire'. This is pretty well identical with Montesquieu's view of the culture of northern countries, where 'imagination, taste, sensibility, and vivacity' are far less in evidence (along with vice) than in southern climes.[22] Goldsmith makes little effort to differentiate his theme from that of Montesquieu, except perhaps insofar as his reference to patriotism (l. 199 ff.) may allude to a long-celebrated national characteristic among the Swiss cantons. Otherwise, the contrast between penurious virtue and self-indulgent opulence (the point of setting Switzerland against Italy) is in essence a development of Montesquieu's typology of northern and southern races.

Another 'turn' is dramatized at l. 239, with France the new centre of attention. This would seem to belong, in strict climatology, to Montesquieu's intermediate category of the 'temperate'. If anything, however, Goldsmith aligns it with the warm-blooded side of his scheme: though warmth is secondary here to light and movement. In fact, this 'Gay sprightly land of mirth and social ease' is characterized very much in terms of the seasonal properties attached to spring. The opening line itself, 'To kinder skies, where gentler manners reign', echoes the very start of Thomson's *Spring*: 'Come, gentle Spring, Etherial Mildness, come.' Again we find an unmistakable convergence of idiom as between *The Seasons* and *The Traveller*, manifest above all in the words which relate to stock properties of spring: *soft* (the crucial single expression), *gay, zephyr, freshen, busy, maze, kind, sportive*.[23] Thomson celebrates 'the Symphony of Spring', and Goldsmith takes over the musical imagery of the earlier poet (*choir, murmur*); in fact, the traveller piping inexpertly for the dancers supplies a comic replay of the pastoral Golden Age of *Spring*, ll. 267 ff. ('For Music held the whole in perfect Peace'). 'Dance and Sport' are common themes: but the double-edged 'social ease' of *The Traveller* has its source, too, in *Spring*, with 'Luxury and Ease'. The epithet *social* occurs on another occasion in Goldsmith's short passage: this echoes several key usages in Thomson, where 'social Feeling' is a key to humanity and understanding of nature. Thomson writes of 'the Spirit of the genial Year', and a whole cluster of ramified associations spill out from 'genial'—parents and children, love, festivity, hospitality, creativity. Goldsmith has much less space and a less complex rhetoric, but he too evokes psychological states by means of seasonal motifs. In his dialectic the French have become too soft, too vain and ostentatious: this is the obverse of their civility and charm. Even Montesquieu had picked out 'the vanity of a Frenchman' as contributing to the energy of the race—his point is taken from Mandeville, that is the idea that vanity, unlike pride, in 'encouraging a trifling turn of mind' serves to increase commercial activity.[24] Although Goldsmith lays his emphasis elsewhere, he draws on the same set of national stereotypes.

Finally in this tetrad (a very common and characteristic formal layout in Augustan literature) comes Holland. Once again the very opening statement incorporates hints of the seasonal lore: 'To men of other minds my fancy flies,/ Embosom'd in the deep where Holland lies' (ll. 281–82). The proleptic hint of Keats's great ode is not wholly fortuitous; Thomson, too, had lit on the expression 'in thy Bosom grow' in the first fifteen lines of *Autumn*, and the significant epithet occurs in expressions such as 'deep-loaded Bough' later in his poem. Goldsmith's lines continue with a number of the terms consecrated to autumn, with *treasure, wealth, gain, cultivated, toil*, amongst others. The argument here is that 'Convenience, plenty, elegance, and arts' have been perverted by the greed of the people; uncorrupted, these were the traditional benefits of a prosperous harvest. At the heart of Thomson's poem is a celebration of the blessings of industry (ll. 44–6):

> Whom Labour still attends, and Sweat, and Pain;
> Yet the kind Source of every gentle Art,
> And all the soft Civility of Life.

Goldsmith refers to 'repeated toil,/ Industrious habits [which] in each bosom reign,/ And industry begets a love of gain'. There is a stronger sense than elsewhere of the land itself, 'the wave-subjected soil'; traditionally autumn was associated with the element of earth, and agricultural rather than broadly pastoral activities were emphasized. Once again Goldsmith forges a negative critique by converting the usual terms of praise to a hostile end; the 'treasures' of autumn, as celebrated along expected lines by Thomson, have become baneful emblems of a nation's greed. The Dutch are seen as 'dull', slow, crafty, hard-hearted. The 'yellow blossom'd vale' no longer connotes laughing Ceres; it links, as the passage develops and opens out imagistically, with the lure of gold. The stagnation of natural feeling among the people derives from a kind of national log-jam, a plethora of commercial bustle. Some of the flatness of the landscape and the temperance of the climate has leaked through into the national character.

122

After this repeated pattern of thesis and antithesis—soft, hard, soft, hard—comes the synthesis. Britain occupies the place which Thomson allots to his concluding hymn in *The Seasons*; and though Goldsmith gives disproportionate space to this section—aesthetically, as well as structurally—he does not achieve such a convincing resolution. Britain is clearly temperate, spring-like, but not enfeebled by social frivolity as France is. The poet uses superlative forms of the semantically moderate epithets that go with these attributes of temperance: 'the gentlest breezes', 'Creation's mildest charms'. The imagery of wheels and the motions of a system (ll. 347–48) is strongly suggestive of Montesquieu; the 'ferments' and 'factions' are those of a free people, not just as Goldsmith sees it, but in the terms Montesquieu had used to analyse British constitution in Books XI and XIX of *L'Esprit des Lois*. In this final section, too, we encounter renewed use of oxymoron (see ll. 398, 400); the contrasts hinge on ideas of excessive hardness and softness, northern and southern attributes as the poetry has defined these: for have we not (ll. 401–4)

> Seen opulence, her grandeur to maintain,
> Lead stern depopulation in her train,
> And over fields, where scatter'd hamlets rose,
> In barren solitary pomp repose?

The opposites which had been played one against another, earlier on in the text, are now thrust together to concentrate the energies of the cultural argument in a single image. It is Britain's mission, so the rhetoric would insist, to steer a middle course between despotism and anarchy, between excessive independence and excessive absorption in 'social' living, between rigour and indulgence. What Montesquieu had set out as a model for the purposes of political explanation, Goldsmith has idealized into a sort of cultural myth. Unlike Carlos Argentino, he has given his survey of the 'civilised' world a shape unrelated to mere topographic connections. *The Traveller* is a reading of contemporary society, sentimental in its ultimate pieties perhaps, but as a poetic argument solid and coherent in construction.

NOTES

1. Jorge Luis Borges, *El Aleph* (Buenos Aires, 1974), pp. 160–61. Translation mine. The collection originally dates back to 1949.

2. Relevant to Goldsmith are such ironic, even sneering phrases as '*luxuria nostra*' (*Germania*, 45); there is some irony directed towards the Germanic tribes, but during the Enlightenment readers were perhaps less disposed to pick up this thread in the argument. A 1760 edition of Tacitus was in Goldsmith's library at his death.

3. Mme. de Staël, *De la Littérature: De l'Allemagne* (Paris, 1935), p. 49. The extract is taken from the opening chapter of Part 1.

4. *The Spirit of the Laws*, tr. Thomas Nugent (New York, 1949), p. 223. As explained in the text, I cite this translation as one almost certainly known to Goldsmith, as well as to his readers. For a more scholarly modern version, see Melvin Richter, *The Political Theory of Montesquieu* (Cambridge, 1977), where, however, this particular paragraph is omitted.

5. For the poetic exploration of these attributes, see my articles, 'James Thomson and the Correspondence of the Seasons', *Revue des Langues Vivantes*, 42 (1976), pp. 64–81; and 'Rhythm and Recoil in Pope's Pastorals', *Eighteenth-Century Studies*, 14 (1980), 1–17.

6. See *Sales Catalogues of Eminent Persons*, VII, 'Poets and Men of Letters', ed. Hugh Amory (London, 1973), 227–46.

7. See *The Poetical Works of Oliver Goldsmith*, ed. Austin Dobson (London, 1906), pp. 162–77; *Collected Works of Oliver Goldsmith*, ed. Arthur Friedman (Oxford, 1966), IV, pp. 245–69; *Selected Poems of Johnson and Goldsmith*, ed. A. Rudrum and P. Dixon (London, 1965), pp. 84–101; and *The Poems of Gray, Collins and Goldsmith*, ed. Roger Lonsdale (London, 1969), pp. 622–57. For the alternative version of the poem, see W. B. Todd's edition of *A Prospect of Society* (Charlottesville, Va., 1956). Quotations in the text are taken from Friedman with references to vol. and page nos.

8. *Goldsmith: The Critical Heritage*, ed. G. S. Rousseau (London, 1974), pp. 29–33, 35–43, 231–34, 283–92.

9. Ibid., p. 283. Books mentioned are: William Black, *Goldsmith* (London, 1878), pp. 75–81; Austin Dobson, *Life of Oliver Goldsmith* (London, 1888), pp. 96–103; John Forster, *The Life and Times of Oliver Goldsmith* (London, rev. ed. 1877), I, pp. 364–76.

10. Ralph M. Wardle, *Oliver Goldsmith* (Lawrence, Kansas and London, 1957), pp. 156–61; Ricardo Quintana, *Oliver Goldsmith: A Georgian Study* (London, 1969), pp. 127–31 (quotation from p. 130); Robert H. Hopkins, *The True Genius of Oliver Goldsmith* (Baltimore, 1969), pp. 66–95.

11. Hopkins, p. 67, quotes the description by Frederick W. Hilles: 'Its balanced discussion (the friendliness or hostility of nature versus the follies or virtues of the natives) reinforces the theme of moderation.' In my view *The Traveller* can properly be called dialectical rather than balanced in structure, since each stage in the argument helps to redefine the terms of the stage just past.

12. *The Poetical Works of Richard Savage*, ed. Clarence Tracy (Cambridge, 1962), p. 97.

13. For Goldsmith's interest in Voltaire as early as 1757, see Friedman, I, 81–2, 95–105. For the background to the *Memoirs*, see Friedman, III, 225–26. Also in the sale catalogue, no. 63 among the octavos, is 'La Pucelle': almost certainly Voltaire's burlesque poem of 1755, highly popular in its time, although not dealt with in the *Memoirs*.
14. Forster, I, 300.
15. Friedman, I, 104–5; Forster, I, 175.
16. A fuller assessment of Goldsmith's relations to the French enlightenment would certainly not eliminate Montesquieu from calculation, even if other sources could be traced. One of the starting points of such an inquiry might be the entry for '*Encyclopédie*' in the index to Friedman, V, 400. A number of articles by R. S. Crane are more helpful in this regard than A. Lytton Sells, *Les Sources Françaises de Goldsmith* (Paris, 1924), though the latter contains some useful information.
17. Alan D. McKillop, *The Background of Thomson's Seasons* (Minneapolis, 1942), pp. 81–8 and *passim*. I should like to record once again my debt to this endlessly fertile work.
18. For *The Seasons*, I refer to the 1746 text as used by James Sambrook in his authoritative edition (Oxford, 1981). For the words cited here, see *Summer*, ll. 67, 213, 346, 461, 512, 632, 706, 861, 1313, 1334, etc.
19. One might perhaps even stretch this idea to include the basic concept of humours: Italy is essentially choleric in its uncontrolled youthful energy and 'plethoric' tendencies (l. 144); Switzerland is wintry, the inhabitants phlegmatic (appropriately in terms of the stock typology of the seasons); France is airy, child-like, in terms of the humours psychology sanguine; Holland has many of the standard associations of melancholy, that is, the self-enclosed, crafty, anal kind of personality described, e.g. ll. 305–12.
20. See, for example, *Winter*, ll. 48, 58, 67, 73, 93, 94, 99, 140, 228, 238, 262, 350, 397, 431, 749, 995, 1024.
21. Tr. Nugent, pp. 222–23: compare Richter, p. 259.
22. Tr. Nugent, p. 222.
23. See, for example, *Spring*, ll. 83, 153, 242, 270, 324, 575, 584, 597, 647, 836.
24. Tr. Nugent, pp. 295–96: note that the section on vanity follows one entitled 'Effects of a Sociable Temper'. For 'honour', central to Goldsmith's argument at ll. 259–66, see Montesquieu, tr. Nugent, I, 25–6.

8

Goldsmith, Swift and Augustan Satirical Verse

by J. A. DOWNIE

In 1796 Dr. John Aikin concluded his 'Critical Dissertation' on the poetry of Oliver Goldsmith thus[1]:

> We have already seen that GOLDSMITH possessed humour; and, exclusively of his comedies, pieces professedly humorous form a part of his poetical remains. His imitations of Swift are happy, but they *are* imitations. His tale of the *Double Transformation* may vie with those of Prior. His own natural vein of easy humour flows freely in his *Haunch of Venison* and *Retaliation*; the first, an admirable specimen of a very ludicrous story made out of a common incident by the help of conversation and character; the other, an original thought, in which his talent at drawing portraits, with a mixture of the serious and the comic, is most happily displayed.

It is hardly surprising that Goldsmith's 'humorous' verse has received very little attention from critics. His reputation as a poet rests firmly on the achievements of *The Traveller* and *The Deserted Village*. And yet the minor poems present in miniature the major problems which beset any attempt to assess Goldsmith's art. To what extent can his multifarious works be seen as original contributions to English literature? How far did he merely follow in the footsteps of the Augustan giants? How accurate is the traditional picture of Goldsmith as an amusing trifler in a variety of genres? Did he, in fact, have a serious purpose underlying the surface of his comedy? Can he be genuinely considered as a subtle exponent of that pervasive Augustan mode—satire—or is his output excessively sentimental, mirroring the change in taste which coincided with the cultivation of sensibility? How much weight should be placed on the fact that Goldsmith, like Keats, died before the full flowering of his genius? 'His *Retaliation*, as a sportive sally of humour, shews him to have been capable of satire', William Mudford observed thirty years after Goldsmith's death.[2] *Retaliation* was his last composition, published posthumously on 19 April 1774. Are we justified in seeing Goldsmith as a late practitioner of Augustan satire, or is he working within a new vein of sentimental humour? These are some of the questions to which I intend to address myself in this short review of Goldsmith's comic poetry.

1

In the *Monthly Review* for September 1757, Goldsmith reviewed Thomas Gray's *Odes*. 'Such a genius as Mr. Gray might give greater pleasure, and acquire a larger portion of fame', he wrote, 'if, instead of being an imitator, he did justice to his talents, and ventured to be more an original.'[3] Strange words from Oliver Goldsmith. However much of an 'original' he proved to be in his private life, however eccentric his appearance on occasion, much of 'Magnanimous' Goldsmith's work is notable precisely because it is a re-working of earlier writings by other authors. His first five printed poems, for instance, published in *An Enquiry into the Present State of Learning* and in *The Bee*, are imitations of Macrobius, an unidentified Spanish source, Bernard de la Monnoye, and Denis Sanguin de Saint-Pavin, respectively (IV, 363, 365, 366). 'Obviously', writes Ralph M. Wardle, 'Goldsmith was not practicing what he had preached in his reviews about the virtues of originality.'[4]

While some critics are disturbed by Goldsmith's shameless borrowing, others are not. 'He regarded his contributions to *The Bee* as pure hackwork', Professor Wardle suggests, 'not literature at all.'[5] And yet the epigraph to *The Bee* is taken from Lucretius: '*Floriferis ut Apes in saltibus omnia libant,/ Omnia Nos itidem.*' As Robert H. Hopkins has pointed out, a contemporary translation of this line (perhaps even written by Goldsmith himself) carries an apt comment: 'You should, like bees, fly from flower to flower, extracting the juices fittest to be turned into honey. The severest critics allow such amiable plundering.'[6] This is an important consideration in approaching Goldsmith's writings, especially his poetry. His behaviour seems to place him, almost by default, on the side of the ancients in Swift's *The Battle of the Books*. '*I visit, indeed, all the Flowers and Blossoms of the Field and the Garden,*' says the bee in dialogue with the spider, '*but whatever I collect from thence, enriches my self, without the least Injury to their Beauty, their Smell, or their Taste.*'[7] The spider possesses that horrid, *modern* characteristic— the obsession with originality. As everybody knows, in the eighteenth century translation and imitation were perfectly acceptable modes of literary expression. Pope spent 'three whole years with Broome' translating Homer, and even longer imitating Horace and Donne. The title-page of Fielding's *Joseph Andrews* proclaims that the novel is 'Written in Imitation of Cervantes, Author of *Don Quixote*'. It is not the *fact* that Goldsmith indulged in 'amiable plundering' that is troubling, but the *manner* in which he borrowed would bear investigation. In dealing with a writer who worked in such a diversity of genres, it is necessary first of all to remove the lumber which he collected from the works of others. Only then can we have a clear view of his own achievements.

Let us take as our starting-point Goldsmith's lines describing an author's bedchamber. Not a major work, admittedly, but Goldsmith flattered himself that the 'manner' of the 'heroicomical poem' was 'quite original'.[8] First published in one of the 'Chinese Letters' in the *Public Ledger*, it ultimately found its way into *The Citizen of the World*. Although he never carried out his earlier plan to expand the poem into a genuine mock epic, Goldsmith appears to have been sufficiently satisfied with the lines, reworking them into *The Deserted Village* (ll. 227–36). A fictional setting is provided by having the lines read by the poet in the club of authors. When the Chinese Philosopher arrives, the poet is trying to get permission to read the 'first book of an heroic poem' to the company, but without much success. Finally, according to club rules, he pays for the privilege of reading his own work. In this 'heroical description of nature', the poem 'begins with the description of an author's bed-chamber', with the poet himself as the hero (II, 128–29):

> Where the Red Lion flaring o'er the way,
> Invites each passing stranger that can pay;
> Where Calvert's butt, and Parsons' black champaign,
> Regale the drabs and bloods of Drury-lane;
> There in a lonely room, from bailiffs snug,
> The muse found Scroggen stretch'd beneath a rug,
> A window patch'd with paper lent a ray,
> That dimly shew'd the state in which he lay;
> The sanded floor that grits beneath the tread;
> The humid wall with paltry pictures spread:
> The royal game of goose was there in view,
> And the twelve rules the royal martyr drew;
> The seasons fram'd with listing found a place,
> And brave prince William shew'd his lamp-black face:
> The morn was cold, he views with keen desire
> The rusty grate unconscious of a fire:
> With beer and milk arrears the frieze was scor'd,
> And five crack'd tea cups dress'd the chimney board.
>   A night-cap deck'd his brows instead of bay,
>   A cap by night—a stocking all the day!

The use of a narrator, the Chinese Philosopher, and a fictional character in the poet Scroggen, necessarily distances us from Goldsmith as poet. Scroggen is supposedly writing about himself, for 'the picture was sketched in [his] own apartment.' But, of course, there is a strong personal element in the poignant circumstances of the indigent poet. Goldsmith's own view of the relationship between author and bookseller undoubtedly informs the lines. As he wrote to his brother Henry, supplying a specimen of the projected 'heroicomical' poem, 'All this is taken you see from Nature.'[9] We might be forgiven for discerning characteristics of Goldsmith himself in the poet in his 'shabby finery', 'his love of fame out-weigh[ing] his prudence' (II, 127–28). I emphasize the autobiographical element not in imitation of those early critics who, as G. S. Rousseau complains, were more interested in 'Goldsmith-the-man' than 'Goldsmith-the-writer',[10] but because I wish to draw attention to the fact that Goldsmith, like his fictional counterpart Scroggen, was pleased with the manner of the description. The Chinese Philosopher's account continues:

> With this last line he seem'd so much elated, that he was unable to proceed; there gentlemen, cries he, there is a description for you; Rablais's bed-chamber is but a fool to it:
>
> *A cap by night—a stocking all the day!*
>
> There is sound and sense, and truth, and nature in the trifling compass of ten little syllables. (II, 130)

In this case, Goldsmith really does appear to have succumbed to the modern pursuit of originality. He really was fond of his line. The rhythm was followed with precision in the corresponding line in *The Deserted Village* (l. 230): 'A bed by night, a chest of drawers by day . . .', while the nightcap motif was pursued in *The Double Transformation* in the 'Five greasy nightcaps wrap'd' around Flavia's head (l. 46).

Roger Lonsdale, however, has pointed out that in Swift's *Cassinus and Peter*, one of the characters is discovered 'just crept out of Bed;/ One greasy Stocking round his Head'.[11] Here we have a possible literary original for both Scroggen's stocking doubling as a nightcap, and Flavia's 'greasy' nightcap. If Goldsmith was as impressed by his own last line as his shabby poet, my attention is drawn instead to an ingenious line which employs the pathetic fallacy in an unusual way. 'The rusty grate unconscious of a fire. . . .' The grate is imbued with sensation, only to emphasize the absence of intellect. Not only is there no fire in the grate, but the rusty grate itself does not know what a fire is. It really is 'unconscious' of the phenomenon, and the reference not merely to English usage but to the meaning of the Latin root as well provides amplified resonance. By these means Goldsmith's line finely catches the pathos of the scene. But if we turn to Swift's *The Parson's Case* we can see that, once again, Goldsmith has been discovered in the act of borrowing[12]:

> Thy curate's place, thy fruitful wife,
> Thy busy, drudging scene of life,
> Thy insolent illit'rate vicar,
> Thy want of all-consoling liquor,
> Thy thread-bare gown, thy cassock rent,
> Thy credit sunk, thy money spent,

Thy week made up of fasting days,
Thy grate unconscious of a blaze. . . .

Goldsmith's wit is not his own. Perhaps in his ten syllables he gains from the 'heroicomical' manner more than simply the addition of 'rusty', and, it is true, the rhyme-word has been changed. But Goldsmith did not bring life to the poet's rusty grate. Swift did. And the description of the author's bed-chamber, for all its vaunted originality, can be recognized as nothing more than a type of the reductive verse satire of which Swift was a past master. The needy writer's plight is merely a version of the 'mangled Plight' in which Corinna, 'Pride of *Drury-Lane*',[13] finds herself in *A Beautiful Young Nymph Going to Bed* or the state of Cassinus as discovered by Peter, or the case of the poor parson.

2

Pointing out possible influences, allusions, verbal echoes, gets us so far, but no farther. It is, I think, important to draw attention to facts such as these, but source-hunting is a means to an end, not an end in itself. Beyond Goldsmith's 'amiable plundering' of Swift is the question of what his own art succeeds in accomplishing. Whilst conceding that Goldsmith 'ow[ed] much to Swift and Pope', Robert H. Hopkins claims that

> it was Charles Churchill and other radicals who imitated Swift and Pope too closely, whereas Goldsmith and Johnson, who would be thought to have more in common with the 'Tory' line of wit, took great pains not to imitate them. . . . If Goldsmith and his contemporaries were to be at all original, they could not therefore merely imitate the matter or forms of their pre-decessors.[14]

On the surface these seem strange claims to make for Oliver Goldsmith. True, neither Swift nor Pope attempted the drama. They did not write sentimental novels. But, as Roger Lonsdale remarks, '*The Traveller* is in fact a late example of a favourite Augustan genre, the Horatian verse-epistle, which had received its classic expression in Pope's *Moral Essays* . . . and *Essay on Man*.'[15] Pope's influence can also be detected in

The Deserted Village, even though its displays an increasing interest in exploring states of mind in a sentimental manner. William Mudford made the point most forcefully in 1804[16]:

> [Goldsmith's] versification has found many admirers; and it has been asserted, that his numbers are the most harmonious of any writer since the days of Pope. This is probably true; but let it be remembered he had Pope for a model. All excellence is great in proportion to its originality; and I do not know that any man deserves extravagant praise for having imitated another.

Again the modern preoccupation with originality is to the forefront, and we might wish to make excuses for Goldsmith. But they would be excuses. There is sound sense in Mudford's comment, if little that is surprising, perceptive or profound.

If, in his serious verse, Goldsmith appears to imitate both the style and forms of Pope, in his humorous verse the most obvious influence is Swift, even though, as Leigh Hunt remarks, his 'pieces in professed imitation . . . possess neither the wit nor the ease of his model'.[17] *A New Simile. In the Manner of Swift* proves, on closer examination, to be modelled not on Swift at all, but on Thomas Sheridan's *A New Simile for the Ladies*. It was sometimes included in collections of Swift's works, and Goldsmith evidently felt, with good reason, that he *was* imitating Swift's manner. He seems to have lifted his 'New Simile' from his source as well. Certainly his comparison of Mercury's wand and the vitriolic pen of the modern author recalls Swift's *The Virtues of Sid Hamet the Magician's Rod* in which the lord treasurer's white staff is compared to the rod of Hermes. Swift's poem also provides the original for the author's snaky behaviour.[18] *The Logicians Refuted*, on the other hand, was actually attributed to Swift when first printed in *The Busy Body*. Whether or not this was a deliberate effort to deceive the reader on Goldsmith's part is difficult to say, but the lines were subsequently collected as his own, with the note, 'In Imitation of Dean Swift'.[19] Roger Lonsdale writes that the poem 'is a careful, if rather wooden, vehicle of attitudes held by Swift', which may not be the work of either man.[20] Although there are distinct echoes of Swift's style, such as the reference to Walpole as 'Bob' (l. 32),[21] *The Logicians Refuted* reads like another studied attempt to write 'In the Manner of Swift'.

In a small way, Goldsmith's imitations of Swift must call into question Professor Hopkins's assertion that he 'took great pains not to imitate' his celebrated predecessor, either in 'matter or forms'. On the other hand, such poems are essentially apprentice-work, in which Goldsmith is searching for his own voice through studying Swift's style. According to Hopkins, Goldsmith, like Smollett, is 'defending the finest values of the disintegrating English Augustan world', and he does this through an 'extraordinary *refinement* of irony'. We are reminded that Swift claimed (ironically?) to be 'born to introduce' irony, and that he 'Refin'd it first, and shew'd its Use'.[22] The argument in favour of Goldsmith's originality, then, is that he took Swift's ironic manner a stage further.

This would not have occurred to Goldsmith's critics in the century after his death. As G. S. Rousseau has noted, 'Goldsmith-the-harsh-satirist is unknown' to these men.[23] *The Vicar of Wakefield* is the battlefield over which controversy principally rages. 'There is scarcely a touch . . . of satire in it from beginning to end', wrote George Craik, 'nothing either of acrimony or acid.'[24] Professor Hopkins's answer lies in the *type* of satire adopted by Goldsmith:[25]

> Rather than labeling Goldsmith as an 'amuser', we may instead interpret him as an amiable satirist. Goldsmith himself . . . would not think of this label as a contradiction in terms. For some, no doubt, satire must be corrosive—must be the lashing mode of Juvenal or Swift—but this is to limit its range too narrowly. Satire should be conceived as a spectrum in which the color is determined by the technique and by the ends for which a particular work is designed. In the past critics have called Goldsmith a comic writer, forgetting that comedy is a criticism of life and ignoring exactly what it is Goldsmith is criticizing. . . . If Swift is placed at one pole of eighteenth-century English satire and Goldsmith at the other, we will have a much better grasp of the mode's surprising range, refinement, and versatility. We will no longer think of Goldsmith as merely an amuser but second only to Chaucer as a master of the art of amiable satire.

Far from Goldsmith imitating Swift in his writings, in Professor Hopkins's view the two are poles apart. Goldsmith is essentially a satirist. That is his 'genius'. But it is not satire in the manner of Swift who, as he put it himself, wrote in a

'hum'rous biting Way'.[26] Goldsmith, it seems, removed the
bite and accentuated the humour.

This can be seen in *The Double Transformation: A Tale*.
'Matrimony was always one of my favourite topics', writes the
vicar of Wakefield, 'and I wrote several sermons to prove its
happiness' (IV, 22). Swift would have relished the irony in this
comment, as the vicar, with a wrong-headed enthusiasm
worthy of the hack in *A Tale of a Tub*, insists on his ability to
demonstrate the felicity of the married state through rational
argument. It exposes the character's foibles in a gentle—or, as
Hopkins would have it, an amiable—way. Marriage as a
theme allows Goldsmith to point up his moral in a humorous
manner. Roger Lonsdale notes that Goldsmith

> appears to have been imitating such poems, dealing lightly in
> octosyllabics with marriage, as Swift's *Phillis, or the Progress of
> Love*, *The Progress of Marriage* and *Strephon and Chloe* (only the
> moral of this last is really comparable), and Prior's *Hans
> Carvel*.[27]

One of these suggestions can be discounted out of hand. *The
Progress of Marriage* was not published until 1765—five years
after Goldsmith's poem was first printed in *The Weekly
Magazine* as *The Double Metamorphosis*. Unless he had seen the
verses in manuscript, which seems unlikely, then they cannot
have influenced his own lines. But his treatment of marriage in
this poem does suggest an acquaintance with *Strephon and Chloe*
which, perhaps significantly, was first published in pamphlet
form together with *A Beautiful Young Nymph Going to Bed* and
Cassinus and Peter; these three poems in particular appear to
have exercised an influence on Goldsmith's attempts to write
satirical verse.[28]

Perhaps Goldsmith's earlier critics recognized an affinity
between *The Double Transformation* and Swift's 'marriage'
poems. Certainly John Aikin saw the similarity between the
poem and the poetic tales of Prior.[29] In *Hans Carvel*, the hero,
'Impotent and Old,/ Married a Lass of LONDON Mould',[30]
only to be led a merry dance. Goldsmith's poem concerns Jack
Book-worm, who is contented with his college life until smitten
with love for Flavia at the age of 36. 'Miss frown'd, and
blush'd, and then was—married' (l. 20). It is a twelvemonth

later that Jack finds 'his goddess made of clay', and here the strategies of Swift's marriage poems are apparent. *Strephon and Chloe* is built around the revelation that Chloe, 'By Nature form'd with nicest Care,/ And, faultless to a single Hair', of whom 'Her graceful Mein, her Shape, and Face,/ Confest her of no mortal Race', is all-too-mortal after all.[31] Goldsmith's poem, too, pursues the (by now) well-worn theme of loving courtship giving way to familiarity and contempt after marriage, just as in Swift's *Phillis, Or, the Progress of Love*, where the heroine and John the groom, having eloped, are soon thinking better of their adventure:

> Phil wish't, that she had strained a Limb
> When first she ventur'd out with him.
> John wish't, that he had broke a Leg
> When first for her he quitted Peg.

Once married, Flavia indulges her taste for society—'In short by night 'twas fits or fretting,/ By day 'twas gadding or coquetting'—until, her complexion seamed by smallpox, she is finally deserted by her 'bevy,/ Of powder'd coxcombs at her levy'. Forced to turn her attentions solely onto her husband, the result is connubial bliss, as 'Serenely gay, and strict in duty,/ Jack finds his wife a perfect beauty.'

The theme of a transformation after marriage, then, is already well developed when Goldsmith turns to it. Does he succeed in handling it in an original way? Is there any evidence of an 'extraordinary *refinement* of irony'? Well, it is undoubtedly true that Flavia's nadir is when she is disfigured by smallpox. Human pretensions are soundly rapped here. And we have seen the reality behind social affectation, as she is pictured 'By turns a slattern or a belle'. But Goldsmith draws the veil over the functions that interest Swift so much. He is content to reveal Flavia as a slut at home who cares nothing for her husband. Thus Jack's goddess is shown to be 'made of clay'. In *Strephon and Chloe* Swift takes the process of deflation a degree further. Strephon is disabused in the wedding-bed itself, as Chloe, distressed by the cumulative effects of twelve cups of tea and a supper of peas, is 'constrain'd . . . to leak'[32]:

135

STREPHON who heard the fuming Rill
As from a mossy Cliff distill;
Cry'd out, ye Gods, what Sound is this?
Can *Chloe*, heav'nly *Chloe* piss?
But, when he smelt a noysom Steam
Which oft attends that luke-warm Stream;
(*Salerno* both together joins
As sov'reign Med'cines for the Loins)
And, though contriv'd, we may suppose
To slip his Ears, yet struck his Nose:
He found her, while the Scent increas'd,
As *mortal* as himself at least.

The crucial difference between Goldsmith's satiric use of the marriage motif and Swift's is not that Swift uses obscenity to press home his point, though this is one way in which Goldsmith's irony is more refined, but that Swift is ultimately concerned with the human predicament *tout court*. The pissing, farting nymph quickly dispels the conceit that she is in any way godlike. Goldsmith's moral is to recommend mutual duty and respect between the marriage partners, just as Swift's ostensible moral in *Strephon and Chloe* is to recommend cleanliness and modesty to future brides.[33] But whereas Swift's satiric treatment of marriage informs a coherent satiric vision, Goldsmith's trite observations are left to stand or fall by themselves. Goldsmith's satiric point is a specific one about the fickle nature of human relationships. The art of Swift's satire, even his humorous satirical verse, is that it extends beyond the immediate subject matter to make telling points about society as a whole.

Swift's satire often works through metonymy and this, it seems to me, is the chief distinction between the verse satire of the two men. Swift's works are never *merely* humorous—the universal application is always there to be made. And it is this which constitutes his 'Augustanism'; with Fielding he could say that he describes manners not men, not individuals but a species. When Swift turns to marriage, it is to draw attention to the range of human fallibility through concentration on one particular aspect of human folly. The institution of marriage and the frailty of human relationships fascinate him, and he returns to the themes time and again. Satire allows him to emphasize the discrepancy between how, ideally, human behaviour is represented, in conventional love poetry for instance, and what, in reality, it is like. True satire establishes an ideal against which the shortcomings of society can be measured. It is the peculiar difficulty of Swift's satire that the ideal is almost always implied, rarely explicit.

Swift chooses marriage not because it is a subject about which it is easy to be humorous (which, I suspect, is the case with Goldsmith), but because it is an institution at the heart of the Christian way of life. The predicaments into which Swift places his unfortunate characters are, indeed, very funny. But the humour, especially the scatological humour, is not there simply for its own sake. Satire exploits the ridiculous for a serious purpose. Swift's success in making us smile or laugh out loud at his poetry often obscures his didactic intent. We must not forget that we are *meant* to respond heartily to the ridiculous. At the same time, his art as verse satirist can only really be appreciated by recognizing his satiric vision in the same way that we would accept it in, say, *Gulliver's Travels*. As he writes in *Phillis, Or, the Progress of Love*, 'See then what Mortals place their bliss in!' (l. 25). The key word is 'Mortals'. Just as Chloe is shown to be 'at least' as mortal as Strephon, so the love Phillis supposedly feels for John is stripped of its pretensions. Instead of their marriage vows remaining sacred, Phillis is forced to break them (ll. 90–4)

> In kindness to maintain her Spouse;
> Till Swains unwholsome spoyld the Trade,
> For now the Surgeon must be paid;
> To whom those Perquisites are gone
> In Christian Justice due to John.

Goldsmith may, as Roger Lonsdale remarks, be imitating poems by Swift 'dealing lightly in octosyllabics with marriage', but the degree of 'lightness' must be in some doubt. Swift's 'hum'rous biting way' raises serious issues. Even the sacrament of marriage itself is turned into a farce by the ridiculousness of that creature, man, as Swift, with bitter irony, suggests that the proceeds of the wife's prostitution are, 'In Christian Justice', due to her husband. 'See then what Mortals place their bliss in!' might serve as the *idée fixe* of Swift's satire.

3

Goldsmith's use of the 'marriage' poem, then, is vastly different from that of Swift. Apart from superficial thematic similarities and possible verbal echoes,[34] there is little resemblance in the *character* of the satire. The savage reminder of man's mortality is missing in Goldsmith's trite moral, and it is the constant reference in Swift's poetry to a coherent satiric vision which constitutes his essential Augustanism. In this sense Robert H. Hopkins is right to point to a distinction between the satiric technique and intent of the two writers, however much Goldsmith's *Double Transformation* imitates a Swiftian form. But the 'moral motives' of the poem are hardly profound or original. Nor is the technique suggestive of subtle irony. Evidence, in the imitations, of a refinement of Swift's irony is missing. It is only in the *Haunch of Venison* and *Retaliation* that an individual comic voice can be heard at all clearly in Goldsmith's humorous verse. In this instance, the early critics, for all their shortcomings, are right.

The Haunch of Venison is one of those pieces which appear to justify the tradition of Goldsmith-the-amuser. Too trivial to be considered as even an exercise in amiable satire, it tells in lively anapaests the fate of a gift of venison. It is curious that even in this poem Goldsmith's originality should be open to dispute. He seems to have derived the idea for his entertaining account of a tedious meal from Boileau (who, in turn, was using Horace), while the opening is influenced by Swift's *The Grand Question Debated*. Not only, as Roger Lonsdale notes, did this *jeu d'esprit* suggest 'the metre and some details of phrasing',[35] but the ironic consideration of the respective merits of turning a large old house into a barrack or a malt house provides the original for the debate over the disposal of the meat. While Goldsmith's wry account of his discomfort during dinner at the house of 'An under-bred, fine-spoken Fellow' accentuates the difficulty critics face when trying to divorce analysis of his works from considerations of his private life, it would be hard to make out a case for a serious moral for *The Haunch of Venison*, even allowing for the fact that, as Professor Hopkins contends, 'comedy is a criticism of life.' The poem is a humorous commentary on human nature, without offering any hint of the genuine reformative impulse at the root of all satire, whether amiable or harsh.

Goldsmith's main claim to any sort of distinction as a verse satirist rests on his *Retaliation*, which 'would have been owned with pleasure by SWIFT himself'.[36] The stimulus for this poem is traditionally supposed to have been Garrick's comic epitaph for Goldsmith:

> Here lies NOLLY Goldsmith, for shortness call'd Noll,
> Who wrote like an angel, but talk'd like poor Poll.

Richard J. Dircks has recently clarified the circumstances of this incident. 'Scholars have been generally reluctant to attribute a mood of general goodfellowship to Goldsmith on this occasion', he writes, 'and inclined to stress too strongly the aspect of "Retaliation" in the poem.'[37] It is clear, however, that the mood was one of gentle raillery rather than an out-and-out battle of words. Mock epitaphs were a regular feature of the 'club of *Beaux Esprits*' of which Goldsmith was a member, along with Burke, Garrick, Reynolds and Cumberland. *Retaliation* was read, in Garrick's absence, to the assembled company at dinner on 9 March 1774. Contemporaries noted that the epitaphs mixed panegyric and satire.[38] The overall tone of the poem resembles Swift's genial attacks on his friends in *Verses on the Death of Dr. Swift*, and, at times, the comments carry the same sting.

Take, for instance, Goldsmith's retaliation at the expense of David Garrick (ll. 101–12):

> On the stage he was natural, simple, affecting,
> 'Twas only that, when he was off, he was acting:
> With no reason on earth to go out of his way,
> He turn'd and he varied full ten times a day;
> Tho' secure of our hearts, yet confoundedly sick,
> If they were not his own by finessing and trick,
> He cast off his friends, as a huntsman his pack;
> For he knew when he pleased he could whistle them back.
> Of praise, a mere glutton, he swallowed what came,
> And the puff of a dunce, he mistook it for fame;
> 'Till his relish grown callous, almost to disease,
> Who pepper'd the highest, was surest to please.

Here we have genuine wit, as Goldsmith, in successive lines, employs metaphors and similes from card-playing, hunting and eating. The pun on 'hearts' is particularly fine, as Garrick is suggestively pictured as a card-sharper dealing with the hearts of his friends, pleased with his own skill rather than simply satisfied with winning the round. The irony here is especially refined, and easily missed. The technique of blame by praise is what most interests modern scholars in *Retaliation*[39] as Garrick is seen courting the applause of dunces. But we should not overlook the playful aspects of the epitaphs. They were not designed to be genuinely provoking. As Richard Cumberland observed, they had 'humour, some Satire and more panegyric'.[40] As well as blame by praise, Goldsmith uses its converse, praise by blame. In the case of Garrick's acting, true panegyric is limited to a succinct but just appraisal of his talent ('On the stage he was natural, simple, affecting'), but the subtle mixture of two types of raillery which colours the rest of the epitaph cannot obscure one fact—Garrick is famous, and rightly so. Hence when he is accused of mistaking 'the puff of a dunce' for fame, he is merely being teased by Goldsmith in much the same way in which Swift playfully attacks Pope, Gay and Arbuthnot in the passage from *Verses on the Death of Dr. Swift* to which we have turned for guidance about satiric technique[41]:

> In POPE, I cannot read a Line,
> But with a Sigh, I wish it mine:
> When he can in one Couplet fix
> More Sense than I can do in Six:
> It gives me such a jealous Fit,
> I cry, Pox take him, and his Wit.
>
> WHY must I be outdone by GAY,
> In my own hum'rous biting Way?
> ARBUTHNOT is not more my Friend,
> Who dares to Irony pretend;
> Which I was born to introduce,
> Refin'd it first, and shew'd its Use.

Praise by blame is a peculiarly Swiftian trait. Arbuthnot, of course, is still Swift's friend, and although he recognizes Pope's poetic flair, his 'jealousy' is simply part of the technique of raillery. Similarly Goldsmith writes of Garrick (ll. 93–6):

> Here lies David Garrick, describe me who can,
> An abridgment of all that was pleasant in man;
> As an actor, confest without rival to shine,
> As a wit, if not first, in the very first line. . . .

In the case of *Retaliation*, however, Goldsmith's wit is not borrowed. There are Augustan elements in his satire, admittedly, but it is his sure-footedness which stands out. He is in control of his materials in this poem, even though it remains unfinished. Oliver W. Ferguson writes that his character-sketches of Garrick and Burke, 'poised exactly between panegyric and satire', are 'especially notable', and 'could only have been drawn by someone who possessed to a remarkable degree the ability to temper the understanding of his fellows with affection'.[42] They are, indeed, fine examples of Goldsmith's mature style, but it is not the judicious balancing act which is most impressive, it is the witty complexity of lines that, through subtle irony, appear to praise and then to blame, or vice-versa, as they strike the reader's eye first one way, and then another. *Retaliation*, as an anonymous contemporary reviewer remarked, is 'delicate satire', and it is in this 'poetical strain', 'in which good humour, and a facetious turn of thought are equally conspicuous',[43] that Oliver Goldsmith finds his own satiric voice.

4

As a verse satirist, Goldsmith's output is slender, and it would be difficult to make a case for his original contribution in this medium. Given his debt to Swift, his poems need to be seen as more than simple imitation if his achievement is to be viewed as other than an anachronistic concern for outmoded Augustan values and forms. 'For the most part', writes Professor Hopkins, 'Goldsmith reserved satire for prose and his poetry for rhetorical persuasion.'[44] This seems to me too ready a distinction. In several poems Goldsmith is attempting to emulate the satiric voice of the high Augustans, but without conspicuous success. *Retaliation* perhaps indicates a sureness of touch which previously had been lacking. However, Goldsmith's comic verse does little to assist those who wish to revalue his achievement as a humorous writer. Even allowing for the fact that satire does not have to administer a sound lashing, Goldsmith's gentle criticism of human folly rarely rises above the level of raillery. Of *The Citizen of the World*, William Mudford wrote that it was 'one of the most delicate, the most refined, and the most correct satires, upon the English nation and its manners, that can be pened.'[45] None of Goldsmith's satirical verse merits such praise, and yet this is suggestive of the character of his satiric vision. When Swift wrote of 'refining' irony and showing its use, he was employing a chemical metaphor. The 'refinement' of Goldsmith's irony is the tasteful elegance of the new era of sensibility. It is not the purifying fire of the Augustans.

NOTES

1. *Goldsmith: The Critical Heritage*, ed. G. S. Rousseau (London and Boston, 1974), p. 236.
2. Ibid., p. 245.
3. *Collected Works of Oliver Goldsmith*, ed. Arthur Friedman, 5 vols. (Oxford, 1966), I, 113–14 (hereafter references are cited in the text).
4. Ralph M. Wardle, *Oliver Goldsmith* (Lawrence, Kansas and London, 1957), p. 103.
5. Ibid.
6. Robert H. Hopkins, *The True Genius of Oliver Goldsmith* (Baltimore, 1969), pp. 96–7.
7. *The Prose Works of Jonathan Swift*, ed. Herbert Davis *et al.*, 16 vols. (Oxford, 1939–74), I, 149.
8. *The Collected Letters of Oliver Goldsmith*, ed. Katharine C. Balderston (Cambridge, 1928), pp. 63–5: to his brother Henry, *c.* 13 January 1759.
9. Ibid.
10. *Goldsmith: The Critical Heritage*, p. 3.
11. *The Poems of Gray, Collins and Goldsmith*, ed. Roger Lonsdale (London, 1969), p. 590n; *The Poems of Jonathan Swift*, ed. Harold Williams, 3 vols. (Oxford, second edition, 1957), II, 594 (hereafter cited as Swift, *Poems*).
12. Swift, *Poems*, II, 676.
13. Ibid., p. 581.
14. Hopkins, p. 8.
15. *Poems*, ed. Lonsdale, p. 627.
16. *Goldsmith: The Critical Heritage*, p. 242.
17. Ibid., p. 317.
18. See *Poems*, ed. Lonsdale, pp. 659–60n.
19. Swift, *Poems*, III, 1141.
20. *Poems*, ed. Lonsdale, p. 765.

21. See J. A. Downie, 'Pope, Swift and *An Ode for the New Year*', *Review of English Studies*, new series, 32 (1981), p. 170.
22. Hopkins, p. 6; Swift, *Poems*, II, 555.
23. *Goldsmith: The Critical Heritage*, p. 12.
24. Ibid., p. 307.
25. Hopkins, pp. 235–36.
26. Swift, *Poems*, II, 555.
27. *Poems*, ed. Lonsdale, p. 583.
28. Swift, *Poems*, II, 580–81.
29. *Goldsmith: The Critical Heritage*, p. 236.
30. *The Literary Works of Matthew Prior*, ed. H. Bunker Wright and Monroe K. Spears, 2 vols. (Oxford, 1959), I, 184.
31. Swift, *Poems*, II, 584.
32. Ibid., p. 589.
33. Swift, in all seriousness, recommended 'Cleanliness' to his own prospective wife, Jane Waring, in 1700 (*The Correspondence of Jonathan Swift*, ed. Harold Williams, 5 vols. (Oxford, 1963–65), I, 36), and in *A Letter to a Young Lady on her Marriage* he advocated that ladies 'allow a suitable Addition of Care in the Cleanliness and Sweetness of their Persons: For, the satyrical Part of Mankind will needs believe, that it is not impossible, to be very fine and very filthy' (*Prose Works*, IX, 87). Once again, the frowziness of Flavia is anticipated.
34. In addition to the 'Five greasy nightcaps', wrapped round Flavia's head, we have the use of the 'civil/devil' rhyme of which Swift was fond (see Downie, 'Pope, Swift, and *An Ode for the New Year*', p. 170), and the contraction of 'physiognomy' into 'phiz'—another Swiftian usage (see *A Concordance to the Poems of Jonathan Swift*, ed. Michael Shinagel (Ithaca and London, 1972), p. 609).
35. *Poems*, ed. Lonsdale, p. 696.
36. Leigh Hunt, quoted in *Goldsmith: The Critical Heritage*, p. 317.
37. Richard J. Dircks, 'The Genesis and date of Goldsmith's *Retaliation*', *Modern Philology*, 75 (1977–78), p. 50.
38. Ibid., p. 49; *Goldsmith: The Critical Heritage*, p. 130.
39. See, for example, Hopkins, pp. 9–11.
40. In a letter to Garrick, quoted in Dircks, 'Genesis and Date of Goldsmith's *Retaliation*', p. 49.
41. Swift, *Poems*, II, 555.
42. Oliver W. Ferguson, 'Goldsmith's "Retaliation" ', *South Atlantic Quarterly*, 70 (1971), 149.
43. *Goldsmith: The Critical Heritage*, p. 130.
44. Hopkins, p. 79.
45. *Goldsmith: The Critical Heritage*, p. 247.

9

Goldsmith in the Theatre

by BERNARD HARRIS

> College Green is a place to linger in, particularly on a summer
> evening when the westering light streams down Dame Street,
> the old High Street of Dublin, plays hide-and-seek in the
> colonnade of Parliament House, and re-juvenates the whole
> great screen of Trinity, with Hogan's beautiful statue of
> Goldsmith standing before it.[1]

A guide-book may aid understanding of Goldsmith, that
much-travelled, well-read, sociable man; though by its means
we scarcely expect to locate him. His effigy has achieved a
final poise, solidly placed within Trinity's railings, where he
seems to pore upon a book, but his gaze is on the passing
traffic. His portrait in the National Gallery of Ireland also
shows divided attention; he clasps a book to his heart but looks
elsewhere. Frank O'Connor catches the elusive stance, and
nails it down firmly in terms of common sense:

> Throughout the eighteenth century, and indeed to our own day,
> Dublin remained provincial. I am not impressed by traditions
> of Garrick or Peg Woffington. . . . After Swift there is no figure
> in its history whom I can visualise, who creates an atmosphere
> of visibility about himself as he does, or as Pepys does. . . .
> Goldsmith, the one Irishman of his generation who could have
> surrounded himself with this atmosphere of visibility, who
> could have made anything which interested him of interest to
> all eternity, could not have made a living here, then or now.

The conjunction of Swift and Pepys is startlingly apt.
Goldsmith made his life between the margins of despair and

gossip. It was a quietly desperate affair, accomplished everywhere but at home, and most securely in the imagination. Goldsmith's sheer versatility is to be respected, not least because it was contrived from necessity. Saintsbury observed an essential, indestructible element in Goldsmith's work—

> most eminently present in that remarkable style of his which is charming and so difficult to characterise. . . . Johnson, Burke, Gibbon, his own contemporaries, can be analysed in this respect. . . . Goldsmith defies analysis, and therefore synthetic imitation.[2]

The most recent editor of Goldsmith's work is not so readily persuaded by those charms:

> Oliver Goldsmith was and is still a paradoxical figure. His contemporaries could not understand why he was a great writer, and neither, apparently, can we.[3]

Those contemporaries who knew him personally were certainly often confused by a discrepancy between his social awkwardness and the manifest ease of his writing. To his reading public he was a popular author who achieved excellence in poetry, essay, novel, drama, all the forms available, and to his friends an incomparable letter-writer. Goldsmith wrote to everyone's satisfaction but not apparently to his own. However, he did not suffer then, as he has since, from the efforts of critics to 'place' him. Evidently, we cannot stomach individuality, but feel an obligation to categorize. The most plausible category available in Goldsmith's case is that of Anglo-Irish literature; and in drama the list seems to write itself—Congreve, Farquhar, Goldsmith, Sheridan, Wilde, Shaw. It is a persistent and false habit of criticism to perpetuate this list, a lazy assumption which derives continuity from casual accidents of birth, or place of education, and a wish to believe in a 'line of wit'. All these dramatists wrote for the London theatre of their respective times, Restoration, Georgian, or Victorian; they do not constitute a 'tradition', they simply adapted their talents to their audience.

There are welcome signs that this conventional view is under challenge:

All but the most obdurate of Gaelic racialists . . . would have to admit the Irishness of Goldsmith as the son of his father; while all but the most insensitive to the display of national characteristics would recognise the sometimes heartbreakingly Irish modes of his behaviour. . . . As subject matter, whether in its corporeal or incorporeal aspects, Ireland might as well have disappeared off the map as far as Goldsmith was concerned after he left the place, never to return, at the age of twenty-two. His career thereafter was that of the London literary gent who was jack of all literary trades. . . . He wrote no *Drapier's Letters*, no *John Bull's Other Island*. He never mentioned Ireland in his well documented conversations with his London literary friends. His ambition was to take rank as the typical English man of letters of his time, an up-to-date critic of thought and manners who was *au courant* with English and Continental life, thought and literary fashion.[4]

Such passages, full of useful intentions however over-quickly some judgements are made, bring us back to a problem. Where, if we are disposed to do so, should we accommodate Goldsmith? 'A.E.' used a different range of names, Berkeley, Swift, Burke, and others. The sheer energy of Goldsmith's writing carries him into different areas of scrutiny. In the case of his plays a fancied, and fanciful, tradition of Anglo-Irish drama is understandable. Critics wish, or will, a sensible history of the drama, wherein epoch follows epoch in orderly process, a kind of evolutionary dream. But though understandable, the ambition is misplaced.

Goldsmith was a sport, displaced by circumstance, an isolated, perhaps neurotic, engaging figure. There is no congruence of opinion about his achievement, nor should we expect one; to manage that would be to acquire full understanding of the social differences of Ireland and England and their cultural distinctions. Criticism of Goldsmith as a dramatist fails to notice that he unites the observation of a stranger to the study of a society of which he wishes to become a member, but in which he is doubtful of acceptance. Within a year or so of learning an acceptable public language, subtle enough to convey self-enquiry and satisfying enough to appeal to a general public, he was dead.

The comment of the American editors of a valuable

anthology of eighteenth-century drama is initially sympathetic, and then, as must have happened so often in his life, dismissive:

> That Goldsmith founded no school, had no successor, produced almost no effect on the drama of his day is perhaps regrettable. More than the two plays of a charming and incomprehensible Irishman were needed to check the course of sentimentalism, and one can hardly expect a dawn of Shakespearean comedy in 'the twilight of the Augustans'.[5]

Did Shakespeare found a school? Or have a successor? The expectations raised in this crude verdict remain a real challenge to be met and answered in any reassessment of Goldsmith as a dramatist. I stress his Irishness not from conventional concerns. He neither founded a school, nor sought to maintain one. His contribution to theatre is a genuine gift: two comedies, one flawed, one perfect; his second play was the last throw of the dice. To understand how he achieved it we must go back to some basic facts.

When Goldsmith returned to London in 1756 the English theatre was backward-looking and insecure, over-shadowed by its past and uncertain of its future. Garrick was supremely an actor-manager; his contribution to the theatre, as actor, manager, playwright, restorer of Shakespeare, promoter of the Jubilee Celebration of 1769—his career was owed to deference. Goldsmith certainly shared that fatal reverence for the past, as 'A reverie at the Boar's Head Tavern, Eastcheap', and much else, shows. But his was an imaginative engagement with an ideal. For Garrick, Shakespeare was an idol, to be restored, exploited as an acting vehicle, revered, promoted. A theatre so dedicated to the preservation of its past, totally bound by commercial considerations, anxious to please a superficially genteel audience, afraid to offend, was an unstable platform for innovative talent. Garrick had many virtues, and much power. Perhaps we should not persist in ignoring the disadvantages of his long reign. (Boswell: 'But has he not brought Shakespeare into notice?'—Johnson: 'Sir, to allow that, would be to lampoon the age.') Allardyce Nicoll observed three facts:

> Although the theatre manifestly flourished during the four decades from 1740 to 1780, there was virtually no new playhouse built in London during those years. . . . With the

partial exception of the King's Opera House in the Haymarket, the various theatres used by Garrick and companions were all designed according to one single plan. . . . Such theatres as were constructed outside of London within the period all followed the same pattern.[6]

R. G. Noyes, long ago, enquiring into the vanished life of the drama of this time, quoted a revealing statistic, and adduced Goldsmith as a witness:

> for the thirty-five years of Garrick's connection with the stage, 1,448 performances of twenty-seven Shakespeare plays were given at his theatre alone.[7]

The quotation is familiar. Dr. Primrose in *The Vicar of Wakefield*, written in 1762, addresses the strolling player:

> I demanded who were . . . the Drydens and Otways of the day.—'I fancy, Sir,' cried the player, 'few of our modern dramatists would think themselves much honoured by being compared to the writers you mention. Dryden and Row's manner, Sir, are quite out of fashion; our taste has gone back a whole century, Fletcher, Ben Johnson, and all the plays of Shakespear, are the only things that go down.'—'How,' cried I, 'is it possible the present age can be pleased with that antiquated dialect, that obsolete humour, those over-charged characters, which abound in the works you mention?'—'Sir,' returned my companion, 'the public think nothing about dialect, or humour, or character; for that is none of their business, they only go to be amused, and find themselves happy when they can enjoy a pantomime, under the sanction of Johnson's or Shakespear's name.' (IV, 96)

This opinion, expressed by a character in a novel, must have been close to Goldsmith's own frustrated sense of opportunities available, and yet denied. There was, of course, an underlying factor which determined many of his literary activities: money. Goldsmith's chronic poverty was due to his faults: compulsive gambling, misplaced hospitality, extravagance of living. We can be sympathetic, smug, and eventually grateful for a condition which brought him insight as well as misery, without falling through a stage-trap of useless pity. His fortunes, like his health, were always precarious.

Pat Rogers summarizes the financial rewards of several

writers in different kinds; after noting the sad comparative sums received by earlier writers, Gay, Fielding, Cleland, he observes:

> Meanwhile Goldsmith was making 20 guineas for *The Traveller* (1764), and 100 for *The Deserted Village* (1770). . . . A play *The Good Natur'd Man* earned him £150; the novel (a short one), *The Vicar of Wakefield* (1776), 60 guineas. . . . Unfortunately Goldsmith had to dispose of his popular comedy *She Stoops to Conquer* (1773) in settlement of a debt to his publisher Newbery; it sold 4,000 copies within three days. (By way of compensation Goldsmith obtained £500 from three benefit performances.)[8]

The economics of eighteenth-century publishing were different from those of theatre production; both were, and are, 'high-risk' businesses. It is not surprising that Goldsmith sought a base of security with Newbery, preferring to supply the market with encyclopaedic knowledge, even, probably, the sickening tale of *Goody Two-Shoes*, rather than risk his pen on more ambitious aims. And he needed time to establish himself in the volatile world of literary London. Boswell, one of his pretended friends, is at his most complacent when describing Goldsmith:

> He, I am afraid, had no settled system of any sort, so that his conduct must not be strictly scrutinised; but his affections were social and generous, and when he had money he gave it away very liberally. His desire of imaginary consequence predominated over his attention to truth.[9]

Was Goldsmith a liar? There are many obscurities in his life which he was careful to preserve. We should not disturb them. A perceptive, lenient, and convincing view of Goldsmith's entry into social favour is provided by Mrs. Parsons:

> The lovable image of Goldsmith pervades The Club, and its brightest memories mingle inextricably with his name. Boswell's phrase about 'honest Goldsmith talking away carelessly' almost equals Griffith's description of him as the 'not unuseful assistant' of the Monthly Reviewers, what time he was boarded in by Mrs. Griffiths on a starvation diet. . . . Goldy was born to be quizzed and utilised by the dull. His Irish brogue provoked their grins, his incorrigible habit of giving himself away by ready words and unready thoughts supplied them with

number-less occasions for belittling report. That wise observer, Reynolds, was of opinion that he purposely affected silliness in order to 'lessen himself,' *i.e.* make himself not feared nor envied, but liked, a very thinkable refuge for sensitive amiability.[10]

If Goldsmith played the stage-Irishman, as he may have done, it was with a purpose. He had no real alternative, since that was the badge of acceptance. Within three years of his arrival in London he had declared his opinion of the drama; it took him a further six years to get a play on stage.

> In one of his earliest works, the *Enquiry into the Present State of Polite Learning* (1759), Goldsmith gave utterance to the thought which was to be his guiding star in the field of the drama. He says: 'Does the poet paint the absurdities of the vulgar, then he is *low*; does he exaggerate the features of folly, to render it more ridiculous, he is then very *low*. In short, they have proscribed the comic or satirical muse from every walk but high life, which, though abounding in fools as well as the humblest station, is by no means so fruitful in absurdity.' It was Goldsmith's mission to render natural the comedy of his time, and strike a decisive blow at the *genteel* or *sentimental* comedy, which he later termed a 'kind of *mulish* production, with all the defects of its opposite parents, and marked with sterility.'[11]

Maybe Goldsmith's friends were no more informed than he was about theatrical matters. The problems which arose over the production of *The Good Natur'd Man* were complicated, and are not to be confidently summed up, though John Ginger has provided an excellent account of the probabilities.[12]

Goldsmith had completed the play by early 1767, and with the encouragement of Sir Joshua Reynolds offered it to Garrick for production at Drury Lane that season. Perhaps it was naïve of Goldsmith to enlist support from a friend of Johnson, since the relationship of the latter to Garrick was one of mutual mistrust. It was a further disadvantage to Goldsmith that the partnership of Garrick and Colman was ending, with some acrimony. Garrick kept the play until the theatre season ended in July. He is unlikely to have found the play to his taste. When Colman persuaded William Powell, leading actor at Drury Lane, to leave for Covent Garden, both the playwright and his play became pawns in a managerial dispute of the kind familiar between the patent houses since the days of Rich and Betterton. Colman was no more interested in an untried dramatist than Garrick had been, but was more precariously placed and hence exposed to pressure from Reynolds and Burke. The Club went into action. Johnson was summoned, and though sick, or perhaps because ill, responded:

> It appears from his notes of the state of his mind, that he suffered great perturbation and distraction in 1768. Nothing of his writings was given to the publick this year, except the Prologue to his friend Goldsmith's comedy of *The Good-natured Man*. The first lines of this Prologue are strongly characteristical of the dismal gloom of his mind; which in his case, as in the case of all who are distressed with the same malady of imagination, transfers to others its own feelings. Who could suppose it was to introduce a comedy, when Mr Bensley solemnly began,
>
> > Press'd with the load of life, the weary mind
> > Surveys the general toil of human kind.
>
> But this dark ground might make Goldsmith's humour shine the more. (i. 365–66)

Boswell did not have the sensitivity to recognize what Johnson instinctively felt; otherwise he would have continued the quotation:

> With cool submission joins the labouring train,
> And social sorrow, loses half it's pain:
> Our anxious Bard, without complaint, may share
> This bustling season's epidemic care.
> Like Caesar's pilot, dignified by fate,
> Tost in one common storm with all the great;
> Distrest alike, the statesman and the wit,
> When one a borough courts, and one the pit.
> The busy candidates for power and fame,
> Have hopes, and fears, and wishes, just the same;
> Disabled both to combat, or to fly,
> Must hear all taunts, and hear without reply.
> Uncheck'd, on both loud rabbles vent their rage,
> As mongrels bay the lion in a cage. (V, 15)

When Goldsmith, not exactly a lion, more an elusive hare, wrote his Preface to the published play, he was notably appreciative of the indifference of Colman, and though reasonably confident (the play had been a qualified success) the tone is hurt, devious and constrained:

> When I undertook to write a comedy, I confess I was strongly prepossessed in favour of the poets of the last age, and strove to imitate them. The term, *genteel comedy*, was then unknown amongst us, and little more was desired by an audience, than nature and humour, in whatever walks of life they were most conspicuous. The author of the following scenes never imagined that more would be expected of him, and therefore to delineate character has been his principal aim. (V, 13)

There seems here a fatal desire to please:

> How frequently in his letters does he inquire for old friends and acquaintances. 'I have disappointed your neglect,' he writes to his old chum, Bob Bryanton, 'by frequently thinking of you.'[13]

Goldsmith certainly looked back with longing to the theatre of a previous age, that of Vanbrugh, Farquhar, perhaps of Steele, and perhaps even more to the audiences they entertained:

> Upon the whole, the author returns his thanks to the public for the favourable reception which the Good Natur'd Man has met with: and to Mr. Colman in particular, for his kindness to it. It may not also be improper to assure any, who shall hereafter write for the theatre, that merit, or supposed merit, will ever be a sufficient passport to his protection. (V, 14)

The last image is a telling one. Goldsmith needed protection.

He waged no war against 'genteel comedy'—a term not so much unknown as totally familiar. Goldsmith was content to work within available terms, while attempting to adjust the conditions they imposed. The subject of sentimentalism, the specific topic of good nature, was a European commonplace of general speculation. Elizabeth Yearling has most recently shown the extent to which Goldsmith, Cumberland and Sheridan all subscribed to the principles of sentimental—in the proper sense of that word—drama, and deplored its decline into sentimentality.[14] What Goldsmith managed to do was simply to reduce lofty concepts to practical outcome.

The famous uproar on the first night of *The Good Natur'd Man* is of no consequence now; the bailiff scene, which had to be temporarily omitted, is one of the funniest in the play.

(Frith's painting is reproduced in Cassell's National Library edition, 1904.) It is improbable that the reaction of the audience was spontaneous. The politics of theatre were evident. Goldsmith was caught in a trap, partly of his own, but largely of his mentors' contrivance. Sentimentalism, or genteelism, was his avowed target. But was he not a recipient of precisely such benefits? There is no way conceivable by which the velvet-slippered manoeuvres of this time could be construed as intellectually motivated. Garrick had anticipated Colman's venture by staging Kelly's play a week earlier. It was a success, but did not entirely defeat Goldsmith's play, for which the reception was mixed and puzzled. It is difficult now to imagine an audience so dense, a critical circle so entirely apprehensive of their popular support, and support so incompetent that it could not distinguish between novelty, fashion and the new.

Boswell, by way of gossip, reports Johnson's opinion:

> Talking of some of the modern plays, he said *False Delicacy* was totally void of character. He praised Goldsmith's *Good-natured Man*; said, it was the best comedy that had appeared since *The Provoked Husband*, and that there had not been of late any such character exhibited on the stage as that of Croaker. I observed it was the Suspirius of his Rambler. He said, Goldsmith had owned he had borrowed it from thence. 'Sir, (continued he,) there is all the difference in the world between characters of nature and characters of manners; and *there* is the difference between the characters of Fielding and those of Richardson.' (i. 367)

Johnson's careful disengagement from Boswell's probing is tactful, thoughtful, and ill-considered. Kelly's *False Delicacy* is admittedly a successful time-serving play, quite entertaining, but dealing in habits of conduct, patterns of speech, conventions of behaviour, already passing into extinction. But for Goldsmith's play to be linked with Cibber's is perhaps sufficient evidence of the failing powers of Johnson's judgement. Cibber's play is a travesty of its author's intentions. Johnson's wits were wandering from his usual sense when he spoke thus. If Vanbrugh's original drift had been discerned, the outcome could never have been condoned. However, the nervous response of Johnson is some indication of what

Goldsmith was about. That Boswell should so easily have been drawn off the scent as to continue 'It always appeared to me that he estimated the compositions of Richardson too highly . . .' is testimony to Johnson's residing acumen. What could he do about a play which came so cruelly near to deciphering the predicament of The Club? It was not a part of their code to mention love. They were in the business of loss. Consider this extended quotation from *The Good Natur'd Man*:

> *Honeyw.*   It's a melancholy consideration indeed, that our chief comforts often produce our greatest anxieties, and that an encrease of our possessions is but an inlet to new disquietudes.
> *Croaker.*   Ah, my dear friend, these were the very words of poor Dick Doleful to me not a week before he made away with himself. Indeed, Mr. Honeywood, I never see you but you put me in mind of poor—Dick. Ah there was merit neglected for you! and so true a friend; we lov'd each other for thirty years, and yet he never asked me to lend him a single farthing.
> *Honeyw.*   Pray what could induce him to commit so rash an action at last?
> *Croaker.*   I don't know, some people were malicious enough to say it was keeping company with me; because we us'd to meet now and then and open our hearts to each other. To be sure I lov'd to hear him talk, and he lov'd to hear me talk; poor dear Dick. He us'd to say that Croaker rhim'd to joker; and so we us'd to laugh—Poor Dick. (*Going to cry.*)
> *Honeyw.*   His fate affects me.
> *Croaker.*   Ay, he grew sick of this miserable life, where we do nothing but eat and grow hungry, dress and undress, get up and lie down; while reason, that should watch like a nurse by our side, falls as fast asleep as we do.
> *Honeyw.*   To say truth, if we compare that part of life which is to come, by that which we have past, the prospect is hideous.
> *Croaker.*   Life at the greatest and best is but a froward child, that must be humour'd and coax'd a little till it falls asleep, and then all the care is over.
> *Honeyw.*   Very true, Sir, nothing can exceed the vanity of our existence, but the folly of our pursuits. We wept when we came into the world, and every day tells us why. (V, 25–6)

These lines are from the first scene of *The Good Natur'd Man*. They show Goldsmith's skill in turning a point, or eloquently extending it. Some critics even now quote Croaker's penultimate remark as though it were Goldsmith's own philosophy. The whole dialogue is a tissue of derivative utterances, never accumulating to a conversation. At this time Goldsmith had not thought of the difficulties of making characters talk to each other. He was relying on his own experience as a journalist, where matters, even of great moment, are reported, not experienced. Goldsmith, in part, had launched upon an analysis of his own personality, but although the theme is rich in potential, that of good nature inseparable from self-indulgence, it is not really dramatic. The material is more suited to an essay, not to a play, and Goldsmith had not yet perceived the difference, nor had he made up his mind to what extent the dénouement should disclose the ambiguity or preserve it. The central character, Honeywood, is never seriously put under pressure; when he is most at risk, he is protected, and by the ingenious intervention of the bailiffs, for whom the 'public' had no place:

> *Honeyw.* Tenderness is a virtue, Mr. Twitch.
> *Bailiff.* Ay, Sir, its a perfect treasure. I love to see a gentleman with a tender heart. I don't know, but I think I have a tender heart myself. If all that I have lost by my heart was put together, it would make a—but no matter for that.
> *Honeyw.* Don't account it lost, Mr. Twitch. The ingratitude of the world can never deprive us of the conscious happiness of having acted with humanity ourselves.
> *Bailiff.* Humanity, Sir, is a jewel. Its better than gold. I love humanity. People may say, that we, in our way, have no humanity; but I'll shew you my humanity this moment. There's my follower here, little Flanigan, with a wife and four children, a guinea or two would be more to him, than twice as much to another. Now, as I can't shew him any humanity myself, I must beg leave you'll do it for me.
> *Honeyw.* I assure you, Mr. Twitch, your's is a most powerful recommendation (*giving money to the follower*).
> *Bailiff.* Sir, you're a gentleman. I see you know what to do with your money. (V, 46)

Here Goldsmith writes from experience, with a sly allusion to Irish improvidence. But even when engaged upon a topic, central to his plot, but perhaps foreign to his own knowledge, the relationship of men and women, he surpasses the manners of his time. Compare these extracts from Kelly, Cumberland and Goldsmith.

Miss Marchmont.   My life was marked out early by calamity, and the first light I beheld was purchased with the loss of a mother. The grave snatched away the best of fathers, just as I came to know the value of such a blessing; and hadn't it been for the unspeakable pleasure of relieving the necessitous, had myself, perhaps, felt the immediate want of bread. And shall I ungratefully sting the bosom which has thus benevolently cherished me? Shall I basely wound the peace of those who have rescued me from despair, and stab at their tranquility, in the very moment they honour me with protection? O, Mr Cecil! They deserve every sacrifice which I can make. . . .
Cecil.   Hortensia, I can't stay with you. My eyes are exceedingly painful of late. What the devil can be the matter with them? But let me tell you before I go, that you shall be happy after all; that you shall, I promise you. But I see Lady Betty coming this way. . . .

(*False Delicacy*, III, ii)

Belcour.   . . . I am in love with you to distraction. I was charmed at the first glance; I attempted to accost you; you fled; I followed but was defeated of an interview. At length I have obtained one and seize the opportunity of casting my person and my fortune at your feet.
Lousia.   You astonish me! Are you in your senses, or do you make a jest of my misfortunes? Do you ground pretenses on your generosity, or do you make a practice of this folly with every woman you meet?
Belcour.   Upon my life, no. As you are the handsomest woman I ever met, so you are the first to whom I ever made the like profession. As for my generosity, madam, I must refer you on that score to this good lady, who, I believe, has something to offer in my behalf.
Lousia.   Don't build upon that, sir.

(*The West Indian*, III, iii)

Honeyw.   I presum'd to solicit this interview, Madam, before I left town, to be permitted—
Miss Rich.   Indeed! Leaving town, Sir—
Honeyw.   Yes, Madam; perhaps the kingdom. I have presumed, I say, to desire the favour of this interview—in order to disclose something which our long friendship prompts. And yet my fears—

Miss Rich. His fears! What are his fears to mine! (*Aside.*) We have indeed been long acquainted, Sir; very long. If I remember, our first meeting was at the French ambassador's—Do you recollect how you were pleas'd to rally me upon my complexion there?

Honeyw. Perfectly, Madam; I presum'd to reprove you for painting: but your warmer blushes soon convinc'd the company, that the colouring was all from nature.

Miss Rich. And yet you only meant it, in your good natur'd way, to make me pay a compliment to myself. In the same manner you danc'd that night with the most aukward woman in company, because you saw nobody else would take her out.

Honeyw. Yes; and was rewarded the next night, by dancing with the finest woman in company, whom everybody wish'd to take out.

(The Good Natur'd Man, IV) (V, 64)

From these encounters Cumberland, I suggest, comes out best. But Goldsmith was already learning to let his performers speak their own minds, and not just his own. This is always a difficult matter to judge, but surely it is crucial in deciding what is a permanent play, and what is an ephemeral one. *The Good Natur'd Man* has a respected history, it is often read, has been broadcast successfully, and qualifications about its double-plot, over-sophistication of action, sheer cleverness, should not prevent its revival. At the same time I think it important to notice the disappointment that the dramatist felt and was expressed by one of his senior players; Bulkley took the then conceived principal rôle of Miss Richland, a part very underwritten by Goldsmith, and was rewarded shrewdly with an epilogue: here is part of it.

> An Epilogue, things can't go on without it;
> It cou'd not fail, wou'd you but set about it.
> Young man, cries one (a bard laid up in clover)
> Alas, young man, my writing days are over;
> Let boys play tricks, and kick the straw, not I;
> Your brother Doctor there, perhaps, may try.
> What I! dear Sir, the Doctor interposes,
> What plant my thistle, Sir, among his roses!
> No, no, I've other contests to maintain;
> To-night I head our troops at Warwick-Lane.
> Go, ask your manager—Who, me? your pardon;

Those things are not our sort at Covent-Garden.
Our Author's friends, thus plac'd at happy distance,
Give him good words indeed, but no assistance.
As some unhappy wight, at some new play,
At the Pit door stands elbowing away,
While oft, with many a smile, and many a shrug,
He eyes the centre, where his friends sit snug,
His simpering friends, with pleasure in their eyes,
Sink as he sinks, and as he rises rise:
He nods, they nod; he cringes, they grimace;
But not a soul will budge to give him place.
Since then, unhelp'd, our bard must now conform
To 'bide the pelting of this pittiless storm,
Blame where you must, be candid when you can,
And be each critick the Good-natur'd Man. (V, 82–3)

It is impossible to know, now, how Mrs. Bulkley spoke these lines; the hesitancy is not only in the syntax. The suave savagery of this thin epilogue should not be unregarded. It was a hasty compilation, admittedly, but the testimony of the stage is quite clear. Goldsmith might pretend wry grace ('What is here offered, owes all its success to the graceful manner of the Actress who spoke it'), but there is no doubting the difficulties he encountered in dealing with theatre people, and they, of course, with him. The blatant citation of *Lear* should not distract us from the practical problems. Goldsmith did not command the confidence of his actors and actresses. He was a competent, professional writer, and must have been disappointed at the diffident response to his first play by those who took parts in it. He had a good company (Shuter as Croaker, Powell as Honeywood, Woodward as Lofty, Bulkley and Green, Pitt and Bensley in important rôles), but their enthusiasm seems to have been cautious.

The pre-history of *She Stoops to Conquer* falls into a similar pattern to that of *The Good Natur'd Man*. Again, lack of confidence in the dramatist's general capability was extensive. Colman, as manager, was reluctant. The company was indecisive. Powell, the star, had deserted; Woodward had declined the rôle of Tony Lumpkin. Goldsmith simply could not manage the relationships inevitably involved in the preliminaries of theatrical production. Prologues and epilogues may seem no more than tedious intrusions upon the directness of our present enjoyment. But in this period, mid-Georgian, they matter more than usual, simply because they are so evidently an intentional rather than accidental part of the whole; theatre was socially stratified, perhaps more completely than at any time in English, or Anglo-Irish, social history. So we need to seek the evidence from every fossil. Garrick composed a prologue, spoken by Woodward—'Dressed in Black, and holding a Handkerchief to his Eyes'—and containing the following passage:

> One hope remains—hearing the maid was ill,
> A *doctor* comes this night to shew his skill.
> To cheer her heart, and give your muscles motion,
> He in *five draughts* prepar'd, presents a potion:
> A kind of magic charm—for be assur'd,
> If you will *swallow it*, the maid is cur'd;
> But desp'rate the Doctor, and her case is,
> If you reject the dose, and make wry faces!
> This truth he boasts, will boast it while he lives,
> No *pois'nous drugs* are mix'd in what he gives;
> Should he succeed, you'll give him his degree;
> If not, within he will receive no fee!
> The college *you*, must his pretensions back,
> Pronounce him *regular*, or dub him *quack*. (V, 103)

J. B. Lyons, in the fullest account of Goldsmith's qualifications, comments: 'This Prologue would have been in the worst possible taste if there was the slightest doubt among Goldsmith's contemporaries as to his possession of a medical degree.'[15] But that seems to me entirely the point of the prologue; it is in the worst possible taste, and calculatedly so. For a comparison we might look at the prologue which, for his friend Cradock, Goldsmith composed:

> In these bold times, when Learning's sons explore
> The distant climate and the savage shore;
> When wise *Astronomers* to *India* steer,
> And quit for *Venus*, many a brighter here;
> While *Botanists*, all cold to smiles and dimpling,
> Forsake the fair, and patiently—go simpling;
> When every bosom swells with wond'rous scenes,
> Priests, cannibals, and hoity-toity queens:

Our bard into the general spirit enters,
And fits his little frigate for adventures:
With *Scythian* stores, and trinkets deeply laden,
He this way steers his course, in hopes of trading—
Yet ere he lands he'as ordered me before,
To make an observation on the shore.
Where are we driven? Our reck'ning sure is lost!
This seems a barren and a dangerous coast. . . .
This is his first adventure, lend him aid,
Or you may chance to spoil a thriving trade.
His goods he hopes are prime, and brought from far,
Equally fit for gallantry and war. (IV, 386–88)

Goldsmith usually wrote better on behalf of another cause than his own. The generosity he extended to Cradock's *Zobeide* was not reciprocated. As Tom Davis notes, 'Goldsmith had considerable difficulty with the epilogue to *She Stoops to Conquer.*' Cradock's epilogue arrived betimes: 'This came too late to be spoken.' Arthur Murphy attempted another, but was rejected. Goldsmith, as Davis notes, attempted three. His first effort, a 'quarrelling epilogue' between Catley and Bulkley, was discarded when the former left the company. His second effort was rejected. His third succeeded.

Why, we may ask, was there all this trouble over a minor matter of the technicalities of production, or presentation? The original intention was to have the epilogue 'To be Spoken in the Character of Tony Lumpkin'. In the event the epilogue was spoken by Bulkley in the character of Kate Hardcastle. Why, we are entitled to ask further, was Goldsmith involved in such confusion, and in an area where he was so competent? I suggest that he was struggling to escape from the demands of his patrons, to announce his true intentions as a comic writer.

Colman, unpersuaded of Goldsmith's ability as a writer, yielded to the power of The Club; he was 'prevailed on at last by much solicitation,' Boswell informs us, 'nay, a kind of force, to bring it on.' Shuter and Bulkley stood their ground, and provided the Hardcastles. Quick, who delivered the prologue to *Zobeide* 'in the character of a sailor' and played the Postboy in *The Good Natur'd Man*, was given the major rôle of Lumpkin. Kniveton, brought in for Catley, proved a better actress and triumphed as Miss Neville. Out of this chaos of competing

160

egotisms, including his own, and in spite of theatrical rivalries which persisted until the opening night, Goldsmith contrived success. Johnson, who had done so much to make it possible, was able to say, with an ease verging on complacency, 'I know of no comedy for many years that has so much exhilarated an audience, that has answered so much the great end of comedy—making an audience merry' (i, 498).

It is peculiarly senseless to attempt to analyse comedy. Tragedy is concerned with death, and necessitates judgement. But comedy depends upon the temporary postponement of disaster, and is concerned with the momentary, not the inevitable. There is no limit to the platitudes which such study may invoke. Johnson recognized this when composing a prologue for a failed comedy by Hugh Kelly, *A Word to the Wise*, for a benefit show on behalf of Kelly's widow and children:

> To wit, reviving from its author's dust,
> Be kind, ye judges, or at least be just. . . .
> Let one great payment every claim appease,
> And him who cannot hurt, allow to please;
> To please by scenes, unconscious of offence,
> By harmless merriment, or useful sense. . . .
> If want of skill or want of care appear,
> Forbear to hiss;—the poet cannot hear.
> By all, like him, must praise and blame be found,
> At last, a fleeting gleam, or empty sound. . . . (ii, 85)

Johnson's habitual melancholy was not in evidence on the occasion of Goldsmith's triumph, but the difference between success and disaster is marginal. Goldsmith was adroit enough to see the complications which the support of his powerful friends had posed for him. He was exposed to their innuendo—he was poisoning himself by wrong prescription—but like the true gambler he put himself at risk, and hazarded all.

The plot of *She Stoops to Conquer* is simple in action, however complex in origin. Susan Hamlyn reminds us that it depends 'on the device of sending Marlow and Hastings to the House of Marlow's intended father-in-law, a place where he would naturally wish to display his best behaviour, on the pretence that it is an inn'. She offers a fresh suggestion for yet another source, a jest from *Quick's Whim*:

A sailor, half-groggy, passing along the street of a certain sea-port town, discovered over an admiral's door an escutcheon, and very naturally took it for an ale-house—the gentleman (a ruddy looking portly man) standing at the door, he clapped him on the shoulder, *Damn it, landlord, you look like an honest fellow, give us a cup of the best.*—The gentleman, to carry on the joke, ordered his servants to bring him some beer, which being done, the jolly tar drank towards the landlord's good health, and enquired what was to pay, which the officer told him he might settle the next time he came that way.[16]

Hamlyn's proposal is initially attractive, mainly because of the connection with Quick. But his book was published more than twenty years after the performance of the play, and may represent not a source but a defeated memory and a vulgarized intelligence. The sources of *She Stoops to Conquer* are legion and are certainly not contained in this slight anecdote. It is richness of allusion, not confinement of anecdote, which endows the play, already robust with references which have escaped successive editors, with popular acceptance. The story which Goldsmith's sister told, that he lodged at the house of a friend in the mistaken belief that it was an inn, has the benefit that it is more associated with folk-lore than a drunken sailor's anecdote. And Goldsmith was drawing on deeper sources than Quick's quips. That the dramatist 'never alluded to this legend and has left no clues as to its authenticity' is no argument. Goldsmith never alluded to a great many matters about which we would wish to have confirmation. As Hamlyn admits of her preferred source, 'authoritative proof that Goldsmith used this, or, indeed, any of them has not been found and is likely to remain elusive.' Goldsmith was always elusive. He was in pursuit of larger matters that great comedy encompasses, not simply farce which diminishes response by hurried manipulation.

The sub-title, 'The mistakes of a night', is an obvious and provocative allusion to *A Midsummer Night's Dream*. But Goldsmith was usually more subtle than even his friends supposed. Here he challenged them to make comparison with the only writer Garrick acknowledged, and though Goldsmith managed to comply with the taste of his age, he also subverted some of its assumptions about class, choice in life, and notions of independence. The eventual title, *She Stoops to Conquer*, was chosen late, but brings with it overtones which we would be stupid to ignore:

> Kneel down and take my blessing, good my girl.
> Wilt thou not stoop?

> You did know
> How much you were my conqueror.

> And can shee, who no longer would be shee,
> Being such a Tabernacle, stoop to be
> In paper wrapt; or, when shee would not lie,
> In such a house, dwell in an Elegie?

The play is haunted by such literary reminiscences, most too familiar to mention, and also by infusions of Irish interest which defy editors, and may be self-indulgent, but never intrude upon the enjoyment of audiences or readers. Goldsmith was writing, in a manner both calculating and inspired, a prose comedy of ideal, romantic love. To do this he needed to create a fresh dialogue, compounded of his own experience, and one which Shakespeare and Vanbrugh had already accomplished, in their own time, and in their own way. They wrote comedies about love, in which the equality of men and women was recognized, whatever expedients were made necessary by social or stage conventions. Deprived of Shakespeare's opportunity to entrust so much emotional charge to the substitution of rôle to boy-players, Goldsmith found a new release: feminine energies would rely on deception, like the basic plot of the play.

Goldsmith had learned from the criticism of *The Good Natur'd Man* to simplify his plot. From the basic misunderstanding of a country house for an inn derive multiple related misunderstandings; Sheridan Morley calls the plot 'the British theatre's first example of a truly triumphant running gag'.[17] In addition to a situation which any audience, even the first one, could grasp immediately, he had also sharpened his style from the convoluted manner of his first play; almost the only device is antithesis, but now unlaboured. The speed of delivery enabled him not only to please an audience, but to divert them from their prejudices. Thus by setting the action in an 'old-fashioned' country house, with servants named Diggory and Pimple,

163

visited by fashionable society intent on despising a household whose ridiculous mistress admits that she has never once been to London and derives her notion of fashion from journals, Goldsmith indulges his audience's prejudices, but contrives their discomfort, as with the characters, when the rural wits prove more than equal to the metropolitan.

Speed alone would result in farce. But *She Stoops to Conquer* is a true comedy because the dexterity of plotting reveals complicated feelings which define individuality, not stereotypes. There are reversals of an audience's expectations. Thus, mindful of the reception of the bailiffs, his 'low' character is a squire of inherited social status; he is the hero, in the practical sense that he sets off the plot, and though a boisterous, hard drinking, song-making, lover of cock-fighting, horse racing man of energy and no thought, illiterate into the bargain, yet he contrives to gain his inheritance and assist the romantic lovers Constance and Hastings in getting their own inheritance and freedom. Lumpkin's sheer energy drives the play along; his vigorous rural vocabulary sets off the formal language of the lovers, though he can mimic polite and sentimental discourse (as in pretending to court Miss Neville) when it suits him to deceive his mother, on whom he takes physical revenge in the wild coach ride. By contrast, Marlow, the play's technical hero, a sophisticated womanizer, is endowed with an endearing and humiliating stammer which inhibits his stilted conversation when with a woman of his own class, but is eloquent in the presence of servants. This confusion of language and class seems to me to get to the heart of the comedy. The mistakes of the night are resolved not by Puck's magic, but by human conspiracy, in which the central agent is the heroine.

The trick by which Kate Hardcastle assumes her rôle of serving-girl (a device as successful as Rosalind's) is made possible not by a stage convention but the idiosyncrasy of her father who prefers her to dress as a maid in the evening. (We need not attribute sinister motives here, though St. John Hankin made a witty playlet about the subsequent married life of Kate Hardcastle and Marlow, in which she rescues their failing relationship by rôle-playing as a maid with cap and broom.[18]) We should not discount unconscious forces in any comedy, but Goldsmith's interest seems more likely to be in the way parental demands, however eccentric, may be honoured by a dutiful daughter; and the false sentiment then discarded:

> *Enter* Miss Hardcastle, *plainly dress'd.*
> *Hardcastle.* Well, my Kate, I see you have changed your dress as I bid you; and yet, I believe, there was no great occasion.
> *Miss Hardcastle.* I find such a pleasure, Sir, in obeying your commands, that I take care to observe them without ever debating their propriety. (III) (V, 157–58)

Such sweet submission should have warned her father that pretended sentiments are sometimes the means of obtaining one's own way. Kate's first reaction to Marlow's halting conversation is laughter:

> Was there ever such a sober sentimental interview? I'm certain he scarce look'd in my face the whole time. Yet the fellow, but for his unaccountable bashfulness, is pretty well too. He has good sense, but then so buried in his fears, that it fatigues one more than ignorance. If I could teach him a little confidence, it would be doing somebody that I know of a piece of service. But who is that somebody?—that, faith, is a question I can scarce answer. (II) (V, 148)

The economy of such language, as with the previous illustration, compresses not only conflicting feelings but the activities which true dramatic language is always required to carry. There is both plot-furtherance in 'he scarce looked in my face'—preparing us for Kate's questioning of her maid 'are you sure he does not remember my face or person?' (III)—and emotional dawning; there is a pun on 'interview' in both scenes, and preparation in 'service' for the eventual dissimulation of being a barmaid. Her question, 'But who is that somebody?', is offered in coquetry to the audience, and is also one she asks herself.

It is only necessary to labour such detail because the 'naturalness' of the result may make us overlook the art. The versatility of Goldsmith's language has never been denied, but the subtlety is still there in simplicity. In one way the comedy trades natural humour in place of the striving after brilliance, and the range of personal relationships is therefore wider than in more sophisticated social comedies. Lumpkin would be no more than a buffoon in such surroundings, not the anarchic principle he is here; Hastings and Miss Neville would be sentimental lovers in more genteel company, but become conspirators here, and form a foil for the more individualistic Kate; the extent to which the play explores family relationships, daughter and father, husband and wife, son and mother, is a more satisfying, fuller concept of comic relationships than in many restricted social comedies, and defies restrictions of the polite, the merely witty. It provides an order of release at various levels, for Kate, for Marlow, for Tony Lumpkin, for the young lovers; even, if harshly, for Mrs. Hardcastle. The play is very much about such liberation, and Goldsmith managed this by not directly challenging too violently the acceptance of his audience, but by subversion, and by capturing a mood in his own society so comprehensively that, in the manner of all truly successful comedy, it remains renewable and available to subsequent experiences in totally different circumstances.

Its spirit has not been caught since. John O'Keefe tried a sequel, *Tony Lumpkin in Town*, produced in 1778 with local success—but his true vein lay in *Wild Oats*, not imitation. And by way of an Irish postscript one might add two revealing anecdotes. In 1929 The Peacock Theatre, Dublin, performed *She Stoops to Conquer* in an Irish translation.[19] The author's introduction is mainly devoted to hostile criticism of just about every aspect of the play, its great length, its mixture of language styles, the presence of many untranslatable idioms, images, references. The play has been translated for 'the benefit of Irish drama producers'. The nature of the translation may be briefly shown:

Mrs. Hardcastle. Ay, *your* times were fine times, indeed; you have been telling us of *them* for many a long year.

'Seadh, nuair a blúos ég! Bhí ana-shasghal agat ansim, go deimhin! Jáimid bodher agat ag cur súos air le sne bliantaibh fada.'

'Aye, when I was young! You'd the grand life then, to be sure, Your descriptions deafen us this many a long year.' (I) (Trans. Sabina Sharkey)

166

In the first fifty years of The Abbey Theatre only one performance of *The Good Natur'd Man* was given, in 1920, and one of *She Stoops to Conquer*, in 1923.[20] Goldsmith had escaped his origins and defeated translation.

NOTES

References in the text are to the *Collected Works of Oliver Goldsmith*, ed. Arthur Friedman, 5 vols. (Oxford, 1966), giving volume and page nos.

1. Frank O'Connor, *Leinster, Munster and Connaught* (The County Books, n.d.), pp. 10 and 26.
2. George Saintsbury, *The Peace of the Augustans* (London, 1946), p. 215.
3. *Oliver Goldsmith: Poems and Plays*, ed. T. Davis (London, 1975), p. xi.
4. Anthony Cronin, *Heritage Now: Irish Literature in the English Language* (Dingle, Ireland, 1982), pp. 8–9.
5. *Plays of the Restoration and Eighteenth Century*, ed. Dougald MacMillan and Howard Mumford Jones (London, 1931), p. 789. Contains *The Clandestine Marriage, False Delicacy, The West Indian*, and much else.
6. Allardyce Nicoll, *The Garrick Stage: Theatres and Audiences in the Eighteenth Century*, ed. Sybil Rosenfeld (Manchester, 1980), p. 22.
7. R. G. Noyes, *The Thespian Mirror: Shakespeare in the Eighteenth Century Novel* (Brown University Studies, Providence, R.I., 1953), pp. 34–5. Quotes G. W. Stone, Jr., 'David Garrick's significance in the history of Shakespeare criticism'.
8. Pat Rogers, *The Eighteenth Century* (London, 1978), p. 55.
9. James Boswell, *Life of Johnson* (London, 1927), i, 277. Subsequent citations in the text refer to vol. and page nos. of this edition.
10. Mrs. Clement Parsons, *Garrick and his Circle* (London, 1906), p. 226.
11. Barrett H. Clark, *European theories of the drama* (New York, 1929), p. 235.
12. John Ginger, *The Notable Man: The Life and Times of Oliver Goldsmith* (London, 1977), pp. 365–66.
13. J. J. Kelly, *The Early Haunts of Oliver Goldsmith* (Dublin, n.d.), p. 78.
14. Elizabeth Yearling, 'The Good-Natured Heroes of Cumberland, Goldsmith, and Sheridan', *MLR*, 67 (1972), 490–500.
15. J. B. Lyons, *The Mystery of Oliver Goldsmith's Medical Degree* (Blackrock, 1978).
16. Susan Hamlyn, 'A new source for the plot of "She Stoops to Conquer"', *Notes and Queries* (May–June 1977), 278–79.
17. *Punch*, 18 August 1982.
18. St. John Hankin, *Dramatic Sequels* (London, 1925).
19. Piaras Béaslaí, *Isliú chun buadha* (Oifig an tSolathair, 1939).
20. Catalogue: *Abbey Plays, 1899–1948* (Dublin, 1948).

10

Goldsmith, Biography and the Phenomenology of Anglo-Irish Literature

by W. J. Mc CORMACK

F. S. L. Lyons, tabulating the achievements of post-war Irish historiography, was prompt to admit a neglect of the whole area of *Kulturgeschichte*.[1] In a humbler capacity I have myself complained of a different but related neglect—that of Anglo-Irish literature generally, by Marxist critics specifically.[2] My intention in this essay is to bring these two issues together, and to relate them to the problem of Goldsmith's biography. Stated plainly, that problem has been the scarcity of reliable material, either released by Goldsmith himself, or collated by his contemporaries, or transmitted by successive nineteenth- and twentieth-century commentators. As the culmination of this articulated silence is Yeats's incorporation of Goldsmith into his 'tradition' of Anglo-Irish literature, the reconsideration of a specific aspect of Goldsmith's biography may subject the entire formation of literary production known as Anglo-Irish literature to a drastic critique. With so specific a focus on the one hand, and with so broad an implication on the other, it is advisable at the outset to note the various stages of the argument which follows. Having expanded on the dual neglect outlined above, I shall discuss Goldsmith's ancestry and the elimination of aspects of this from his biography. Then, I will turn to Goldsmith's place in eighteenth-century literary relations between England and Ireland, gradually concentrating on variants of a famous passage in *The Deserted Village*. The final stages of the essay will discuss Goldsmith's contribution to the early stages of a romantic formulation of the artist-as-genius, the simultaneous development of biography as a critical practice, and—at last—the phenomenological procedures upon which Yeats's Anglo-Irish tradition is based, Goldsmith providing the principal evidence here.

1

Irish historians have been busy since the inauguration of the Irish Free State, and especially so since the end of the Second World War. On the whole, however, they have declined to offer any detailed historical account of Irish literary production despite its high reputation in the world. In this they have not revealed a lack of personal interest in literature or culture generally—as incidental work by Louis Cullen and Oliver Mac Donagh testifies impressively.[3] What has caused the historians' reticence to enter this area is, in my view, the uncertainty as to what Anglo-Irish literature *is*. No such ontological reservations have affected the literary critics, of course, and the classic work of A. N. Jeffares, T. R. Henn and their followers proceeds on the assumption that the existence and being of Anglo-Irish literature is entirely unproblematic—and this despite the awkwardness and revealingly schismatic hyphenation of the very term employed. With the new left movement in the sociology of literature, however, a different reaction is obvious, a surprising silence on the colonial or neo-colonial status of the Yeatsian or Joycean context, and a complementary excision of the colonial and imperialist dimension to that 'English' culture upon which the New Left intermittently concentrates.[4] Given the nature of these complaints, I should emphasize that this present essay is intended as a Marxist corrective to the English Marxist neglect of the entire area of *British* culture and its penumbra known as Anglo-Irish literature, and intended also as an initiative towards a properly dynamic Irish literary history.[5] Of course it would be entirely feasible to designate Goldsmith as naming the site of a conjuncture between eighteenth-century writing practices and a Lacanian discourse constructed to eliminate the transcendental reading subject, or to recuperate 'Goldsmith' to the functions of a revolutionary seminar. However, my complaint effectively is that such approaches (?) deny access to history, and such access is necessary to the full admission of the colonial condition of Anglo-Irish cultural relations. What English Marxist criticism urgently needs is a confession (and subsequent practical purging) of its own patronizingly colonial perspective on this issue, for it is central to the political crisis of the British state in the late twentieth century just as it has been central to the understanding of 'English' modernism since the publication of *The Wanderings of Oisin*. Adventures with the Transcendental Signifier, and questions as to whether Mrs. Hardcastle *is* or *has* the Phallus may be safely left for discussion on some other occasion.

2

In dealing with Goldsmith's biography there are two crucial historical moments. The first of these is the collection of documents preserved in Trinity College Dublin, and known as the 1641 Depositions. I shall be concerned to exhume material from the Rev. John Goldsmith's account of his sufferings during the Irish rebellion of that year and to relate the suppression of such genealogical traces to the question of the construction of a Goldsmith biography. The other historical moment is likewise textual, the following lines of Yeats's:

> Oliver Goldsmith sang what he had seen,
> Roads full of beggars, cattle in the fields,
> But never saw the trefoil stained with blood,
> The avenging leaf those fields raised up against it.[6]

The historical Goldsmith stands midway between these two moments, but the ideological nature of the biographical enterprise in this specific case is best caught in the preface to the 1871 edition of John Forster's *Life and Times of Oliver Goldsmith*. When Forster had earlier published a life of the poet he had been attacked by a rival biographer, James Prior, essentially on a charge of plagiarism. Returning to the question in 1871, Forster declared that the attack had been on

Prior's part 'nothing less than the claim to an absolute property in facts'.[7] As to his own work, he continued:

> Not only are very numerous corrections to every former publication relating to Goldsmith here made, and a great many new facts brought forward, but each fact, whether new or old, is given from its first authority.[8]

This talismanic addiction to facts (and to the word 'fact') permits Forster to ignore entirely the question of Goldsmith's origins and the larger perspective of his place in the formation of Anglo-Irish society. His characteristic Victorian method is the positivistic obverse side of that gnostic contempt for historical specificity to which I have already adequately alluded. And the Victorian Goldsmith (like the Victorian Swift) is one source for the Yeatsian model of the same name. The task of the literary historian is to render totally accessible the practices by which the succession of re-makings produces both the 'original' Goldsmith and the 'objective' Goldsmith of our superlatively new critical procedures; that historical undertaking simultaneously establishes a critique of the texts concerned and the texts themselves. The attempt to establish such a totality necessarily reveals the *lacunae* by which we identify past significance and present meaning, and distinguish between them. In the course of attempting to apply such a historical criticism to Goldsmith we may be able to rediscover a more dynamic notion of 'text' itself in a specifically Anglo-Irish context.

The lines I have quoted from 'The Seven Sages', in common with Yeats's other placings of Goldsmith, are explicitly dramatic. Goldsmith is seen or accounted for in dramatic relation to Swift or Burke. He represents the happy imperception of imminent revolution which is counterbalanced by Swift's involuntary witnessing of 'the ruin to come' in 'The Words Upon the Window-Pane'. The Irish Augustan tradition which Yeats evolves requires each figure to act in complementary relation to others, and Goldsmith is consistently seen 'sipping at the honey-pot of his mind'.[9] The Yeatsian universe is always a matter of antimonies, and Goldsmith's permanent, partial function is to embody a transitory unity between antimonies. Thus he unites expression and perception,

171

sings what he sees, and his vision specifies the beggars as well as the noblemen. Goldsmith, in Yeats's system, contributes permanence with inadequate acknowledgement of that process inherent in permanence; Swift, one might say, stands for the reverse—an excessive awareness of the process of imminent 'ruin' unchecked by the actual. Unable to see the bloodstained trefoil (shamrock and gallows?), Goldsmith embodies a state of prelapsarian harmony, pristine innocence, the perfect conjunction of word and object, signifier and signified. As against this, we see Swift as fallen, knowing, self-divided, ironic, savage.

It is worth emphasizing at this point the degree to which this Yeatsian view of the Irish eighteenth-century is a Romantic construct, in which both a Victorian positivism and a Nietzschean opposition of knowledge to power are all but explicit. That Yeats celebrates the age as 'that one Irish century that escaped from darkness and confusion' is no abdication from such a dualism.[10] Swift and Berkeley, Goldsmith and Burke may be recruited as *dramatis personae* in an enactment of this play, yet it is admitted (tacitly) that they too were a reversal of the age, that Swift was evicted from court circles, Berkeley sequestered in remote Cork, Goldsmith jeered into eccentricity, and Burke held in perpetual opposition. Thus, while the eighteenth century shows up the 'darkness' of the nineteenth, Swift and Goldsmith by their knowledge and innocence show up the tawdry mechanical achievements of the Augustan hegemony. By such a symmetry, we come finally to recognize the intensity of ideological investment in this myth.

The Protestant tradition which Yeats thus creates is to be seen in the historical moment of its articulation and not of its alleged setting alone. That is to say, it belongs with the dead Parnell, and the exertions of Augusta Gregory and Horace Plunkett at the turn of the century. It contributes a family tree to that version of Victorian philanthropy which Yeats disguises as aristocratic service. This 'non-political' service may be elevated into a tradition by the invocation of a sequence of such figures—from Swift to Burke. The contradiction at the centre of this formation is precisely this, that its sequence is not historical but mythic, and its order dramatic rather than diachronic. Add to this, the by now self-evidently oppositional nature of this 'service', and Yeats's tragic aesthetic is seen as the vehicle by which a specifically *fin de siècle* social dichotomy is provided with a resonant 'history', an Edenic past from which it is a falling-away nobly transformed.

Here, we may resume contact with the issue of Goldsmith's biography and its metamorphosis. Yeats's categorization of Irish society, like his periodization of its history, required polar terms, and these he found in the Catholic/Protestant antagonism. From the 1790s onwards, these terms had gradually shifted from a relationship of complementary hostility (i.e. rival versions of the same creed) to one of mutual exclusivity. In this the deployment of sectarian feeling contributed to the perception of a rigidly stratified class system in Ireland, in which class is intensively perceived as a category rather than as a formation. Goldsmith, within the Yeatsian schema, while embodying an innocent harmony of the 'seen' and the 'sung', is required to remain within a backdated eighteenth-century reflection of this essentially post-revolutionary sociology.

In concentrating on Yeats's dramatic placings of Goldsmith, I do not intend to imply that our task today is to 'recuperate' some pristine, original Goldsmith who might be disinterred from the fossil banks. Nevertheless, it is worth stressing that Marxist hostility to empiricism as a theory of knowledge does not necessarily lead to a dismissal of research; on the contrary, the dialectical movement of thought (understood within a materialist philosophy) may at every stage require, transform or annihilate the results of 'empirical' research. Consequently, in drawing attention to the details of Goldsmith's ancestry preserved in the transcript of the Deposition of 1643, I want to emphasize the dialectical manner of its implementation. Neither that document nor Yeats's dramatic poem should be seen as an unmediated source, and the responsibility of criticism is to recover the fully articulated history which lies between these nodal points.

It is surprising that the resemblance of the Rev. John Goldsmith's experiences in 1641 to the conventional view of poor Noll has not been noted. To have had three-and-a-half years' notice (on good authority) of a rebellion universally

173

execrated for its precipitative treachery, and yet to have been
pathetically embroiled—this indeed is worthy of Oliver Goldsmith's reputation for thriftless vulnerability. That the document was known to Goldsmith's biographers almost from the
(admittedly delayed) outset cannot be denied: James Prior
cites it at some length in the opening pages of his 1837 *Life*.[11]
Prior, however, was also the biographer of Edmund Burke
(1824) and well aware of Burke's contemptuous dismissal of
the Depositions as propaganda.[12] It is in this light that we now
read the opening passage of the Rev. John Goldsmith's
narrative:

> John Goldsmith, parson of Burrishoole, in the county of Mayo,
> sworn and examined, says that between three and four years
> before the last rebellion in Ireland began Francis Goldsmith,
> the deponents brother, who is a Romish priest of good account,
> living at and being Capitan Maior [*sic*] of the castle of Antwerp
> in Brabant, wrote and sent a letter to this deponent . . . which
> was delivered to him, this deponent, by one Father Richard
> Barret, a Jesuit and Spanish preacher. . . . This letter, as this
> deponent has heard, was first delivered at Antwerp aforesaid to
> Malone, the arch-Jesuit that dwelt in Dublin . . . he is hereby
> persuaded that the said Malone had forewardly revealed the
> intended plot of rebellion to this deponents said brother which
> induced him so earnestly to write for this deponent, his wife and
> children to leave the kingdom and so escape the danger thereof
> which this deponent did not suspect, nor in any way under-
> stand, until the latter end of July next. . . .[13]

This, together with the subsequent confession of 'having been
formerly a romish priest and converted to the protestant
religion by the light of God', establishes our poet's family
origins as including active Catholics. Sir John Temple, who
employed this evidence as early as 1646, omits these Catholic
associations in the case of John Goldsmith but is not averse to
including them in describing the qualifications of other
witnesses.[14] Moving on to the poet's biographers, we have
already noted that Prior uncritically cites the Depositions in
1837 but that John Forster has eliminated them by 1848.
Forster's laundering of Goldsmith's ancestry, while it superficially appears to remove innuendo and self-contradictory
evidence, is a far more damaging blow to genuine historical

veracity than Prior's unanalytical citation of the Depositions. However, the onward march of a sectarian sociology of Ireland (together with a romanticizing of the eighteenth century in retrospect) required the elimination of the admission that Goldsmith's ancestor had been a Catholic priest, and that in the 1630s there had been affable correspondence between the Goldsmith brothers in which the now-Protestant John was warned by his Catholic kinsman in Antwerp of imminent rebellion. The folly of the Rev. John's behaviour (if the warning were genuine), or the improbability of the warning itself, is nothing compared to the admission of an active Catholic ancestry for Oliver Goldsmith. It is true that the poet and his brother told Thomas Percy about a forebear called Juan Romeiro, a Spanish tutor who settled and married a good Protestant Miss Goldsmith.[15] That 'tradition', of course, is a conveniently narrative explanation (John the Swordfish) of a more significant social transformation occurring between the early seventeenth and late eighteenth centuries. The late Gerard Simms observed in this connection that 'Oliver Goldsmith's Irish background was very different from that of Jonathan Swift. . . .'[16] In the fashionable argot of today we might speak of the deconstruction of Yeats's tradition; accordingly the specific historical distinction which Simms makes may be recovered from the psycho-symbolic rôles of the Yeatsian drama. However, such exercises are meaningless if they do not also establish the historical continuity which led to the Yeatsian model. Instead of Yeats's Goldsmith, we substitute no seemingly pristine Goldsmith's Goldsmith, but instead seek to recover every stage of the process by which Johnson, Percy, Prior, Forster, and others contribute to the neo-romantic Goldsmith of 'The Seven Sages'. Our reading of the poet does not itself recover that figure, rather it contributes a further element to the object of its own attention.

3

'Poor Dr. Goldsmith! Lord bless us what an anomalous Character was his.'[17] Conventional wisdom has accepted Mrs. Thrale's opinion as somehow literally accurate, with a reactive discounting of Goldsmith's observations on his own condition.

175

If, for example, he employs the term 'industrious poor' in outlining the prospects of his nephew, we are required to see this as evidence of his quaint unreliability as a witness to his own circumstances, of his pathos or exaggeration.[18] Yet the question remains unasked as to what norm Goldsmith's anomalous character related, and beyond that the more pressing question as to the significance in cultural history of Goldsmith's 'anomalies'. At this point, some attention may be paid to the colonial relationship between England and Ireland existing in the eighteenth century. Goldsmith was born and educated in Ireland, and spent his career in England. Notoriously he demonstrates the conditions for success and failure in Grub Street prevalent in London—rather than Dublin. If we now bear in mind our renewed apprehension of his ancestry, then the account he gave to his brother Henry of his feelings in England takes on a new significance:

> I have passed my days among a number of cool designing beings and have contracted all their suspicious manner, in my own behaviour. I should actually be as unfit for the society of my friends at home as I detest that which I am obliged to partake of here. I can now neither partake of the pleasure of a revel nor contribute to raising its jollity, I can neither laugh nor drink, have contracted an hesitating disagreeable manner of speaking, and a visage that looks illnature itself, in short I have thought myself into settled melancholy and an utter disgust of all that life brings with it. Whence this romantic turn that all our family are possessed with, whence this love for every place and every country but that in which we reside?[19]

It has been customary among critics of Anglo-Irish literature to read such passages as evidence of what Yeats called 'Anglo-Irish solitude' or, less resonantly, the distemper of the colonial settler in the face of decadence in the metropolis. Yet Goldsmith's position was far more complex than that of *colon*, and one level of his social experience recorded here is surely the revelation of *colon* society to the *colonisé*, a revelation which is carefully suppressed 'at home' in the colony. Ireland and England differ, not *per se*, but by their embodying aspects of a single colonial system which employs difference as bond.[20] To put it in psychological terms, Goldsmith's perception of this depends on his position as a *colonisé* in the process of

176

absorption into a categorized sectarian colonialism. That process is of course only in its early stages in the 1750s, and Goldsmith's social status is more complex and problematic than the borrowed terminology of *colonisé* and *colon* can indicate. It nevertheless becomes imperative—as the sectarian sociology of the 1790s onwards gains ground—that Goldsmith's biography should exclude his papist ancestry. Thus amputated from one aspect of history, he may play the rôle of insouciant in the ultimate Yeatsian drama.

Answering Mrs. Thrale on the level of cultural theory, one might pompously demand of her some indication of the norm she saw Goldsmith deviating from, for the conjuncture which he inhabits renders it impossible to declare him in some unproblematic way either English or Irish. Indeed, his significance lies precisely in the extent to which the suppressed relations symbolized in his biography and in the official constitutions of Britain and Ireland must be made manifest and subjected to analysis if his 'anomalies' are to be examined. The notion that Goldsmith was unhappy away from his beloved and possessed Ireland has led to a singularly sentimental reading of *The Deserted Village*. Auburn (one is repeatedly told) is Lissoy, his birthplace, or (by a rival school of local patriots) Ballymahon. Accordingly, the declension of the harmonious past into a luxuriating and mercantile present is but the passage from one island to the other. Here, the central notion of 'text' is as much in need of radical re-definition as the double dynamic of colonialism. The following lines from *The Deserted Village* well illustrate the point (ll. 225–36):

> Imagination fondly stoops to trace
> The parlour splendours of that festive place;
> The white-washed wall, the nicely sanded floor,
> The varnished clock that clicked behind the door;
> The chest contrived a double debt to pay,
> A bed by night, a chest of drawers by day;
> The pictures placed for ornament and use,
> The twelve good rules, the royal game of goose;
> The hearth, except when winter chill'd the day,
> With aspen boughs, and flowers, and fennel gay,
> While broken tea-cups, wisely kept for shew,
> Ranged o'er the chimney, glistened in a row.[21]

At first sight, the passage is characterized by a modified Augustan antithesis which runs through all its details—balance, contrast, binary expression are pre-eminent. But underlying this general pattern, there is a more specific antithesis between ornament and use—which is of course the poem's larger theme. Interpretation of *The Deserted Village* has at times divided along similar lines—to some critics Goldsmith denounces expansionist imperialism abroad and its consequences at home, to others he enacts a latterday imitation of conventional classical motifs.[22] To squeeze up our eyes in a determined attempt to scan this puzzling set of lines is, however, to adopt a drastically over-simplified notion of poetic text though one sanctioned in this century by the practices of the New Critics. Edward Said has recommended (and Lucien Goldmann has impressively demonstrated) a more dynamic approach to the task of de-fining the text.[23] In accordance with their practice, I would not assume the exclusion from *The Deserted Village* as text of the following passage from Goldsmith's letter to his brother; he had asked the Rev. Henry for an opinion of the 'heroicomical poem which I sent you':

> You remember I intended to introduce the hero of the Poem as lying in a paltry alehouse you may take the following specimen of the manner; which I flatter myself is quite original. The room [in] which he lies may be descri[bed] somewhat this way.
>
> [A] Window patch'd with paper lent a ray,
> That feebly shew'd the state in which he lay.
> The sanded floor, that grits beneath the tread
> The humid wall with paltry pictures spread.
> The game of goose was there expos'd to view,
> And the twelve rules the Royal Martyr drew.
> The seasons fram'd with listing, found a place,
> And Prussia's Monarch shew'd his lamp black face.
> The morn was cold he views with keen desire,
> A rusty grate unconscious of a fire.
> An unpaid reck'ning on the freeze was scor'd,
> And five crack'd teacups dress'd the chimney [board].
>
> And Now immagine [*sic*] after his soliloquy the landlord to make his appearance in order to Dun him for the reckoning,
>
> Not with that face so servile and so gay

178

That welcomes every stranger that can pay,
With sulky eye he smoak'd the patient man
Then pull'd his breeches tight, and thus began, &c.
All this is taken you see from Nature.[24]

What we have here is not a different text, hermetically distinct from *The Deserted Village*, but rather—to use a familiar metaphor—the textual obverse of a renowned passage, that is, of a passage renowned in one familiar and partial aspect. It is futile to protest that this 'paltry' version exists merely in private correspondence, intended purely for domestic consumption, for Goldsmith employed these lines (with a few variants and a few additional framing lines) in the thirtieth letter of *The Citizen of the World*.[25] Here, the context is explicitly that of a Poet's living conditions, as reported from Europe by Lien Chi Altangi to his friends in China. The georgic tone of *The Deserted Village* is extended, qualified, and intensified by these less frequently cited aspects of the text. Nor is Goldsmith's incidental commentary on the lines merely incidental or conveniently external to some purist definition of text; in writing to his brother Henry, he had observed that 'All this is taken . . . from Nature' and Nature here is ironically identified with that (Irish) society the Goldsmith brothers had in common. The projected heroicomical poem of 1759, its employment of Irish 'Nature' as symbolic of the Grub Street author's experience of English society, the satirical perspective of *The Citizen*, and the soft nostalgia of the canonical *Deserted Village*—all these are dynamic aspects of a single textual conjuncture. In addition, the modes of publication successively employed in disseminating Goldsmith enter into this textual conjuncture also. Collected editions, for example, isolate the *Citizen* lines and establish them as the independent poem 'The Description of an Author's Bed-chamber'.[26] The precarious status of the author in Grub Street, as witnessed in the 1759 letter to Henry Goldsmith, is structurally paralleled and parodied in the splendid isolation of the poem *per se*, cut off now from the larger interpretive framework of *The Citizen*'s oriental satire and from the ironic interchangeability of Nature and Society in the Anglo-Irish colonial nexus.

4

Ideally, one should proceed from here to demonstrate how the career of Goldsmith's text offers an opportunity to examine the real interrelation of altering literary practices with the modes of production and consumption operating in eighteenth-century Anglo-Irish colonialism generally. Unfortunately, Marxist historians who have specialized in Irish history and historiography have concentrated on the period of democratization and the issues of nationalism and independence, to the neglect of the eighteenth century and earlier eras. This has left us without any detailed terminology or typology with which to distinguish the changing economic, social and political relations which characterized the two kingdoms and their colonial bond during Goldsmith's lifetime. I have already conceded that *colon* and *colonisé* inadequately describe these relations, for the simple reason that such terms tend to particularize in an excessively personalized way relations which were necessarily repressed, abstratized and impersonal. However, we can resume contact both with the problem of Goldsmith's biography and its successive forms and with the larger question of a homology between literary and social structures.

Once again, *The Deserted Village* and its marginalized aspects can shed some light on the matter. In an elegy for Goldsmith, Courtney Melmoth seized upon Goldsmith's style to render his own response:

> The village-bell tolls out the note of death,
> And thro' the echoing air, the length'ning sound,
> With dreadful pause, reverberating deep;
> Spreads the sad tydings, o'er fair Auburn's vale.[27]

This is at once a horrid failure to realize the most elementary features of *The Deserted Village* and a sinister appropriation of the poem's fiction as the world of the poet himself. Just as successive editions of the poems splendidly isolated certain aspects of the text to stand in place of those extensive and dynamic relations of which the text is, so to speak, symbolic, so here we find the poet reduced to being a function of his own fiction. To take a ludicrous but revealing parallel, it is as if T. S. Eliot were eulogized as a long-suffering Monsieur

Sosostris or Yeats granted citizenship of Istanbul. For what is at work in Melmoth's negligible tribute is more significantly observed in the altering force and meaning of the word *genius*, classically defined as the informing or indwelling spirit of place or whatever, but romantically to re-emerge as 'extraordinary capacity for imaginative creation' (*O.E.D.*). While seeming to intensify individuality, the change actually renders that individuality more abstract because less specific, less relational. The Goldsmith of Irish 'Nature', the satirist of *The Citizen of the World*, and the author of those closing lines of *The Deserted Village* in which expansionist economics in the Americas is exposed to view—all these aspects of Goldsmith are subsumed in the propagation of the genius of Auburn. At the risk of prolixity we can quote as a consequence of this reformulation of Goldsmith lines from a Canadian poem *The Rising Village* written early in the nineteenth century by a kinsman and namesake:

> Behold! the savage tribes, in wildest strain,
> Approach with death and terror in their train;
> No longer silence o'er the forest reigns,
> No longer stillness now her pow'r retains;
> But hideous yells announce the murd'rous band,
> Whose bloody footsteps desolate the land;
> He hears them oft in sternest mood maintain
> Their right to rule the mountain and the plain:
> He hears them doom the *white man*'s instant death,
> Shrinks from the sentence, while he gasps for breath;
> Then, rousing with one effort all his might,
> Darts from his hut, and saves himself by flight.[28]

If the descendant of Father John Goldsmith, and the uncle of the industrious poor, may yet become symbolic of Protestant Ascendency, so too may a univocal and decontextualized *Deserted Village* inspire a provincial identification of the Red Man and Whig luxuriance. Nevertheless the function of literary history remains the elucidation of precisely those strategies of interpretation which render tradition so unconsciously ironic.

Writing his *Life of Richard Nash*, Goldsmith perceptively located the social material to which the new art of biography related:

> I profess to write the history of a man placed in the middle ranks of life; of one, whose vices and virtues were open to the eye of the most undiscerning spectator, who was placed in public view without power to repress censure, or command adulation, who had too much merit not to become remarkable, yet too much folly to arrive at greatness.[29]

Unlike Goldsmith's better known *Life of Thomas Parnell*, and unlike those early classics of the biographical art, Johnson's *Lives of the Poets* and (more crucially) Boswell's life of Johnson himself, the life of Beau Nash is not centrally concerned with the individual as author. It is this marginal relationship between Goldsmith's subject and the conventional eighteenth-century biographical sketch which, in part at least, requires Goldsmith to spell out the 'middle ranks' station and its characteristics. It is tempting to interpret Goldsmith's analysis of Nash's social impotence as autobiographical—'too much merit not to become remarkable, yet too much folly . . .'—but more important to emphasize that Goldsmith is a pioneer among eighteenth-century biographers, though by no means among the greatest. Thus, the problem of his own biography reflects upon the larger issue of the emergence of biography as a critical practice. The convergence of 'life' and 'work' in this kind of criticism is itself another stratum of that altering sense of genius which is characteristic of, and also parasitical upon, the romantic poets.

We can say, then, as a reasonable and indeed tiresome generality, that Goldsmith's biographical exercises form part of the material which eventually coheres as the biographical individual. By the middle of the eighteenth-century, this individual is (not surprisingly) bourgeois, 'of the middle ranks of life'. Why then should Goldsmith supply such unsatisfactory details to Thomas Percy when the latter decided in April 1773 that the author of *She Stoops to Conquer* deserved some commemoration of his life? Mrs. Thrale's insistence on Noll's eccentricities will not suffice as an explanation for, though the poet gave Percy the first hint of the Romeiro ancestry as a suitable variant upon native recusancy, it was Maurice Goldsmith, the poet's cabinet-maker brother, who corrects and extends this pretty story:

> The Doctor's great grandfather Juan Romeiro came over to Ireland as private tutor to a Spanish nobleman in the last century, who was then on his travels.[30]

In positivist style, we could respond to this claim by proudly establishing that the Goldsmiths' great-grandfather was precisely the ex-Catholic priest whose record in the Depositions undergoes such interesting sea-changes in later biographies of the poet. For, as late as 1974, A. Lytton Sells accepts the Romeiro story at face value and proceeds to identify the Spanish tutor with the Rev. John Goldsmith, an exercise which obliges him to suppress the papist brother in Antwerp.[31] However, the restoration of some pristine Goldsmith is not a priority here. If we accept the cultural weight behind Joshua Reynolds's observation that Goldsmith, while knowing himself to be a distinguished writer, also was conscious of having 'lived a great part of his life with mean people', then we may be able to approach an answer to our question about Goldsmith's unsatisfactory memorandum dictated to Thomas Percy. As the examination of those marginalized aspects of *The Deserted Village* testify, Goldsmith knew two kinds of 'mean people', two kinds of social deprivation. The better known of these is the author's bedchamber, somewhere behind Grub Street; the lesser known, the more totally marginalized, is colonial Ireland as experienced by lower Protestant clergy descended from persecuted Catholic priests. It will remain an urgent task to elaborate the extent to which the eighteenth-century biographical individual depends, as an ideological construct, on the suppression of British colonialism as a central feature of 'English' society and culture. The problem of Goldsmith's biography therefore is valuable precisely because the anomalies and contradictions discernible in it render the continued suppression of that feature difficult if not impossible.

5

So much for Goldsmith, so much for biography; what then, you may ask, should be said on the topic of 'the phenomenology of Anglo-Irish literature'? I fully intend to justify, if only briefly, that element in my title—but not just yet. There remains an issue raised indirectly by Mrs. Thrale's apostrophe on Goldsmith's anomalies—the issue of an implied norm from which Goldsmith deviated in his anomalous conduct. Of course, the record suggests that Goldsmith's behaviour and attitudes were inconsistent, that is, anomalous one to another. Yet the conventional view of eighteenth-century Anglo-Irish writing from Jonathan Swift to Edmund Burke (and including Berkeley, Goldsmith and Sheridan) has stressed the centrality of irony and satire. And, in neo-classical terms at least, irony and satire presuppose some norm which is either positively or negatively manifested by ironic distortion or satiric portraiture. In the first book of *Gulliver's Travels*, the Lilliputians are a model of what humankind is and should not be; in the second, the Brobdignaggians are (conversely) a model of what humankind is not and should be. So, at least, a universalist and anti-historical criticism would have us believe. In the third book, and even more drastically in the last, the models, standards and norms upon which such a concept of satire depended are progressively exposed as inadequate, redundant, or simply non-existent. Reading Swift, we are made uncomfortably aware that the Absolute has abdicated. Officially, of course, Swift continued to trust in Christian stoicism and a rather ferocious version of Augustan commonsense as surrogate Absolutes, but in the larger battle of the books his Moderns have in fact won the day. It is as well to remember that Augustan universalism was a more limited matter than was officially admitted and that the Absolute had never enjoyed more than a relative sovereignty. Humankind, for example, might be more precisely defined as European *man*kind of a certain social standing. And, as J. K. Walton has demonstrated, Swift's satire is directed specifically against social *élites* rather than against humanity.[32] This digression by way of Swift has its direct relevance to a discussion of Goldsmith in that it serves to confirm the problematic nature of a norm within the eighteenth-century colonial bond of England and Ireland. The colony is intended to be an imitation of the colonializing society, to be modelled upon metropolitan norms, but by reason of its need to incorporate the *colonisés* as well as the *colons* the intention is distorted. More drastically, however, the metropolitan society is itself altered by its colonial enterprise, though altered in ways which it cannot fully articulate. Hence, in modern European colonial cultures we find an accelerating and intensifying relativization of values. In the Augustan age, it is precisely Swift (with his Irish marginality) and Pope (with his stigmatized Catholicism) who provide not only characteristic satirical perspectives but also subversive revelations of the constraints within which satire may operate. There is therefore a case to be made for reading *The Deserted Village* as ironic satire—though it is a case more attractive to an Irish peasant or a Cherokee than to an English Whig. One can therefore identify quite precisely the political necessities lying behind the critical insistence on a definition of text which is exclusivist, de-historicized and limited to a formal structure.

The complex and incompletely expressed nature of the real relations existing between England and Ireland in the eighteenth-century resulted in some cumbersome linguistic formulae.[33] Behind these there were two principal experiences of Ireland from the English point of view: on the one hand, Ireland was the wilderness, an unregenerate and in a sense unknowable Nature; on the other, it was quintessentially artificial, a model of society rather than the reality of society. Henry Grattan, complaining of the impotence of Irish politics in 1792, characterized his society as 'theatric representation', not the real thing.[34] Thus, the horrors of colonialism are a combination of palpable and violent existence with a formal unreality. The problem of Goldsmith's biography serves to articulate this paradox by drawing our attention to the *lacunae*, the silences, the omissions necessitated within a colonial culture.

The historians' polite neglect of Anglo-Irish literature in their massive revision and extension of the field now looks rather less innocently polite. But if one emphasizes the dual nature of colonialism, its effect both 'at home' and in the colony, is it legitimate to isolate Anglo-Irish literature (as conventionally defined) as a proper object of study? Here, we should recall that the formation known now as Anglo-Irish literature dates from the period of High Modernism rather than the Augustan era. More urgently, a reconsideration of the Irish contribution to 'English' Modernism is required, not so much by some remote archaeological problem lodged in the past, as by the central place of contemporary poetry (notably, but by no means exclusively, Seamus Heaney) in the present crisis of the rancid British state. Literature has long been the primary export of the Irish ideological economy operating within the penumbra of Britain. In theoretical terms, the position is

185

expounded with admirable concentration by Walter Benjamin in the 'Theses on the Philosophy of History' written in the last year of his life:

> A historical materialist cannot do without the notion of the present which is not a transition, but in which time stands still and has come to a stop. For this notion defines the present in which he himself is writing history. Historicism gives the 'eternal' image of the past; historical materialism supplies a unique experience with the past. The historical materialist leaves it to others to be drained by the whore called 'Once upon a time' in historicism's bordello. He remains in control of his powers, man enough to blast open the continuum of history.
>
> . . . Thinking involves not only the flow of thoughts, but their arrest as well. Where thinking suddenly stops in a configuration pregnant with tensions, it gives that configuration a shock, by which it crystallizes into a monad. A historical materialist approaches a historical subject only where he encounters it as a monad. In this structure he recognises the sign of a Messianic cessation of happening, or, put differently, a revolutionary chance in the fight for the oppressed past.[35]

With this distinction between the historicist who seeks indiscriminately to relate and accumulate, and the historical materialist who distinguishes in order to transform and totalize, we can approach at last the phenomenology of Anglo-Irish literature.

I have no wish to escape from the decorative treadmill of Anglo-American formalism only to take up dumb-bells in Professor Heidegger's *gymnasium*, and the term 'phenomenology' is to a degree used heuristically. The particular conditions of the argument which justify its employment are precisely those of colonial Ireland's appearance as artefact, as work of art. Since Burke's *Reflections* the application of aesthetic terms to the description of society had become something of a commonplace, but in the case of Ireland its function was precise and distinctive—to insist on the unalterable character of Ireland within the United Kingdom, by endowing it with the immutability of art. But if the Victorians invested heavily in Immutability as a virtue in art, they also were obliged by their positivism to concede its non-reality, its exclusion from everything that is the case. As I have observed elsewhere, throughout the nineteenth century no novelist speaks of Irish society as a totality, for they either defined that society as explicitly a dual system of rival ideologies or as an integral if threatened part of a larger British society. I called that state of affairs the 'coexistence of non-congruent worlds', though it might be more fully analysed in terms of uneven development.[36] In the period of the late nineteenth century, when W. B. Yeats inaugurated the Celtic Revival the procedures he adopted—which I have called here phenomenological— were particularly appropriate in the cultural conflict engendered by these developments. It is conventional to emphasize the extent and intensity with which Yeats's poetry exploited the Irish landscape. Locally, of course, this tactic can be satisfactorily explained in terms of natural beauty or the intimacies of an associated folklore. Less familiarly, one could cite Heidegger's definition of his phenomenology, 'to let that which shows itself be seen from itself in the very way in which it shows itself from itself'—which is less attractive to tourists than Innisfree.[37] The opening pages of John Synge's *The Aran Islands* (1907) provide perhaps the best example of this technique—comparable to the neo-formalist notion of *ostranenie*, or defamiliarization. What prevents our recognition of this procedure in the work of the Revival authors is precisely the deployment today of their work as part of a cultural politics devoted to reintroducing and reinforcing the aestheticized immutability of Ireland. What was once a cultural assault upon the imposed homogeneity of the United Kingdom is turned now by seminar and summer school into the symbolism of integration.

Yeats's attitude to Oliver Goldsmith may serve to illustrate some aspects of this question, while at the same time reinforcing our sense of the value of the biographical problem which the eighteenth-century poet represents. In May 1904, defending Lady Gregory's *Gods and Fighting Men* as dealing admirably with 'the heroic foundations of the race', he dismissed Swift, Burke and Goldsmith 'who hardly seem to me to have come out of Ireland at all'.[38] In America in 1911, he illustrated his theory of 'two opposite types of characters in Ireland' by citing Goldsmith as an example of the first:

One is the gentle, harmless—you might call it saintly—type, that knows no wrong, and goes through life happy and untroubled, without any evil or sadness. Goldsmith was an Irishman of that type, a man without any real knowledge apparently of sadness or evil. And that kind of Irishman is common in Ireland. . . .[39]

We do not need to wait till the 1930s, and the introduction to 'The Words Upon the Window-Pane', for Yeats's dramatic juxtaposition of *psyches* is already at work here. In 1934, Yeats's presentation of his new Augustan tradition embodies in its very rhythms an enactment of this notion of dramatic juxtaposition:

> I turned from Goldsmith and from Burke because they had come to seem a part of the English system, from Swift because I acknowledged, being a romantic, no verse between Cowley and Smart's *Song to David*, no prose between Sir Thomas Browne and the *Conversations* of Landor. But now I read Swift for months together, Burke and Berkeley less often but always with excitement, and Goldsmith lures and waits. I collect materials for my thought and work, for some identification of my beliefs with the nation itself, I seek an image of the modern mind's discovery of itself, of its own permanent form, in that one Irish century that escaped from darkness and confusion.[40]

'Now I read Swift for months . . .', by its arrangement of the instant and duration in a single phrase, mimics Swift's prophetic vision in the play. 'Goldsmith lures and waits . . .' embodies both the attraction of that figure's innocence and its inaccessibility, its formality. The political context of this renewed commitment to the Irish eighteenth century is more readily seen in *On the Boiler*, where, in an otherwise routine citation of his Augustans, Yeats notably omits Goldsmith:

> I write with two certainties in mind: first that a hundred men, their creative power wrought to the highest pitch, their will trained but not broken, can do more for the welfare of a people, whether in war or peace, than a million of any lesser sort no matter how expensive their education, and that although the Irish masses are vague and excitable because they have not yet been moulded and cast, we have as good blood as there is in Europe. Berkeley, Swift, Burke, Grattan, Parnell, Augusta Gregory, Synge, Kevin O'Higgins, are the true Irish people,

and there is nothing too hard for such as these. If the Catholic names are few history will soon fill the gap. My imagination goes back to those Catholic exiled gentlemen of whom Swift said that their bravery exceeded that of all nations.[41]

It is hardly necessary to add that what Yeats finds as an image of the modern mind's discovery of itself is an anti-democratic politics—power . . . blood . . . hard. . . . The admiration of Mussolini and Hitler has been sufficiently well chronicled to require no further summary here.[42] What is more to the point is the extent to which Yeats's attitude may be directly contrasted with Walter Benjamin's, for the violent exclamations of *On the Boiler* are in many ways the antithesis of 'Theses on the Philosophy of History'. A comparison of the two figures is attractive and admonitory: we are looking here virtually at the last words of each; each will shortly die in the south of France, Yeats in convalescent old age, Benjamin (less than 50) by suicide to avoid the Gestapo. The frenzy of Yeats's last work deliberately renounces a present which may come to a Messianic halt, refuses to blast open history's continuum, which for Yeats is Nietzschean, circular, recurring. Moreover, though he had no appetite for German philosophy, Yeats goes out of his way in *On the Boiler* to condemn as false Hegel's historical dialectic and to recommend Edmund Husserl's *Ideas* as a modern restatement of Berkeley's immaterialism.[43] Rather than advance some case seeking to prove direct allegiances between the phenomenology of Husserl (or, more closely, the teaching of his disciple, Heidegger) and the practices of National Socialism, it is preferable to stress that historically the rise of Nazism drove a wedge between thinkers like Theodor Adorno and Walter Benjamin whose Marxist affinities are intensified and elucidated by the world crisis, and ontologists and phenomenologists whose anti-historical bent suited the requirements of the thousand-year *Reich*. That there *were* subterranean connections between phenomenology and fascism is the substance of a penetrating critique of Husserl (a non-Aryan, himself) written by Adorno during the period of his exile from Nazi Germany.[44] Fascism, following on the example of Louis Napoleon as described by Marx and by the Goncourt brothers, puts on the theatrical robes of ancient events to dignify its spurious authority.[45] At one level, one might relate Yeats's celebration of Irish Augustan dignity as an attempt to appropriate for his opposition to the filthy modern tide some similar 'historical' resonance. The cluster of names which 'are the true Irish people' are, for the most part, cited to bolster up the position of Kevin O'Higgins, the Irish Free State's strong man of politics. But—to use Benjamin's fine distinction— Yeats is a thorough-going historicist, is neither historical materialist nor Heideggerian ontologist. O'Higgins is dead by the time he is bolstered up, is already part of that litany of dramatically ordered citations which constitutes the past for Yeats. For Yeats, it is the present which is restlessly time-filled.

Not all of what is known as Anglo-Irish literature would come under the implied accusation outlined above; Joyce certainly, and Synge also, would require very different readings. But as it is Yeats who launches the manifesto from which these and others subtly diverged, it is fitting that the argument should focus on Yeats. Fitting also because it is he who strives to provide a mythic proto-history for his tradition. However, I do not intend simply to let the argument rest with some static tabulation of Yeats's politics. The texts we conveniently call *Yeats* are more truly and extensively relations—relations between canonical and marginalized aspects of poems and novels; between the social production of texts symbolized effectively as the author and the social consumption (reception and reproduction) of texts by reader, critic and historian, together with all the complex and changing mediations between those two poles; between, ultimately, past and present and future. If one were concentrating on the Yeatsian tradition, then 'the phenomenology of Anglo-Irish literature' is a valid description of a function of British culture. In saying this I have no wish to appear in a revisionist light, depriving a subject nation of its national culture. On the contrary, one discovers the degree and intensity of subjugation by discovering how far that literature is implicated in the dual bonds of colonialism.

Is then Yeats to be rewritten as a rather too-long-lived member of the tragic generation, a *fin de siècle* poet on pension? Is he to be dismissed as a poet because of his fascist sympathies?

Is not all this irrelevant anyhow to the problem of Goldsmith's biography? The answer to all these questions must surely be negative. If it is true that Yeats forged an eighteenth-century tradition which is fundamentally untenable as history, it is also the case that his tradition admits its own inauthenticity. In *On the Boiler* he set out to record the 'two certainties' of his mind: the first concerned blood and breeding; the second . . . is apparently forgotten, unrecorded, absent. To this possibly trivial omission, add a further one—Goldsmith's absence from the lists of Kevin O'Higgins's cultural forebears. Yeats does not omit Goldsmith simply because honey-pots are poor storm-troopers; there were moments when he could see that, like Wordsworth and Keats, Goldsmith had a 'fiery and brooding imagination'.[46] But there is a point beyond which the past cannot fit the requirements of a frenzied, unstable present in its search for imperial clothes: Goldsmith, for Yeats, is that point. 'There is no document of civilization which is not at the same time a document of barbarism', Benjamin wrote in the seventh thesis.[47] If Yeats is a very great poet, playwright and prosewriter (as I fully believe), and if he stands guilty under the charge of the most barbarous sympathies, literary history may yet be able to discriminate properly and comprehensively between aspects of his work by attending to those lacunae and silences which contribute to the Goldsmith of tradition.

NOTES

1. *Ireland Under the Union: Varieties of Tension; Essays in Honour of T. W. Moody*, ed. F. S. L. Lyons and R. A. J. Hawkins (Oxford, 1980), p. 24.
2. In a paper entitled '1792, the Origins of Protestant Ascendancy' read at the sociology of literature conference on 1789 at the University of Essex, July 1981.
3. See, for example, L. M. Cullen, 'The Hidden Ireland: Reassessment of a Concept', *Studia Hibernica*, 9 (1969); and Oliver Mac Donagh, *The Nineteenth-Century and Irish Social History; Some Aspects* (Dublin, 1971).
4. Anthony Easthope's paper on Wordsworth's Lucy poems (read at the conference referred to in n. 2 above) is a representative example of a method which relies heavily on theoretical apparatus acquired from Althusser and Lacan and a notion of 'text' which would not embarrass the least practical of Practical Critics. It should be observed that,

191

although the English Left seems unduly influenced by the gnosticism of Paris, American Marxist criticism is concurrently energetic, generous and exploratory; see in particular the work of Fredric Jameson and (in a less radical mode) of Edward W. Said.

5. I use the term 'literary history' in the dynamic sense elaborated in Robert Weimann's *Structure and Society in Literary History: Studies in the History and Theory of Historical Criticism* (London, 1977).

6. W. B. Yeats, *Collected Poems* (London, 1963), p. 272.

7. John Forster, *Life and Times of Oliver Goldsmith* (London, 6th edn., 1875), p. vii.

8. Ibid., p. ix.

9. Yeats, *Collected Poems*, p. 268.

10. Yeats, 'Introduction to "The Words Upon the Window-pane"', *Explorations* (London, 1962), p. 345.

11. James Prior, *The Life of Oliver Goldsmith* (London, 1837), I, 2–3. Prior's source may well be Sir John Temple's *Irish Rebellion* of 1646, a highly influential and grossly prejudicial account of events in which Temple had lost a great deal of money.

12. Burke to Richard Burke Jnr., 20 March 1792—'the rascally collection in the College relative to the pretended Massacre in 1641'. *The Correspondence of Edmund Burke*, ed. P. J. Marshall and John A. Woods (Cambridge, 1968), VII, 104.

13. Transcribed from the original manuscript in the Library of Trinity College, Dublin.

14. Sir John Temple, *The Irish Rebellion; or, an History of the beginnings and first progress of the general rebellion raised within the kingdom of Ireland, upon the three and twentieth day of* October, *in the year 1641. Together with the barbarous cruelties and bloody massacres which ensued thereupon* (London, 1646), pp. 67, 116–18. The most dispassionate analysis of Temple's unreliability, and of the Depositions generally, is still W. E. H. Lecky in his *History of Ireland in the Eighteenth Century* (London, 1896), I, 72–6.

15. See Katharine C. Balderston, *The History and Sources of Percy's Memoir of Goldsmith* (Cambridge, 1928), p. 13. In a useful article drawing together a variety of printed and oral folk-lore sources Patrick Murray has surveyed the factual problems of the poet's biography, though he is not concerned to draw any interpretive conclusions. See 'Goldsmith's Ancestry: Fact and Tradition', in *Irish Midland Studies: Essays in Commemoration of N. W. English*, ed. Harman Murtagh (London, 1980), pp. 147–58.

16. I am grateful to Dr. Hugh Shields who provided me with a copy of an unpublished paper (from which I quote here) delivered by his father-in-law, the late Professor J. G. Simms, at a Goldsmith centenary celebration in 1974.

17. See Ralph M. Wardle, *Oliver Goldsmith* (London, 1957), p. 1.

18. See *The Collected Letters of Oliver Goldsmith*, p. 59.

19. Ibid., p. 58. The letter can be dated to *c.* 13 January 1759.

20. Two points might be made here at a more general level. First, by emphasizing the colonial relationship between Britain and Ireland I do

not diminish by one jot or tittle the validity of a class analysis; on the contrary, I specify a particular extension of class developments in Britain which, if ignored, can only lead to a simplified and misleading analysis. Second, the practice of some of the British literary left in their criticism constitutes a form of imperialism occasionally tinged with religious humility. As an indigenous Marxist tradition it is about as convincing as a bottle of Chateau Lacan in a Cotswolds supermarket.

21. *Collected Works of Oliver Goldsmith*, ed. Arthur Friedman, 5 vols. (Oxford, 1966), IV, 296.

22. See H. J. Bell Jnr., '*The Deserted Village* and Goldsmith's Social Doctrines', *PMLA*, 59 (1944), and Leo F. Storm, 'Literary Convention in Goldsmith's *Deserted Village*', *Huntington Library Quarterly*, 33 (1970).

23. See Edward W. Said, *Beginnings: Intention and Method* (Baltimore and London, 1975), esp. p. 234: 'the practical notion of "text" is obliged to include a very wide network of relationships; between notes (for instance) and a "final" version, between letters and a tale, between revisions and early drafts, and so on.' Lucien Goldmann's study of Pascal and Racine (*Le Dieu Caché*) opens with a chapter, 'The Whole and the Parts', which includes a practical demonstration of the fruitfulness of such open definitions of *text*. See *The Hidden God: A Study of Tragic Vision in the Pensées of Pascal and the Tragedies of Racine*, trans. Philip Thody (London, 1964), esp. pp. 3–21.

24. *The Collected Letters of Oliver Goldsmith*, pp. 63–5.

25. Friedman, II, 128–29.

26. See ibid., IV, 374–75, though the practice runs right back to the late eighteenth-century collected editions.

27. Courtney Melmoth, 'The Tears of Genius', included in *The Poetical and Dramatic Works of Oliver Goldsmith Now First Collected* (London, 1780), I, lii. See also *Goldsmith: The Critical Heritage*, ed. G. S. Rousseau (London, 1974), p. 162.

28. *The Rising Village: A Poem*, by Oliver Goldsmith; with a preface by the bishop of Novia Scotia (London, 1825), p. 19.

29. Friedman, III, 291.

30. The memorandum is printed in full in *History and Sources*, ed. Balderston, pp. 12–17, with Maurice Goldsmith's corrections.

31. A. Lytton Sells, *Oliver Goldsmith: His Life and Works* (London, 1974), p. 23. John Ginger's *The Notable Man: The Life and Times of Oliver Goldsmith* (London, 1977) is to be preferred in its treatment of this question, quoting the Deposition directly (p. 35) and referring to both Goldsmith brothers (John and Francis) as priests.

32. J. K. Walton, 'The Unity of Swift's *Travels*', *Hermathena*, 104 (1967), 5–50.

33. I discuss some of these problems in the second chapter of *Ascendancy and Tradition in Anglo-Irish Literature from Edmund Burke to James Joyce*, due from Oxford University Press in 1984.

34. *Irish Parliamentary Debates* (Dublin, 1792), XII, 7.

35. Walter Benjamin, *Illuminations*, trans. Harry Zohn (Glasgow, 1973), pp. 264–65. The passage as quoted comes from theses xvi and xvii.

193

36. See W. J. Mc Cormack, *Sheridan Le Fanu and Victorian Ireland* (Oxford, 1980), p. 255.
37. Martin Heidegger, *Being and Time* (Oxford, 1973), p. 58. I sympathize both with those who find the style of much radical criticism a terminological chaos and with those who distrust felicitous appreciations of an intellectual landscape. Heidegger offers an unhappy medium.
38. W. B. Yeats, *Uncollected Prose*, ed. John P. Frayne and Coulton Johnson (London, 1975), II, 328.
39. Ibid., p. 403.
40. W. B. Yeats, *Explorations*, pp. 344–45.
41. Ibid., pp. 441–42.
42. The classic statement is Conor Cruise O'Brien's 'Passion and Cunning: an Essay on the Politics of W. B. Yeats', in *In Excited Reverie: A Centenary Tribute to William Butler Yeats 1865–1939*, ed. A. Norman Jeffares and K. G. W. Cross (London, 1965), pp. 207–78. This provoked a number of outraged responses, but its thesis remains largely unshaken—unless it has been shaken by its author's subsequent right-wing drift. The most recent study is Elizabeth Cullingford, *Yeats, Ireland and Fascism* (London, 1981).
43. See Yeats, *Explorations*, pp. 429, 435. Little has been written on this connection, but see Frank Lentriccia, *After the New Criticism* (London, 1980) pp. 67–8.
44. Theodor Adorno, *Zur Metakritik der Erkenntnistheorie* (Stuttgart, 1956); see Martin Jay, *The Dialectical Imagination: A History of the Frankfurt School and the Institute of Social Research 1923–50* (London, 1973), pp. 68–70.
45. Marx's concentrated study of the aestheticizing of politics is 'The Eighteenth Brumaire of Louis Napoleon'; see Karl Marx, *Surveys from Exile: Political Writings*, ed. David Fernbach (London, 1973), II, 143–249. For the Goncourt brothers' observations on the theatricality of Louis Napoleon's coup see *Pages from the Goncourt Journal*, ed. Robert Baldick (Oxford, 1978), pp. 1–2.
46. W. B. Yeats, *Memoirs*, ed. Denis Donoghue (London, 1972), p. 203. This comment appears in Yeats's journal for 1909.
47. Benjamin, *Illuminations*, p. 258.

Notes on Contributors

JOHN BUXTON is Reader Emeritus and Emeritus Fellow of New College, Oxford. He has been a Visiting Fellow at Wesleyan University, Connecticut, and delivered the Warton Lectures at the British Academy in 1970. His many publications include *A Tradition of Poetry* (London, 1967), *Byron and Shelley* (London, 1968) and *The Grecian Taste* (London, 1978) as well as numerous essays. With N. Davis he is General Editor of the Oxford History of English Literature.

DONALD DAVIE is Andrew W. Mellon Professor in Humanities and English at Vanderbilt University in Nashville, Tennessee. He has held academic posts at universities in Ireland, England and America. His volumes of poetry include *Collected Poems 1950–1970* (London, 1972), *In the Stopping Train* (Manchester, 1977) and *Collected Poems 1970–1983* (Manchester, 1983); he is author of *Purity of Diction in English Verse* (London, 1952; reissued 1967), *Thomas Hardy and British Poetry* (London, 1973), *A Gathered Church: the literature of the English dissenting interest 1700–1930* (London, 1978) and editor of several anthologies, including *The New Oxford Book of Christian Verse* (Oxford, 1981).

SEAMUS DEANE is Professor of English and American Literature, University College, Dublin, and was formerly Visiting Professor at the University of Notre Dame, Indiana and at the University of California, Berkeley. He is author of two volumes of poetry, *Gradual Wars* (Shannon, 1972) and *Rumours* (Dublin, 1977), and has edited Thomas Holcroft's *The Adventures of Hugh Trevor* (Oxford, 1973). He has written widely on eighteenth-century topics, the modern novel and twentieth-century Irish writers.

J. A. DOWNIE is Lecturer in English, University of London Goldsmiths' College. He is co-editor of *The Scriblerian* and author of numerous studies of eighteenth-century literature and politics, including *Robert Harley and the Press: Propaganda and Public Opinion in the Age of Swift and Defoe* (Cambridge, 1979). He is currently writing a critical biography of Jonathan Swift.

BERNARD HARRIS is Professor in the Department of English and Related Literature, University of York. He is a member of the *Shakespeare Survey* Advisory Board and Associate Editor of the *New Cambridge Shakespeare*. With John Russell Brown he was formerly joint general-editor of *Stratford-upon-Avon Studies*. He has edited plays by Marston, Vanbrugh and Shirley as well as publishing numerous essays on the drama.

D. W. JEFFERSON taught English Literature in the University of Leeds and retired in 1977 as an Emeritus Professor. His publications include *Jane Austen's 'Emma'* (London, 1977), two books on Henry James and essays on Milton, Dryden, Swift, Sterne, Scott, Dickens and other authors.

W. J. Mc CORMACK has published *A Festschrift for Francis Stuart* (Dublin, 1972), *Sheridan Le Fanu and Victorian Ireland* (Oxford, 1980) and edited (with A. J. Stead) *James Joyce and Modern Literature* (London, 1982); he is currently completing a study entitled *Ascendancy and Tradition in Anglo-Irish Literature from Edmund Burke to James Joyce* (Oxford, 1984). He has edited several novels for Oxford's World's Classics and is General Editor of its Centenary edition of Anthony Trollope's Palliser novels.

JOHN MONTAGUE is Lecturer in Poetry, University College, Cork. His more recent volumes of poetry include *Tides* (Dublin, 1970), *The Rough Field* (Dublin and London, 1972) and *The Great Cloak* (Dublin, 1978); he has also edited *The Faber Book of Irish Verse* (London, 1974) and other anthologies of poetry and criticism. He has taught at the University of California, Berkeley.

GRAHAM PARRY is Lecturer in English, University of York; he has been Visiting Professor at Toulouse and City College, New York, and at Doshisha University, Kyoto, Japan. Publications include *The Pre-Raphaelite Image* (Leeds, 1978), *Hollar's England* (Wilton, 1980), *The Golden Age Restor'd: The Culture of the Stuart Court* (Manchester, 1981), and various articles on antiquarianism.

PAT ROGERS is Professor of English, University of Bristol. His many books include *Grub Street* (London, 1972), *The Augustan Vision* (London, 1974), *Introduction to Pope* (London, 1975), *Henry Fielding: A Biography* (London, 1979) and he has edited the *Complete Poems of Jonathan Swift* (London, 1983) for Penguin English Poets. He is President of the British Society for Eighteenth-Century Studies.

Notes on Contributors

ANDREW SWARBRICK graduated in English from the University of Leeds where he subsequently completed research on the poetry and criticism of Donald Davie. He has edited Anthony Trollope's *Can You Forgive Her?* (Oxford, 1982), and (with W. J. Mc Cormack) J. S. Le Fanu's *Uncle Silas* (Oxford, 1981) for World's Classics. Essays and reviews have appeared in *Critical Quarterly*, *Long Room*, *PN Review* and elsewhere.

Index

198

Index

Goldsmith, Henry, 72–3, 111, 129, 176, 178, 179
Goldsmith, Rev. John, 170, 173–75, 183
Goldsmith, Maurice, 182
Goldsmith, Oliver: *The Rising Village*, 181
Goldsmith, Oliver: *An Account of the Augustan Age of England*, 71, 72; *The Bee*, 72, 127; *The Citizen of the World*, 13, 33–49, 73, 77, 97, 98, 128, 142, 179, 181; 'Description of an Author's Bed Chamber', 97, 129, 179; *The Deserted Village*, 13, 15, 32, 72 *et seq.*, 82 *et seq.*, 90–104, 126, 128, 130, 132, 169, 177 *et seq.*; *The Double Transformation: a Tale*, 130, 134–38 *passim*; 'The Effect which Climates have upon Man', 118; *An Enquiry into the Present State of Polite Learning in Europe*, 18–20, 37–8, 39, 71, 93, 103, 113, 116, 127; *A General History of the World*, 37; *The Good Natur'd Man*, 33, 44, 150 *et seq.*; *The Grecian History*, 69–70; *The Haunch of Venison*, 138; 'The History of Carolan', 104; *An History of the Earth, and Animated Nature*, 12, 51–67, 71, 94, 95, 117; *The History of England . . . to the Death of George II*, 71; *The History of Little Goody Two-Shoes* (attrib.), 149; *The Life of Bolingbroke*, 20, 48–9; *The Life of Richard Nash*, 20–3, 33, 45, 72, 181–82; *The Life of Dr. Parnell*, 182; *The Logicians Refuted*, 132; *Memoirs of M. de Voltaire*, 115; *A New Simile. In the Manner of Swift*, 132; *The Proceedings of Providence Vindicated. An Eastern Tale*, 35; *Retaliation*, 12, 72, 80, 98, 127, 138, 139–41; 'A Reverie at the Boar's Head Tavern, Eastcheap', 147; 'The Revolution in Low Life', 92, 93, 95; *The Roman History*, 69, 71; *She Stoops to Conquer*, 90, 158–67; *The Traveller*, 13, 15, 57, 72, 79 *et seq.*, 92, 93–4, 96, 98, 102, 108–23, 126; 'Upon Political Frugality', 98; *The Vicar of Wakefield*, 13, 18, 23–32, 33, 44, 48, 76, 86–8, 90, 95, 98, 133, 148
Grattan, Henry, 185
Graves, Robert: *The Crowning Privilege*, 91–2
Gray, Thomas, 20, 127; *Elegy written in a Country Churchyard*, 76
Greene, Donald: *The Politics of Samuel Johnson*, 88
Gregory, Lady Augusta, 172; *Gods and Fighting Men*, 187

Hamlyn, Susan, 161–62
Hankin, St. John, 164
Hazlitt, William, 11, 74
Heaney, Seamus, 185
Heidegger, Martin, 186, 187, 189
Helvétius, Claude Arien: *De l'Homme*, 115
Henn, T. R., 169
Hesketh, Lady Harriet, 88
Holcroft, Thomas, 44
Hopkins, Robert H., 24, 112–13, 127, 131, 133, 134, 138, 141
Horace, 75, 138
Hume, David, 71
Hunt, James Henry Leigh, 112, 132
Husserl, Edmund, 189

Irving, Washington: *Sketch Book*, 30

James, Henry, 11, 14
Jeffares, A. N., 169
Johnson, Samuel, 11, 14, 17, 18, 37, 48, 59–60, 69, 71 *et seq.*, 86, 112, 147, 150 *et seq.*, 175; *Dictionary*, 111; 'Introduction to the Political State of Great Britain', 18; *Life of Savage*, 21, 22; *Lives of the Poets*, 182; *The Rambler*, 24; *Rasselas*, 37, 47
Joyce, James, 190
Juvenal, 75

Kavanagh, Patrick: *The Great Hunger*, 93
Keats, John, 73, 122, 127, 191
Kelly, Hugh: *False Delicacy*, 153, 156; *A Word to the Wise*, 161
King, Edward, 73
Kniveton, Mrs. Priscilla, 160

Langer, Susanne: *Feeling and Form: A Theory of Art*, 14
Langhorne, John, 112; *The Country Justice*, 92
Lawrence, D. H., 103
Leibnitz, Gottfried Wilhelm, 54
Literary Magazine, 18
Linnaeus (Carl von Linné), 61
Lloyd's Magazine, 93
Lonsdale, Roger, 111, 113, 117, 130, 131, 132, 134, 137, 138
Lucretius, 127
Lyons, F. S. L., 168
Lyons, J. B., 159
Lyttelton, Lord George, 34

McKillop, Alan D., 117
McLuhan, Marshall, 114
Macauley, Lord Thomas Babington, 90–1
Mac Donagh, Oliver, 169
Mackenzie, A. M.: *Slavery; or, the Times*, 41
Mackenzie, Henry: *The Man of Feeling*, 44
Macrobius, 127
Mandeville, Bernard de, 121
Mandeville, Sir John, 58
Mason, Rev. William, 36, 79
Melmoth, Courtney, 180, 181
Milton, John, 73; *Lycidas*, 73, 74; *Paradise Lost*, 74; *Paradise Regained*, 110
Momboddo, Lord James Burnett: *Origin and Progress of Language*, 61–3
Monnoye, Bernard de la, 127
Montague, John: *The Rough Field*, 104
Montesquieu, Charles Louis de Secondat de, 35, 47, 72, 115–16, 118 *et seq.*; *L'Esprit des Lois*, 110, 116, 120, 123; *Lettres Persanes*, 34, 37, 116
Monthly Review, 21, 34, 112, 116, 127
Morley, Sheridan, 163
Mozart, Wolfgang Amadeus: *The Magic Flute*, 115
Mudford, William, 127, 132, 142
Murphy, Arthur, 160

Newbery, John, 33, 116, 149
Newell, R. H., 91

199